The

IAO
MILLENNIUM
BOOK

with a foreword
by
The Archbishop of York

edited by
Paul Hale

First published by the Incorporated Association of Organists July 2000.

The moral rights of the authors have been asserted.

British Library Cataloguing-in-Publication Data
A catalogue record for this book is available from The British Library.

ISBN 0 9538711 0 X

Made and printed in Great Britain by Warwick Printing Company Limited, Theatre Street, Warwick CV34 4DR.

CONTENTS

FOREWORD

by The Archbishop of York
the Most Reverend David Hope, KCVO

Whilst delighted and honoured to be invited to produce this Foreword, I could not but wonder, 'Why me?' – whose keyboard skills extend little beyond the simplest of hymns, and who numbers himself among those who are pressed to distinguish between a stopped diapason and a blocked drain! – except that whilst at All Saints Margaret Street and having been introduced to William Lloyd Webber a former organist, I was also introduced by him to the stop called "ophicleide".

But then I took courage, for the realisation dawned that technical expertise might not be the real requirement: there is, after all, a dazzling enough display of that in the pages which follow. Perhaps a more appropriate qualification would be the simple layman's love of good organ music. And here, I am on much firmer ground: for this is a love which has been with me for just about as long as I can remember. It is a love which was born in my days as a boy chorister in Wakefield Cathedral, for it was there that I was introduced to a rich and varied diet of organ music. (The organist of those days I understand had come with the reputation of "organ buster" – such was the enthusiasm of his playing!)

In the years which have followed, I have been privileged to hear some of the greatest living exponents of this most majestic of instruments, who have widened and enriched the horizons of my understanding and appreciation.

Here then in this **IAO Millennium Book** is a splendid collection of essays, providing an informed, informative and multifaceted overview of both the instrument and its music in the 20th century – a fascinating and hugely attractive, if at times highly technical, account of a remarkable century of creative endeavour and social change. Hackneyed though the phrase may be, there is, indeed, something here for everyone: whether amongst the technically competent and therefore (unlike me!) in no danger of getting lost in the pneumatic nomenclature, or merely someone for whom it is pleasure enough simply to wander through this world of music. Either way, we sense that amongst these pages, we are also among enthusiasts and friends who have much to share with us.

From Patrick Burns, who takes us on a guided, if slightly surreal, tour inside the world's largest organ (and, yes, a 64 foot diapason – stopped or otherwise – really does defy the imagination!), to Kevin Bowyer's toast to the 20th century (where, for me, the unsung hero of the piece is the Yorkshireman who commands his bar like a captain on the bridge of his ship!). From Peter Williams and John Butt who remind us that Bach is, above all, the born survivor whose genius will come through almost any treatment with flying colours, to Richard Shephard's self-deprecating recognition that only the very best of 20th century church music will survive (but who rather wishes that these same might also be true of architecture!).

And how those of us who have been compelled to listen to those who *thought* they could – but *actually* could not! – will warm to Pierre Cochereau's advice about self-discipline, in David Briggs' piece on improvisation.

And not forgetting of course the theatre organ too, Reginald Dixon on the Blackpool Tower organ with his "Oh I do like to be beside the sea-side" which gave and continues to give so much pleasure to so many and to stir many a memory, though Roy Bingham wryly comments "not all performers of this style match up to the quality of the style's originator".

But it is Lionel Dakers who leads us into my own world of church music, and who makes his eloquent plea for the 'high flourishes' of worship – challenging the 'dumbers-down' to remember that excellence is not elitism. His tribute to those cathedral Deans and Chapters (and there are so many parishes also to commend here) who have done so much to preserve that inheritance of musical excellence is well-directed. As, indeed, are his comments about 'difficult organists' and 'autocratic clergy' – and I have known both! If there is just one area which might have merited a little more exposure, it is the ongoing 'pipe versus electronic' debate – where, for churches in straightened circumstances, the justification for spending huge sums on organ rebuilds may not always be entirely self-evident!

What *is* self-evident, however, is the enormous debt which the Church owes to the whole history and culture of the organ. It has been an enormous influence in the shaping and sustaining of our churches' worship. We recognise, too, our huge indebtedness to those many hundreds of organists and choir trainers who serve our churches today. Though their skills may vary, the loyal and dedicated commitment of these men and women does not. Without their offering, the life and worship of our churches would be impoverished indeed.

Nor should we forget the painstaking and delicate skills of the organ builders and organ tuners, some of whom I meet as I visit churches at the dedication of a new or refurbished organ.

It is perhaps paradoxical that the best expressed purpose of the organ I know and with which I conclude is most effectively told by one of the very number who sought to abolish the organ and organ playing in our churches and throughout the land. John Milton speaks of the "pealing organ" and "the full voiced choir" who in "service high and anthems clear ... dissolve me into ecstasies, And bring all heaven before mine eyes".

PREFACE

Paul Hale

*T*he *IAO Millennium Book* has sought to assemble the views of a group of distinguished writers, all known for being both leaders in their fields and also blessed with penetrating philosophical insight into the possibilities which lie before us.

Although written to be read today, as we somewhat warily cross the threshold of the third Christian Millennium, the book is also designed to be a social statement, a snap-shot of a significant area of our culture as it existed or was perceived to exist at the end of the twentieth century. It is therefore an inclusive collection of essays, seeking dispassionately to embrace many aspects which defined twentieth century organ or church music life. There is some slight overlap between articles and indeed not all authors hold the same point of view: who would expect them to?

In celebrating the 250th anniversary of the death of J S Bach, we seek to reflect the huge strides in scholarship which the twentieth century embraced. Professor Peter Williams and Dr John Butt both present us with the prospect of a 'post-authentic' future, an ever-widening variety of performance styles informed by the knowledge we now possess, but employing this with freedom of expression and choice to create a new raft of dynamic and creative possibilities, no longer feeling that good performance practice implies a straight-jacket.

My hope is that such creative common-sense will also prevail in the 'heritage' aspect of organ building; the risk of fossilisation in our 'historic' organs and church buildings is very real. No other generation seems to have been so loath to apply the value-judgements of common sense to its inheritance – just what *is* worth preserving as it stands or as it was built, and what should be replaced or – yes – improved? What organ-builder ever left a new organ fully satisfied with his work? Few would not have liked to have returned with improvements as their techniques developed. Just how many original examples do we need of the work of each builder? Father Willis had no such doubts – his melting pot was always hot; and in due course, a generation later, thousands of his own pipes ended upon on the voicing machines at Durham. Cavaillé-Coll, on the other hand, greatly respected the work of Clicquot, preserving many of his ranks in numerous otherwise new organs.

The Renaissance saw a glorification of and fascination with the cultures of the ancient Greeks and the Romans. From that fascination grew something entirely new and wonderful, with huge cultural gains and the creation of such genres as opera. Is the time not ripe now for a second renaissance? Let us not timidly be a generation of copyists: let us learn from the past, and then, inspired, go forth to create the future.

The appetite for sheer size in organs, as exemplified *par excellence* by the Atlantic City giant, may not appeal to many readers, neither may the very particular tones of the cinema/theatre organ, but as there is no denying that these were central and unique elements – indeed for a time, dominant ones – in twentieth century organ culture, I make no apology for covering them here; we censor history at our peril, for there are lessons to be learnt from everything that has gone before. Thus Patrick Burns shares some personal first-hand enthusiasms for the great Midmer-Losh and its 64ft Diaphonic Dulzian, along with the complete stop-list and many unique photographs, and Roy Bingham delves deeply and perceptively into the clever art of registration and playing techniques 'at the mighty Wurlitzer'.

The organ scene in the twentieth century is covered in **The IAO Millennium Book** by the experienced and deeply knowledgeable trio of John Norman, Canon Nicholas Thistlethwaite and Stephen Bicknell. As Stephen rejoices in the inspiring quality of contemporary organ-building in the USA, particularly of those craftsmen working in an historically-informed style, one might wonder why so few historical copies are commissioned in the UK. The answer, I feel, lies not simply in a lack of vision, curiosity or funding, nor principally in academic institutions not being interested, but reflects the proximity of the UK to continental Europe, a proximity which enables any interested organist to visit, hear and play with relative ease any significant historic organ. This facility is largely denied Americans, other than those on the Grand European Tour, or the obligatory Parisian study sojourn. Thus, I suspect, their more ready determination to re-create at home that which they cannot otherwise readily experience.

Professor Thomas Murray offers a refreshingly different view of how the organ scene might develop, observing an international reawakening of true romanticism in organ playing and building, and outlining some significant symphonic tonal developments. Is this a dead-end or a new beginning? Judge for yourselves. From virtuoso Kevin Bowyer we have a chapter – unique in style – which throws light on the whole range of twentieth century organ music, each facet of which receives perceptive comment. As an authoritative overview of a century of achievement it has no obvious peer.

For church music – and I mean essentially the choral tradition of the Church of England – the twentieth century proved an extraordinary era of growth in standards of music-making and of numbers in choirs, partly fuelled by the inspiring influence of the rapidly developing recording industry; Ernest Lough's *O for the wings of a dove* appeared at a pivotal time, as for players did HMV's *Great Cathedral Organs* series a generation later. Terry Hoyle observes how throughout the whole history of recorded sound its influence on singers and organists has been paramount. Yet in recent years there has been an equally remarkable four-way split – standards and aspirations in cathedrals and college chapels steadily rising, standards and numbers of musicians in parish churches rapidly falling away, choral societies just about holding their own, and small specialist singing groups of the highest professional standards burgeoning. Lionel Dakers explores this whole area with his customary thoroughness, while Richard Shephard adds a perceptive chapter from the composer's perspective.

Acknowledgements

I would like to thank all authors for so generously offering their time and expertise, and am especially grateful to the Most Reverend and Right Honourable Dr David M Hope, KCVO, Archbishop of York, Primate of England and Metropolitan for graciously contributing the Foreword.

Thanks are due in no small measure to the staff at the Warwick Printing Company, particularly Paul Yates and Jon Clucas, and to the IAO Council and Executive for commissioning and underwriting this significant publishing endeavour.

Are We Any Closer To Understanding J S Bach, The Organist and Organ-Composer?

by

Peter Williams

Prelude

Consider the *St Matthew Passion*. One sometimes hears it said that performed without an hour-long sermon between the two parts, it cannot be 'heard' correctly, whatever authentic sounds today's well-informed musicians are able to reconstruct. Also, it could well be that listeners now are less likely to be caught up in the story than formerly or to be content to sit in old box-pews to hear it, though more are able to improve their social status, read what they like, go and hear other performances, live longer, re-marry while a spouse is alive, bathe more regularly, keep their teeth, and study the *Passion* in an inexpensive score. All this is obvious enough, but I think there is something more crucial: a *Passion* narrating the story of a trial and public execution had an immediacy quite unimaginable today, because most of the people then present (including the composer and performers too, presumably) had witnessed or at least knew about public executions. To argue the finer points of who plays what kind of recitative-chords in the *Passion* or how the string-players should articulate their parts or how many singers there should be in the two choirs – are any of these surface details really bringing us nearer to experiencing the *Passion* as the composer or his listeners experienced it?

Or consider *Messiah*: how on one or other occasion Handel heard the work – its timbres, ensemble, instrumental tone, volume-level, pitch, key-characteristics, tempi, techniques of articulation and enunciation, kinds of expressiveness – would clearly be worth studying or trying to recreate. But every performance of *Messiah* from Dublin in the 1740s to the American Bible Belt in the 1990s has had elements fully 'authentic' to its own culture, and although few of these were Handel's, re-creating original conditions of performance may hinder one or two that were. While it is true that the massive choirs and ugly organs of the Bible Belt reflect a taste for massive choirs and ugly organs unknown to Handel, its congregations' intimacy with *Messiah's* texts – they knew that Revelation's words 'Worthy is the lamb', were first sung by 'ten thousand times ten thousand' angels – might bring it closer to what Handel felt than what today's enthusiasts for early instruments and small choirs feel, if anything. So which is more authentic?

One of the ways in which the study of history has progressed during the twentieth century is in a more frequent look at what *is* history, what it is to look at something in the past, to try to 'form a picture of it' on the basis of what still exists in the form of documentation or physical remains. As we reconstruct a historical event of any kind – Waterloo, Viking depredations, the discovery of longitude, Lloyd George's amours, last Tuesday's PCC meeting – we can do so only according to our own understanding, our grasp of what a 'fact' or an 'event' is. Even being present at one of these no more ensures freedom from our own inevitable intellectual limitations and experience than not being present at it. Probably less, if anything, for our memory is likely to be wilful. All history is a construct, and I believe we cannot avoid it being so even when we are not deliberately misusing it in order to prove a point. All use of the past is a misuse, and it takes great effort to minimize the inevitable distortion and humbly to push back the point at which we exercise our opinion on any issue.

For the organist this is not quite the counsel of despair it seems, however, because one can draw a distinction between studying a great composer (trying to understand everything one can about him, his time and his music) and playing the same music in public (communicating with listeners of the day through the live artistry of performance). I am not even sure the two musical activities of *playing* and *studying* in this sense are even compatible, except now and then in the case of contemporary music, and a lot of the disagreement in the various authentic movements of today derives from a confusion between those two activities. Early music groups rush to judgment in order to prepare the next concert or recording; scholars avoid judgment if they can, and snipe from the sides. From my own experience, I would say that the most productive and helpful coming together of historical study and live playing happens when what one is studying is not books or even scores but an historic instrument. An old instrument is something one can respond to in a very live way, given a desire to learn, whereas an old theory-book or an old musical source is always at least one step removed from real experience. The revelation that comes from playing a great composer's music on an instrument of the kind known to him is unrivalled and irreplaceable.

As they have developed at their best by the year 2000, performance practice studies are not simply about putting on concerts: they are about studying music in its own right, trying to understand what happened to it over history, what it was its composers had in mind, what they knew, what they assumed, how they heard, and (ideally) how their music was heard by others. Performance practice studies might bring fringe-benefits in the form of introducing or re-revealing catchy sounds – fresh ways of playing or singing, based on old methods and old instruments – and these new sounds will attract a refreshed, CD-buying public. Similarly, now that higher education has to prove itself and offer a marketable end-product for those who invest time and money in it, it will often produce practical success and equip the advanced student with marketable skills. But that is not the aim, or at least the sole aim, of real study. Study does not have to lead either to practical advantage (such as giving one enlightened preferences or heightened pleasure) or to practical disadvantage (such as making us dislike the inauthentic and decline to participate in it). To study is merely to try to understand, to alert oneself to the issues.

Nevertheless, no one wants to feel they are being purely theoretical or 'merely academic', so I hope there may be some details in the following remarks that have some practical use for those playing the music of one distant and complex composer. In the effort to understand him, people often make bold (wild?) speculations about him, reminding one a little of the Shakespeare situation: the creative genius whose works we have but about whom we know very little personally, and whose world becomes increasingly remote from his admirers as the centuries pass.

Bach and the 'Bach organ'

As far as I know, the issue was seldom raised within the first century after his death. Wesley or Kittel or Vogler or Mendelssohn played where and how they liked, spreading the Gospel (as they saw it) in whatever way was effective. In the mid-nineteenth century, however, new scholarly work for the Griepenkerl/Peters and Bach Gesellschaft editions began to supply the background for a new understanding, and by the time the biographers Hilgenfeldt and Bitter were writing (see FN 1), two basic approaches to the Bach organ had clearly emerged. These are: either try to understand and even reconstruct what he knew and liked; or try to create a fine instrument in the taste of the day and play his music according to the sound-world of the day.

Hilgenfeldt reminded readers that there existed one particular instrument praised by the composer and long remembered by him, i.e. St Catharine's, Hamburg, associated with Adam Reincken and thus representing the North German tradition and the fully baroque organ-conception of Arp Schnitger (these are not Hilgenfeldt's words). Now lost for ever, this organ was still then fairly reliable as a historical document. In contrast, Bitter gave more attention to describing a modern instrument, the rebuild of Bach's youthful organ in Arnstadt as 'restored' by the firm Hesse & Meissner in 1864-78, and enlarged to sixty stops, with remote action, detached console and altered case. Not much of this could be described as Bachian but satisfied the then current approaches to the composer.[1]

During most of the twentieth century, practising organists and advisers reforming the organ – from Albert Schweitzer through the German *Orgelbewegung* to the 'authentic copies' of the last few decades – have argued most about the second of these approaches. This must be partly because the organs that resulted have had more duties to perform than merely play Bach chorales and fugues, authentically or otherwise. Nevertheless, the movement towards today's more 'authentic copies' is to take more of the first approach – find an organ Bach knew and then imitate it, in as many ways as skills and sensibilities allow, accepting its limitations in the interest of approaching a specific sound-world, and happily reducing its versatility in the process.

For most of the twentieth century, organists, editors, musicologists, historians and organologists have thought a great deal about 'Bach's ideal organ', proposing for this honour various extant old instruments directly or indirectly associated with the composer (Hamburg Jakobi, Freiberg Dom, Dresden Hof, Rötha, Naumburg, Störmthal, Altenburg, Waltershausen, Lahm in Itzgrund, various smaller Thuringian organs). That these are extant has naturally increased their value for these purposes, and any documented approval of them by Bach himself has inspired people to see direct connections between them and his music. More recently, it has sometimes been pointed out that indeed there is no 'ideal Bach organ' and would not be, even if his own instruments (Arnstadt, Mühlhausen, Weimar, Leipzig) or those he is known to have played (Lüneburg Michaelis, Halle Liebfrauen, Kassel Martini, Potsdam Garnison, Dresden Sophien) did still exist in reliable form. The reasons for this are simple: not only would no single organ have shown all of this music at its best but any great composer is likely to work to a platonic ideal that could never exist.

In any case, there are problems with giving priority to any of these organs. The first is that Bach never presided over any of the great organs of the day, as his *Obituary* already reports him as frequently remarking.[2] Furthermore, it is difficult to see how there could be one single ideal instrument, because the repertory itself, from the early chorales and praeludia to the late Leipzig works, spans almost half a century. Not only is this the very period when the organ had a parting of the ways and changed as far beyond recognition as it could before nineteenth-century technologies laid out other paths for it, but no great composer is likely to keep the same ideals of sound for half a century. A comparable glance at any other great body of music and questions about its instrument – such as Beethoven's sonatas, and whether he had the same kind of 'ideal piano' in mind for both his earliest and latest works – shows how implausible the whole notion is.

The most recent contribution to the thinking about a Bach organ is materializing in St Thomas's, Leipzig as I write. The collapse of the Berlin Wall has opened up the city to, amongst other things, genuine international musicology and organ-building, as a consequence of which the outmoded *Orgelbewegung* organ built for St Thomas's in the 1960s by Alexander Schuke (Potsdam) is now being superseded by a new organ in the north gallery, complementing the Sauer organ at the west end and giving the church something to serve as a 'Bach organ'.[3] By *Orgelbewegung*, I mean the German Organ Reform Movement of the late 1920s, a half-hearted return to basics, reacting to the heavy factory-organs of the time, flavoured with a nationalist bias from which its leading lights did not escape contamination, and surviving to govern the building techniques and stoplists of new organs in both parts of postwar Germany.[4] The Leipzig Schuke was too, in its way, a historical monument, built to play Bach according to the notions of the day, and no doubt serving as some kind of Mecca for young East German or visiting American organists. The *eminence grise* behind much of the Reform Movement's aesthetic was J S Bach and his music: these were the ultimate authorities for most musicians and builders, and partial though their fidelities might have been, later enlightenment was hardly possible without them.

At the turn of the millennium it is the Sauer west-end organ which is now being accorded status as a historic organ, being closely associated with Max Reger's compositions and Karl Straube's Bach-performances, both highly valued in Germany to this day. And it is to match the Sauer, restored in 1991-93, that the new sixty-plus stop organ has been designed for St Thomas's by Gerald Woehl of Marburg, based on his understanding of one particular Bach organ – not St Thomas's (which can not be reconstructed) but the organ in the University Church, built by Scheibe in 1717 and tested by the ducal organist of Weimar, J S Bach, who was not yet a Leipziger himself.[5] The University Church existed until the 1960s, destroyed not by bombs but by socialists of the renamed 'Karl Marx University', who wanted no university church, whatever its associations. As its walls fell, so a Bach-connection was lost. After his appointment to the Thomaskirche in 1723, Bach had come into contact again with the church and its organ, not only performing special cantatas there but even, for all one knows, conceiving and playing some of his mature organ-masterpieces at the Scheibe keyboards. It is certainly possible that here he taught pupils (students, graduates, visitors), since the organs in St Thomas were more frequently in need of attention and the church itself was no doubt busier.

The idea of the Woehl organ is bound to have elements of compromise, if only because there is no question, it seems, of returning to the old galleries and gallery-plan in St Thomas. Also, the Scheibe organ, in any case not one of the prettiest-looking organs of Saxony, may not have been a particularly fine-sounding instrument. One could read Bach's 1717 report in various ways, though a positive light has been put on it.[6] While in the literature much has been made of Bach's expertise in organ-building, and his reports naturally scrutinized for every little hint they give of his preferences and knowledge, it is more than likely that he wrote this particular document in deference to Johann Kuhnau, his predecessor at St Thomas and at the time chief musician in Leipzig. They had worked together recently on a report for the new organ of the Liebfrauenkirche, Halle (a church closely connected with the young Handel twenty years earlier), and presumably, Kuhnau could not himself report on the new Leipzig organ.

That Bach was invited to do so may have been a compliment less to his knowledge than to his position at a ducal court. Furthermore, his report was conventional, relying heavily on the points and some of the very words published by Andreas Werckmeister in his treatise of 1698 (the revised *Orgelprobe*, or 'How to test an Organ'). This had been even more the case at Halle, so there remains a question just how far an educated *director musices* would be familiar with technical and mechanical matters, or want to show that he was.

Either way, the result of such considerations is that one can be sure neither of what Bach thought of the instrument nor indeed how intimate he was with the arts of organ-building. Doubtless he knew something, brought up as he was with an elder brother then very much involved in a major organ-project of his own, but an apprentice-mastercraft like organ-building was distinct from the crafts of town musician. Nevertheless, three of Bach's instruments (Mühlhausen, Weimar and Leipzig St Thomas) were involved in major rebuilding work during the very years he presided over them, and both Weimar and St Thomas were out of commission for some crucial years – at Weimar, probably during the very composition of much of the *Orgelbüchlein*. Much of the work done on these organs was presumably owing to Bach's requests and directions, and must have been inspected or otherwise watched over by him, who would therefore know many a local builder. It is the local builders with whom Bach had closest and longest contact, not the Silbermanns or Schnitgers at work in the great provincial capital cities. What the new Woehl organ in Leipzig does do to every musician's benefit now is re-direct attention away from these star builders, towards the more homely instruments produced by builders in Thuringia and Saxony in the first part of the eighteenth century.

These often large instruments were furnished with an array of colour-stops – not so much subtle mutations or fine manual reeds *à la parisienne* but interesting flutes and strings (various *viola* types), deep pedal basses, strong pedal reeds for *cantus firmus* and supporting the *plena*, echo effects, inbuilt secondary manuals (no separate chair organs), tierce ranks for the colours admired in Lutheran chorales (Sesquialteras), and even a few toy-stops of the kind evidently despised by Silbermann. The search for new colours like overblowing flutes was active during the years of Bach's maturity, and he must have heard many experimental sounds of the kind one can still hear in the region around Brunswick and Eisenach.[7] The bigger organs of Thuringia also had to accompany choir and instruments in the role of *basso continuo*, and so, because pitch was usually high, needed either a low-pitch rank or two of sweet-sounding wooden Gedackts or (preferably?) a tuning that allowed all of the organ to be played a whole tone lower. Much is often made of Bach's avowed regard for strong fundamental tone down to 32', a taste reflecting the gradual shift towards the powerful bass that affected western music in general and eventually became indispensable to the symphonic orchestra of the nineteenth century. All these characteristics will be found on the new Leipzig instrument, which will stimulate a new understanding of the problems of the 'Bach organ'.

Problems in this conception will remain if only because there is another factor in trying to understand any great music in relation to its instrumentation: one looks for as perfect a sound as possible, for sheer beauty of tone not merely according to personal taste but to that mysterious effect which certain quality of fine sound has on the listener, lifting the music on to another level. With organs, I have felt this most often with Silbermann's instruments, in both sophisticated music (exquisite effects of a Sonata movement or an *Orgelbüchlein* chorale played with 8ft stops only) and in more naïve works (the G major Concerto played on 8.4.2 Principals), although I know that the actual link between Silbermann and Bach is not straightforward.

One could say similar things about an early Bach work such as the *Ein feste Burg* fantasia played with the forthright sounds of a Schnitger organ, say at Norden or Stade: it gains a striking immediacy and sibilance, just what a 'northern' toccata or long chorale-fantasia needs. The very works of Bach one sometimes hears being criticized or rated less than highly – organ-chorales without sophisticated harmony or sense of coherent buildup, concerto transcriptions with tiresome sequences, scrappy moments in some of the early preludes and fugues, etc – will positively spring to life and give a fresh delight when played on 'early sounds' of the kind familiar in 1700. If they do so less and less on later organs, as I believe they do, the problem lies with the latter.

Conversely, whatever scholarship suggests, and however good a case is made today (by producers of CDs, for instance) for a close connection between Bach and certain extant organs like Waltershausen or Lahm, only dissatisfaction results if they do not delight listeners or convey the quality of the music, as these two seldom do. Not all old organs are worthy of Bach. One has to be careful with subjective notions of beauty, of course, and not forget that in the nineteenth century countless fine old organs (in England and France, even Germany) were wrecked forever in the desire to make them fit for playing Bach's works. Nevertheless, one also has to be careful with objective historical reasoning, and not project something we call 'Bach's ideal organ' merely on the basis of what, from a pitifully small amount of documentation, we think he thought and felt. By 2000 so much will have been written about Bach, and so much will have been recorded and played so often, that admirers might feel they are nearer some truth about it all. So they might well be, but knowledge built up over recent decades has better exposed the questions than solved them.

The music

There are several issues arising here from time to time, including questions of authenticity, of variants (differences between one early copy or version and another), of function, and of course of chronology. On all of them, knowledge has increased dramatically since World War II.

On authenticity: the project of the *New Bach Edition* (NBA) to issue a further volume of all chorales ever attributed to J S Bach at one time or another in the last 250 years but not yet accepted as 'genuine', ought eventually to give any musician second thoughts about what is obviously inauthentic or 'what can not possibly be the work of Bach'. There can be few players who have not had ideas about this. The volume of so-called *Neumeister Chorales* published for the first time in connection with the tercentenary of 1985 already raised such questions, of course, and the intervening years have not see them very satisfactorily answered, in my opinion. Rather than reject them outright ('these don't sound like Bach', 'they are not good enough') or accept them on the basis of assertive and positivistic scholarship ('the way they have come down to us suggests a direct line to the composer, who is named in the manuscript'), I think the best approach is still to accept them as above-average minor works of a local Thuringian organist in about 1700-05 – but also to accept the probability that the local Thuringian organist was the teenage Bach.

Either way, they are chorale-settings of some interest, and if some or all of them are the work of J S Bach (and whether *all* of them are, is a separate question), they are fascinatingly suggestive about what he knew as a boy and how the 'wild' side to him was to develop into the composer of the *Orgelbüchlein* and the Passacaglia in C minor. The *Neumeister* chorales have many little wildnesses quite unknown in, for example, otherwise comparable chorales in the same manuscript album attributed to Sebastian's first father-in-law, Johann Michael Bach.[8]

Quite apart from these and other chorales attributed to Bach on uncertain authority, there remain many further knotty problems. Some concern the origin or genre of a composition, such as the best-known of all organ works, the Toccata and Fugue in D minor BWV 565 – who composed it? For what instrument? In what key? What was it called? It is easy to show this work as having features hard to attribute either to Bach or to the usual organ music of the time, though of course the exceptionally gifted composer can always surprise us and do unique things. In the case of the *Schübler Chorales*, the questions are slightly different: five are transcriptions of known Bach arias but who made the transcriptions? Is the second of them an original work? Are they true transcriptions or merely scored-up arias? If there exists an original print of them with a few 'corrections' made by the composer, as there is, does it prove that he had anything to do with the publication?

In the case of the so-called *Deathbed Chorale*, 'Vor deinen Thron tret' ich' BWV 668, the questions concern its origins: was anything at all dictated by the dying man (the preface to the posthumous *Art of Fugue* says nothing about his dying, only that he was blind), and if so, was it this? Or, since some of the substance of this composition appears in a much earlier version, did someone else re-compose and copy it, or did he? I will return to this last piece below, for it typifies some of the many approaches to Bach. So in a lesser way do the *Eight Little Preludes and Fugues*, to attribute which to Bach is in effect to underrate some of his quite competent contemporaries.

The notable thing about many questions of this kind is that only the late twentieth-century's increase in information, and the ease with which one can now check on sources or compare documentation, brings them into existence: knowledge has raised questions, not necessarily answered them. Meanwhile, many of the works listed or recognized in the major nineteenth-century editions as dubious – various preludes, chorales, trios etc. – have been assigned over the years to one or other composer of the eighteenth century. A few have been shown to have no verifiable connection with Bach at all, such as the Aria in F major derived (by whom?) from a chamber work of François Couperin. Occasionally, as with the Concerto in D minor, a work has been re-associated with Bach when for long it was thought to be the work of someone else. Such re-assignments are the positive results of modern research, but even more important are the bigger questions it opens up.

One of these is: was the separate large-scale prelude and fugue of the Bach type really developed out of the multiform praeludia of Buxtehude, as books used to suggest? Or did they take this form for the composer to use as separate pieces in services or concerts, i.e. the prelude at the beginning and the fugue at the end? Or is the question itself old-fashioned, based on a textbook misunderstanding of how Bach was influenced, which assumed quite wrongly that a major composer like Buxtehude was a bigger influence than a minor like J K F Fischer or Kuhnau? A separated prelude and fugue appear in *Clavierübung III*, of course, and the very difference in musical character between two powerful movements such as the 'Wedge' (Prelude and Fugue in E minor, BWV 548), might well suggest that the custom was to treat them as a framework around other pieces. Perhaps that is the reason why someone (not the composer?) paired other works like the great G minor Fantasia or the F major Toccata with their respective Fugues: were these 'pairings of convenience', so to speak, which reflected the use made of them by organists, including Bach himself? How many of the pairs accepted as normal in recital-programmes today are firmly established by the sources?

Again, I think the main point of interest for the student is not the practical consideration – whether, for example, to programme dubious works in concerts or services, or to split up genuine pairs like the Wedge or the B minor, BWV 544. Rather, improved knowledge has gradually shown that the whole idea of a recital-series called *The Complete Works Of Bach* is one of practical compromise, indeed an anachronism, something that belongs to the modern world of secular public concerts and based on the nineteenth-century idea of the Complete Edition. This presented 'authenticated' works in fixed versions and brought together works in a common format such as the composer himself never knew. The very similarity presented to readers of the modern printed page by quite different works is itself misleading: we can always approach Bach better, I think, by being aware of the different way that different music of his looked on the page.

The ready availability by now of facsimiles of the *Orgelbüchlein*, all four parts of *Clavierübung* (at least two complete sets available as I write), the *Six Sonatas*, the *Leipzig Chorales* (formerly called 'The Eighteen'), *Schübler Chorales* (at least two) and the *Canonic Variations* (ditto), gives the modern organist some notion of what an organist of the time had in front of him. Only now and then, I think, would organists today actually want to play from these facsimiles – some of the *Six Sonatas* and *Clavierübung III*, perhaps – but they do convey a feeling of intimacy with the music such as no modern edition will give. They can also explain some knotty little problems, such as why one of the 'Nun komm' settings in 'The Eighteen' ends with a minor chord (there was no room left for the b-natural?) or why 'Gott durch deine Güte' BWV 600 has a kind of registration (to clarify the pitch-level in a confusing two-stave layout?), even perhaps why *Clavierübung III* includes the Four Duets (to make good use of empty pages?).

A general point is that one learns by asking the many questions that arise. Clearly, only by knowing of the problems of authenticity and chronology can one begin to deal with such questions as, How did the composer differ from his contemporaries, how did his incomparable talent emerge? How can he have conceived such a work as the *Passacaglia* in his early twenties? What gave him the uncanny and (for that period) unique grasp of diatonic harmony that allowed him to produce the *Orgelbüchlein* within a few years of his early chorales? Was it acquaintance with French music and its handling of accented passing-notes? Did he know much more music than we are now aware of? Conversely, did he really need to know

Vivaldi's concertos before he could plan big ritornello movements? What exactly did he mean with his longer chorales? – were they preludes, interludes, postludes, hymn-substitutes or meditative pieces for recitals? How was it that he took the fully developed prelude and fugue so much farther than any of his contemporaries or even pupils? It is puzzling how even an intelligent musician like J L Krebs seems not to have grasped the structural principles mastered by his teacher. Did Bach not teach them?

On the variants: a major problem of the nineteenth-century Complete Works, and subsequent editions operating under the same philosophy, is that its fixed text transmitted some misleading impressions, especially with the collections of chorales and the big free works. Only gradually have players come to realize that the pairing of several big preludes and fugues is not as straightforward as it seems, that a case can be made for playing certain famous works in other keys (the G minor Fantasia, the E major/C major Toccata, even the E flat Prelude and Fugue), that some works are surely arrangements of some kind made by somebody else (the C minor Praeludium BWV 549, the Toccata in D minor, the 'early' version of the D major Fugue or 'late' version of the Legrenzi), that several have equally authoritative versions, and that not a few ought to be called something else (the 'Fantasia' in G major, the 'Passacaglia', the 'Eighteen', the so-called 'Chorale Partitas'). The notion of the collated edition, in which a musical text is derived from several copies, can easily lead to an end-product representing no single original state of the piece.

Though to many musicians most of the details emerging from such considerations can seem secondary, I find that they open up fields of speculation and so are useful and suggestive. For example, we have come to regard transcriptions, transpositions and so-called original versions as minor branches of any repertory, the first of them not always even quite respectable. And it is true that a full-dress organ prelude, a full-dress violin sonata and a full-dress harpsichord toccata look and sound like a totally distinct genre, abused when transcribed. But they were not entirely separate for Bach and his contemporaries, and on these grounds alone, the idea of *A Complete Edition of the Organ Works of Bach* is misleading. It could be that the *Schübler* are only the tip of an iceberg; that versions in two keys speak for many other examples now lost; and that when written out on five-line staves, early works originally notated in tablature lost their versatility of layout, manual-changing, registration, use or non-use of pedal, etc.

Knowledge of sources helps to suggest possibilities. Is the interesting D minor Prelude and Fugue BWV 539 the transcription of a violin or a lute piece or neither? Were either or both of these also transcriptions, and if so, of what? Is it possible that Bach, like Handel too perhaps, had one or two pieces in his 'portfolio of work in progress' which he could adapt to any instrument at hand? And would it therefore be a justified speculation to work out an organ version of the two other violin fugues (C major, A minor)? In the case of the transcribed *Schübler Chorales*, the least one could do on grasping how tenuous was Bach's connection with them, is to try some such arrangements of one's own: a question of finding suitable arias in three or four parts and laying them out on three staves. In principle, this is different from the kind of Romantic organ-arrangements we might feel happy to have left behind, for even in 200+ cantatas there are not many arias, I think, suitable for the treatment particular to *Schübler*. As to the question of three staves in early sources: even to know that the big pedal preludes and fugues were notated on two staves helps one to recognize that keyboard music does not always present a stark choice between pedal and no pedal. Conversely, open scores like the *Art of Fugue* and the *Ricercar à 6* from *Musical Offering* can easily become true organ-music.

I have wondered whether Bach's failing to give a title to the set of *Six Sonatas*, to *The Eighteen Chorales* (Seventeen? Fifteen?), the *Orgelbüchlein* at first (what was it to him before he gave it this title, matching the *Clavierbüchlein W F Bach*?), the *Art of Fugue* (a set of fugues for organ?), the *Advent & Christmas Fughettas* (a set of chorales for harpsichord?) and other potential sets, was more than a form of professional modesty. Why, probably, did he never assemble the big preludes and fugues into sets? Did he ever collect the concertos, and if so, for publication? Or intended to, making a set of six? Is omitting a title or titlepage much the same kind of thing as never giving registrations, except for *organo pleno* and *a 2 clav* and a few pitch-levels? Is never specifying whether or how to use two manuals in the big ritornello movements, unless there are hand-crossings (Dorian Toccata) or an echo (E flat Prelude), a sign that scores are 'blanks', to be filled in as circumstances suggest?

On the function: distinguishing between the music's very varied purposes and origins leads one to think of pieces differently according to whether they may have been intended for publication (the *Six*

Sonatas), or as studies in composition (the Passacaglia, the varied ritornello fugues), for practical support in the Lutheran service (*Neumeister Chorales?*), for liturgical contemplation (the longer chorales), for a personal agenda of pious self-instruction (the *Canonic Variations*, the Four Duets), for recitals or auditions of various kinds (several, perhaps most, major preludes or toccatas and fugues), and for an intricate combination of all of these (*Clavierübung III*). The listener may not hear much difference in even a knowledgeable player's approach to an early genre-imitation like the C major Praeludium BWV 531 and a mature work of complex number-ratios like the E minor Praeludium BWV 548. But the player will think of them differently and, being alerted to their respective position in the oeuvre as a whole, have different inner experiences of them, often quite private. Not everything has to be made explicit and shared with listeners, even if it could be.

In one's attempt to make as much use as possible of all the available knowledge today, there is another way to look at much of Bach's organ music, especially considering that the composer's duties at Leipzig did not include playing for services: that whatever the surface reasons why this or that work was composed, there is a private act being played out, an act of piety as so understood by an orthodox Lutheran. Your duty as a Lutheran is to return the talents God gave you as fully and with as much 'interest' as possible: you obey the Law joyfully, exploring and developing your gifts as fully as you can, working to create the best, taking no short cuts in doing your job to the best of your ability. Reasoning in this way, one can see that Bach would be at his most dutiful as a Believer precisely when writing his most complex music. Inverted augmented canons or Golden Mean complexities were not acts of everyday cleverness but acts of intense piety.

The aesthetics of our post-Beethoven age finds religious and other sentiments more powerful or striking when the music is sensually beautiful than when it is intellectually ingenious. One worships or expresses belief in higher things with the sheer beauty of 'O Mensch bewein' or 'Gelobet seist du' better than with the sheer cleverness of the big 'Vater unser' or 'Aus tiefer Not'. But I am not at all sure this was true for a Lutheran *director musices* knowing the scriptures and Luther's writings intimately, as he undoubtedly did.

The performance

Granted that for the moment the question is what we understand about Bach rather than what to do about day-to-day situations in which organists may find themselves, there is surely now, particularly since East Germany has been opened up, less and less difficulty in learning about the organs originally involved in his music.

For present purposes we need to start here, even while recognizing how limited this background may be in creating the 'ideal Bach sound' and the 'ideal Bach performance' many of us will have in our imaginations. For example, I look forward to the time when for recordings people will use several instruments which reflect the background and chronology of the Bach repertory as a whole, such as playing the *Orgelbüchlein* at a higher pitch than the later *Clavierübung III*, or finding an older or a less equal temperament for the early C major Praeludium BWV 531 than for the mature C major Praeludium BWV 547. Counsel of perfection in most cases, of course, but perfectly feasible in recordings. It is a question of distinguishing between different works by means of the different kinds of organ originally involved in them, and this seems to me no longer impossible or impractical. The differences are not merely those of period but of geography: an average Thuringian organ of 1750 (several exist in reliable form) may not have the colours and brilliance of earlier organs around Hamburg or Dresden but could well give a more realistic idea of how the *Orgelbüchlein* sounded in 1715. And if the sound is less enthralling (as it will be too on most organs any of us ever play), all the more interesting is the challenge to convey some of the spirit of these chorales!

Instruments govern the technical details of playing. If we could suppose ourselves at the keyboards of the Ducal Chapel in Weimar in 1715 playing, say, the A minor Concerto transcription of Vivaldi, we would surely have an 'older' technique (fingering, articulation) than if we were at the keyboard of Altenburg twenty-five years later, playing the E flat Prelude on *organo pleno*. On the Arnstadt organ in 1705, it is unlikely we would have used heels in those early hymn-like harmonizations; but when Wilhelm Friedemann played the great G major Praeludium BWV 541 as his audition piece at the Dresden Sophienkirche in 1733, it is more than likely that he did. Somewhere between these two

25

Example 1
The opening of the Praeludium in D major, BWV 532, and part of the opening pedal solo of the
Toccata in C major, BWV 564i

occasions – perhaps to play the opening pedal-scale in the startling D major Prelude, or for those exceptional little slurred motifs in the pedal-solo of the C major Toccata – Bach could well have developed heel-playing. Doubtless, toes-only on the right kind of pedalboard is possible for the music of Example 1. But the point of using heels, as when composers like Rameau advocated using all five fingers equally, would have been not merely to increase agility and improve technique but to develop a new taste in playing *legato* lines and slurring certain motifs – musical details not so appropriate to Bach's earlier works. In such cases, understanding both the instruments and the musical sources, both the physical attributes of one and chronology of the other, is now sufficiently in reach of thinking organists that they can soon become aware of the scope and stylistic variety of this music. One learns to see the repertory in terms of different kinds of organ and different kinds of playing technique: there may be little choice of either in one's daily circumstances, but that does not lessen the principle at stake.

Other points could be made about several playing techniques over the half century in question: they surely changed, and the idea that there is a single thing called 'early fingering' is no more plausible than that a mordent or an *appoggiatura* was always played in the same way irrespective of the type and date of the piece. The first half of the eighteenth century might well have seen as great a change in technical details of performance – organ-sound, temperament, registration, fingering, pedalling, articulation, ornamentation – as in any comparable period before or since. As the Bach chronology has become clearer and the sources of music (including the activity of particular copyists) better understood, so the idea of a single organ, a single playing technique and a single purpose for the music has receded.

Only superficially does the modern recital of Bach, in which the player intermingles the various kinds of music – a toccata, some short chorales, a sonata or concerto, some longer chorales, a big prelude and fugue to end – resemble anything that Bach himself is likely to have presented. For although it could well be, as often suggested, that *Clavierübung III* is a model organ-recital of the kind heard here and there, with its massive framework around a liturgically arranged set of chorale treatments, the pieces in it seem to have been composed at much the same time. There is no attempt to arrange in sequence works from different periods, as modern recitals almost always do. The plan of *Clavierübung III* is spiritual not secular: this is no mere organ-recital planned for passive, listening audiences such as they are today, all of us used to public concerts in which our attention might wander if there is not enough variety. *Clavierübung III*, perhaps like 'the Eighteen', is planned as a kind of pilgrimage of orthodox belief, not merely as an array of musical styles.

Many of the questions still unanswered by current research naturally attract various answers but cannot be regarded as solved. For example, I have become less and less convinced by the usual arguments against using two manuals in the bigger preludes and fugues. Can any of the information usually drawn from theorists of the time, or surmised from the absence of information in the copies, or derived from parallels made with other repertories, really prove that J S Bach and his pupils never took the option when available to play episodes in the big ritornello movements on a secondary manual? And were the scores then as sacrosanct as they are to us? Can we know for certain that organists would never have made certain little modifications in the scores as we have them, to enable changing manuals?

Continuity of the kind we assume now to be necessary might be quite a modern idea, unless the music consciously made a point of it, as it does in a *perpetuum mobile*. On the other hand, when echo-phrases are implicit or explicit (one finds them in the C major Toccata, the E flat major Prelude, and some verses in the Chorale Variations) this means neither that a second manual is necessary at this point nor that it is forbidden for any episodes elsewhere in the movement. The E flat major Prelude can be 'scored up' on three manuals, but the composer is not going to demand three manuals in a printed edition because few organists had such a thing. And besides, the point here is what is *optional* not what is *required*. I cannot believe that one did not optionally 'score up' the big works in relation to the organ at which one found oneself. This would be especially so in the big preludes, and perhaps any reluctance we now have to look similarly at fugues (despite the fact that they too are ritornello structures like the preludes) arises only because we have been taught that fugues are uniform constructions, as indeed they usually are in the *Well-tempered Clavier*. But the *WTC* is unique.

Not only the kind of organ affects the details of performance: so do the editions we use. It seems to me a strange decision of the *New Bach Edition*, and others in the same line, to group the free works in order of keys – C major, then C minor and so on. Why start at C major and not the traditional first key, D minor? Because of the *Well-tempered Clavier*? What has that to do with church organ music? Although keys may have certain characteristics preserved over the decades, the *NBA* order is notional rather than musical, and it takes great efforts of imagination and arduously acquired knowledge for a player now to apply different playing techniques (such as fingering and articulation) to adjacent works in the same volume. The early and late works in G major require quite different playing techniques, and only in a twentieth-century volume are they close to each other! Even numbering the dubious C minor Praeludium "BWV 549" and the earlier and genuine version in D minor "BWV 549a" affects some players' view of their relative authenticity. (Here, by the way, is an unusual case in which one's playing could show, by registration and subtle differences of articulation, that the two versions are probably separated by several decades.)

An important future project would be to produce an edition of Bach's organ works arranged in chronological order. Enough is now known for this to be possible in broad terms, and it would stimulate productive thought about the oeuvre as a whole. One needs more than a merely vague outline of chronology in one's mind to consider tricky questions like, How can one show that for J S Bach, C-time was probably slower in his youth than in his maturity? Or, Was the crotchet in 2/4 (the newest of the basic metres, used for the great 'Wir glauben') slower than in 4/4? (And why did he write C and not 4/4?) Or, Are *notes inégales* or unequal quavers ever appropriate, for example in the Weimar chorales in 3/4 time such as the sarabande settings BWV 652-654, produced at a time when the composer was particularly aware of French idioms? Or, Was the three-stave layout of the *Six Sonatas*, a layout usually found only in trio chorales, intended to allow Wilhelm Friedemann to visualize the lines independently? Their very sophisticated italianate chamber style requires the maximum 'counterpoint by articulation' between the three independent parts, all of them melodic in their way, all marked by characteristic motifs requiring distinctly slurred or *détaché* articulation as the case may be. The motivic detail is very carefully thought through and requires alert sensibility from the player.

Not only can the modern edition blur distinctions but there is a further hindrance for players of today: they are often seduced by fanciful ideas that a certain piece 'symbolizes' something, or 'expresses' some article of faith, or 'illustrates' some arithmetical or geometric complexity. These are common approaches to J S Bach, since he of all post-medieval composers seems to be asking for complex interpretation: a fanciful hermeneutic that sees a 'symbol' or an 'agenda' around every corner. And there certainly are many intricate instances of proportion or symmetry in his music, as in the Golden Mean structure of one cantata aria after another. However, even this simple numerical observation can never be truly scientific, for there will be no means of showing that its opposite is false. I think myself that an organist or choir director reacts instinctively to the Golden Mean by recognizing in a performance that 'something is happening' at the pivotal moment approximately two-thirds of the way through a movement – some special climax, convolution of counterpoint, special modulation, etc.

On the other hand, even when simple numbers can be supposed to have been in the mind of the composer, as in the number of pieces in *Clavierübung III* (27 = 3x3x3, an allusion to the Trinity or perhaps to the books of the New Testament?), this is hardly a practical matter. One might count the 27 as one plays or hears the volume complete, but there is no obvious way in which it influences performance or is otherwise reflected in it. But with other associations or supposed significances, there may well be a practical outcome: a performer playing the chorale BWV 668 is likely to be affected one way or another by knowing or not knowing the deathbed anecdote about it.

This 'final work' is a useful example of a common tendency to opt for mystical interpretation of Bach and, in the process, remove oneself farther from him by missing ascertainable, down-to-earth details. The author of a coquettishly named book, *Bach and the Dance of God*, says this about the Deathbed Chorale:

> At the end of his life, he made this other setting [of the melody], drawing on its title from another stanza of the hymn – Vor deinen Thron tret' ich ['Before your throne I stand']. Clearly he regarded the piece as a last testament which, his eyes failing, he dictated to a copyist from his sick-bed, if not at death's door. The autograph which appears in the same volume as the short score of the Canonic Variations, breaks off at the twenty-sixth bar.[9]

There is warmth here, but unfortunately it interferes with the facts: virtually every phrase in it is either speculative or wrong – even the last, for we do not know that it did break off at this point. A similarly fanciful approach appears in the same book in an account of another work, the B minor Fugue in the *Well-tempered Clavier* Book 1, part of whose uncanny quality arises from its simple episodes, shown here as Example 2. These episodes are called 'rather sensuously satisfying' (as they are) and 'no longer distraught' like the long subject (but is it?); they are 'ceremonial', and the gracious nobility of these 'bowing' figures [upper parts?] seems to sing of man's attempt at heroic resolution, which is recurrently undermined by memories of the lamenting fugue (p.245).

Example 2
Recurrent episode from the Fugue in B minor from The Well-tempered Clavier, *Book 1*

Though scholars might avert their eyes from such writing, many Bach-lovers would not. And why should they, when so many approaches fashionable today and taught in our universities – a graphic analysis of the fugue's twelve-note theme, a semiology of its motifs, some politically correct theory of music's narcotic function – are just as fanciful and much less charming?

But there are problems with it. In the first place, I doubt if more than simple association, hindsight coloured by familiarity with much later music, gives one the idea that this fugue is 'distraught' or 'lamenting'. B minor was serious, as organists playing the Praeludium BWV 544 know well, but labelling its effect as a 'lament' is unjustified. A yet more serious problem with programmatic interpretation – as would be the case too if one saw the organ Praeludium in these terms – is that all such approaches ignore what *is* verifiable about the piece. For example, these fugal episodes in the last Example are conventional: one had appeared already in its Prelude (bar 24), and there are others in Example 3, including a well-known organ-piece of Bach. So are these too signs of heroic resolution? If not, why not?

Example 3(a)
Recurrent episode from Domenico Scarlatti's Fugue in D minor Kk 417

Example 3(b)
Recurrent episode from the Fugue in G minor, BWV 542ii

A second 'warm' writer to discuss the Deathbed Chorale responds feelingly to it as a last musical testament:

> *Gleichmäßig pochende Achtel durchziehen das ganze Stück vom Anfang bis zum Schluß – als wollte es nicht enden. Dieses gleichmäßige Pochen ist wie ein Habhaftwerden der Zeit. Die unaufhörliche Wiederkehr, dieses Merkmal der Zeit, wird hier 'verauschaulickt'.*[10]
> "Uniformly beating quavers interlace the whole piece from beginning to end, as if it wanted not to stop. This uniform beating is like the catching hold of time. The incessant returning, this distinctive feature of time, is here made manifest".

Music as an event in time is nicely implied here, but why Georgiades takes this particular music and exaggerates its ticking quavers – in fact they are not actually unbroken – must be its Deathbed associations. Would he speak of its 'epic demeanour' *(epische Haltung)* otherwise? There are centuries of German *Geist* behind such notions. In 1754, a version of the same organ piece was already cited to prove that there was such a thing as Soul and to confound the 'champions of materialism'.[11] And in 1990, an American aesthetician used it to examine 'profundity' in music, unwisely relying on Schweitzer for biographical details.[12]

Understandably, associations lead to attitudes. Would the first author have made Virgilian allusions to the B minor Fugue's episodes had he not assumed B minor to be its original key and thus saw similarities between its theme and the first Kyrie of the *B minor Mass*? Alas, the Fugue was not composed in B minor but (probably) G or A minor. When another modern writer claims that the *Deathbed Chorale* contains within itself strong evidence of Bach's belief in God, and calls this an aspect of the piece more important than its objective function or musical expression,[13] he too is warmly speculating. Though entitled to speculate, one ought then to answer such a question as, Why in that case would a dying composer evince 'belief in God' with a piece whose version here is actually more archaic than one composed much earlier? (The version in the *Orgelbüchlein*, 'Wenn wir in höchsten Nöthen sein', BWV 641, succinct, modern.) Doubtless an answer could be contrived, but the question cannot be ignored.

While 'warmth' in writing about music makes a good impression, it can deflect from the music itself, neglecting details that are truer if more mundane than a composer's supposed dying thoughts. In this case, though 'free of the conditions of speech', as Georgiades puts it – i.e. played not sung, an organ piece not a hymn – the *Deathbed Chorale* looks very much like an actual model of how a four-part hymn was performed at the time in the church service: the melody is in long notes (thus as sung by the congregation, taking gaps between the lines), with introductory bars, interludes and postlude, all in the customary manner of organ accompaniment. It presents an invaluable *record* of the conventions of chorale-singing at the time, so true to its type that in certain details it is rather similar to other Bach organ chorales that have no special association. Compare its closing bars, for instance, with those of another chorale, 'Aus tiefer Not' from *Clavierübung III*, BWV 687, which in principle has the same shape and conception.

In the German quotation above, fancy is also outpacing fact when it couples the idea of a *continuum* (constant quavers producing a continuous flow of music) with the *basso continuo* (the 'underlying harmony centered on the bass'), although I think neither has much to do with the other, here or in any other piece. The author is allowing a pun to imply a significant relationship, attractive but unjustified. The winsome idea of quavers 'catching hold of time' arises in the chorale's associations (death = mutability = time), and if the author had had this idea from hearing a slow, subdued performance of the chorale, it would only mean that the performer was conjecturing along similar lines. Organists too speculate on the puzzling expressiveness of great music, but no more than a writer's words would their playing 'prove' that this chorale was composed on a deathbed. To study this piece's history and technique is inevitably to regard it more neutrally, and in general, it seems that the fanciful and the factual tend to demote each other.

Despite all this, writing such as Georgiades's does express great warmth, and his phrase 'great music, full of meaning' is impossible to take exception to. Music's significances may be difficult to formulate, but not looking for them seems hardly a useful alternative.

Coda

Reading what is written here might lead one to say 'No: we are very little closer to understanding Bach', but I think that would not be right. Learning is asking, not answering; to learn to ask the right question requires study and a reluctance to rush to judgment. The more one knows these works and the factors involved (their source, chronology, function, organ-type and the givens of their performance), the more interesting the questions about them become and – or so I personally find – the less insistent or pressing becomes the need to answer them. The study is ongoing, every performance a novelty. What is instructive is the discussion, and discussion is not always helped by answers: they can close it off, not open it. After all, not a few questions one might have could not have been answered by Bach himself.

References

[1] C L Hilgenfeldt, *Johann Sebastian Bach's Leben, Wirken und Werke* (Leipzig, 1850), p 50. Carl Heinrich Bitter, *Johann Sebastian Bach*, vol. IV (Berlin, 2/1881), pp 48-52.

[2] Translation in ed. Hans T David & Arthur Mendel, rev. C Wolff, *The New Bach Reader* (New York/London, 1998), p 307. Of course, like many an organist today, Bach and/or his *Obituary* writers may have had particular (political) reasons for saying such things.

[3] St Thomas, Leipzig, has a disorientation, so *west* and *north* here are liturgical not topographical terms.

[4] *Orgelbewegung* ('organ movement') is a shorter form of the original *deutsche Orgel-Erneuerungsbewegung* ('German movement for organ-renewal'), where the terms had nationalist associations. There were other political 'movements' of the time, and *die Bewegung* was the title of a Nazi newspaper. See my essay 'The idea of Bewegung in the German organ reform movement', in ed. B Gilliam, *Music and Performance during the Weimar Republic* (Cambridge, 1994), pp 135-153 and 208-214.

[5] As I write, the fullest account of the project so far seems to be Ullrich Böhme's informal article 'Thomasorganist und Thomasorgeln', in *Musik und Kirche* 69 (1999), pp 231-239.

[6] For this report and comments on it, see my *The Organ Music of J. S. Bach*, vol. 3 (Cambridge, 1984), pp 149-53.

[7] John Snetzler, who began work in England during the years of Bach's maturest organ music, brought what was originally an overblowing rank of the new, colourful kind: the Dulciana.

[8] That the early organ works of Bach could often be recognized for a certain 'youthful fire' in them was already recognized in Hermann Keller, *Die Orgelwerke Bach* (Leipzig, 1948), for example on p49, quoting Spitta's biography.

[9] Wilfrid Mellers, *Bach and the Dance of God* (London, 1980), p298

[10] Thrasybulos Georgios Georgiades, *Nennen und Erklingen: die Zeit als Logos* (Göttingen, 1985), p92

[11] Hans-Joachim Schulze, *Dokumente zum Nachwirken Johann Sebastian Bachs, 1750-1800* (Leipzig, 1972), p73

[12] Peter Kivy, *Music Alone. Philosophical Reflections on the purely Musical Experience* (Ithaca NY, 1990)

[13] Hans Heinrich Eggebrecht, *J S Bach's The Art of Fugue. The Work and its Interpretation*, trans. J L Prater (Ames IA, 1993), p34

The historical performance movement; Bach and the organ in 2000

by
John Butt

The last major commemoration of the year of Bach's death in 1950 occasioned two diametrically opposed opinions on Bach and the way his music should be performed. On the one hand, the composer, performer and early-music specialist, Paul Hindemith advocated the wholesale restoration of the instruments and performing practices of Bach's own age: 'We can be sure that Bach was thoroughly content with the means of expression at hand in voices and instruments, and if we want to perform his music according to his intentions we ought to restore the conditions of performance of that time. Using the harpsichord as continuo instrument would not be the only step in this direction. Other kinds of strings would have to be used on our stringed instruments. The wind instruments must be built like their predecessors in size and sound. Even the distinction between choral pitch and chamber pitch should be restored.'[1] On the other hand, the philosopher and music critic Theodor W Adorno poured scorn on historical reconstruction: only the 'improved' modern performance resources could reveal the full import of Bach's music which stood head and shoulders above the pitiful concerns of its own age.

Speaking at a time when the early-music movement was still in its infancy, but when western Germany was undergoing an enormous process of rebuilding and restoration he suggests that 'the neo-religious Bach is impoverished, reduced and stripped of the specific musical content which was the basis of his prestige. He suffers the very fate which his fervent protectors are least willing to admit: he is changed into a neutralized cultural monument, in which aesthetic success mingles obscurely with a truth that has lost its intrinsic substance. They have made him into a composer for organ festivals in well-preserved Baroque towns, into ideology.'[2] Adorno's specific comments about 'historical' performance and, particularly, the Baroque organ sound very much like the types of criticism that have become familiar over the last few decades: 'Mechanically squeaking *continuo*-instruments and wretched school choirs contribute not to sacred sobriety but to malicious failure; and the thought that the shrill and rasping Baroque organs are capable of capturing the long waves of the lapidary, large fugues is pure superstition. Bach's music is separated from the general level of his age by an astronomical distance. Its eloquence returns only when it is liberated from the sphere of resentment and obscurantism, the triumph of the subjectless over subjectivism. They say Bach, mean Telemann and are secretly in agreement with the regression of musical consciousness which even without them remains a constant threat under the pressure of the culture industry.'[3]

Whatever we might think of Adorno's views, he does raise some important questions, taking the debate well beyond the somewhat simplistic antiquarianism of Hindemith. An emphasis on historical correctness – which so often replaces the subjective with the objective – can indeed lead us away from a deeper concern with music's relevance and spiritual content (whatever that may be); on the other hand, this view presupposes that great music is always – and unequivocally – independent of performance and its medium, a view that takes us away from music's traditional and essential embodiment in actual sound and towards a neo-platonist conception of music that is perhaps more ideally seen on paper than heard.

Purists of historical performance sometimes veer towards another type of absolutism: if you haven't heard the music on the right instruments with the right performance practice, then you haven't actually heard it at all – changing the modes of performance is as bad as changing the notes and the correct performance is actually part of the definition of the work concerned. But this view is surely belied by the simple fact that Bach has been highly appreciated through the 'wrong' sort of performance, indeed that his reputation was created in the nineteenth century (with a degree of fanaticism that is not necessarily so evident today) with very little regard for the original performing conditions.

Nevertheless, many people claim today that hearing a restoration of the original performance and instruments comes as a revelation, that they hear things in the music and a certain spirit that they could not have known of before. One simple truth might be that the emphasis on historical performance results in a greater depth of knowledge, a greater saturation in the style than was hitherto the case, and, in the hands of performers who are already talented, this must often have some beneficial effect on the performance. But there is also the niggling notion that we like historical performance because we think we ought to. It seems clear to me that the early-music movement corresponds almost exactly with the wider 'heritage industry'; the idea that we should faithfully preserve what we receive from the past – almost indiscriminately – and that everything should be recycled, given that resources are dwindling and that the wheel of fashion moves ever faster. The standard negative judgement on all this is that we've lost confidence in progress and development, that the modern world has rendered us derivative and unoriginal, that there's nowhere to go except backwards. A more positive view might be that our interest in heritage reflects the very triumph and consequences of modernity: having (at least in the West) virtually all the technology we can possibly need we've reached a certain threshold of progress; the amount of industry we have is already damaging the environment and our ability to replace entire cityscapes within a week or two renders us strangely disorientated. Travel, electronic communication and the vertiginous mutability facilitated by a full capitalist economy start to efface our sense of time, history and our own rootedness; we begin to lose the feeling of own origins and cultural identity. A concern for history, preservation and restoration might thus enable us to recapture some of that security. And, in an interesting twist, it is the very advance in technology that allows us to undertake restoration projects with such precision. In the musical world, this includes the forensic advances in manuscript study, the tremendous progress in instrument building (particularly the analysis and reproduction of historical models) and – most important of all – the developments in recording technology that create a market for all kinds of music on an unprecedented scale. Moreover, many early instruments and types of ensemble that were never designed with the modern concert hall in mind, frankly enjoy a much greater advantage on CD than in actual performance.

The last 50 years have, of course, seen an incredible development in the restoration of historical performance – probably far beyond what Hindemith hoped for or Adorno feared. Certainly, Adorno's belief that historical fidelity could lead to lifeless literalistic interpretations has been confirmed by some styles of performance in recent years, but he would surely have been impressed by some of the traditions and individuals who have been inspired by historical reflection. If it is true that the historical organs and harpsichords lack the dynamic capabilities of the modern piano, many players have developed other aspects of expression and interpretation to a degree that would not otherwise have been conceivable. An emphasis on an infinitely graduated system of articulation, together with agogic accentuation clearly enforces a greater attention to certain aspects of the music than would be the case where dynamic shaping comes as second nature. In other words, the very limitations of the earlier instruments engender a greater refinement of other aspects of performance, just as blind people often develop more acute hearing, the deaf a better sight. Indeed, one essential aspect of Bach's own compositional success was his ability to work with the limitations of the age (both in terms of performance resources and actual musical style); had he had the same range of historical and stylistic resources that are available today he may not have been inspired to write music of such depth and intensity. Adorno may be right to suggest that 'Bach's music is separated from the general level of his age by an astronomical distance', but it is surely also the case that he achieved this within and not without the possibilities of the age. Indeed, this historical consideration might render his music even more remarkable than if we view it as the project of abstract genius that effortlessly travels from one age to another.

If this argument for historic instruments is so far plausible in a negative sense – that the limitations of the instruments encourage us to think again and more deeply about how to perform – there are surely positive benefits as well. Certain types of music might be so closely designed for the instruments that they actually seem to become better pieces of music when restored to the original medium: French Baroque organ music is an obvious case in point and Italian and Iberian music – that may sometimes look unadventurous on paper – often comes alive with unequal temperament and the timbres specific to the instruments of the age. Bach is an interesting case, given that his music does indeed seem able to transfer from one performance medium to another; virtually no other composer survives such 'punishment' – provided the notes are more or less right, at least something seems to come across in performance. There is thus a dichotomy, or at least an irony, in the fact that while aesthetic respect for Bach can lead to a fanatical concern for historical accuracy in performance, his music – of all 'early music' – may seem the least to be affected by the choices of performance. Does this then reinforce the view that historical performance is only for the lesser composers (even if we were to agree with the notion that all his contemporaries were lesser, for the sake of argument)? Not necessarily: many of the instrument makers of his age were also artists of the highest calibre and, like him, learned to push the existing technology to its very limits. Organs were often built with astonishing care (some builders moving their entire workshop to the church concerned in order to ensure an absolute match for the acoustical environment) and, as Christoph Wolff's new biography of Bach makes clear, Bach himself had an extremely detailed knowledge of organ building and concerned himself with every aspect of the art until his dying days. Organ pipes were usually voiced to mimic specifically human qualities with great attention to the consonants and vowels of a pipe's speech; moreover, voicing over the entire compass took into account not only the acoustics of the building but also the peculiarities of average human hearing.

Nonetheless, might it not still be the case that all this is basically irrelevant to the overall quality of Bach's music? Much might depend on how one assessed this quality. If the music is viewed simply as an excellent finished product, then the instrumental context may indeed be irrelevant. But if instead (or in addition) we see this music as issuing from a complex compositional process deeply informed by Bach's personal experience, the original performing environment becomes rather more important. Perhaps the very medium of performance was part of the cause and intentional process of the composition; simply put, with different instruments Bach might have written different music. Certainly our knowledge of this creative process and the infinite give and take between composer and medium can only be conjectural, but it does allow us to view the music in a more harmonised way. Bach and his work become the product of a real human situation in which he had to react to whatever was before him. Thus an interest in historical performance should perhaps be directed somewhat away from the issue of a composer's precise intentions and instructions (which after all might change with time and environment) and more towards how the music came to be composed in the first place. Indeed, in repertories where the performer's improvisational interaction with the composer was crucial (e.g. Baroque opera and virtuoso instrumental music) the music might be entirely misunderstood if viewed as abstract composition. Admittedly, in Bach's case the music is so strong as abstract composition that this is often a happy misunderstanding, but there is still a sense in which he has even more to offer if we put ourselves into his shoes.

Bach was, after all, valued more highly as a performer than composer during his own lifetime and it is unlikely that he ever composed entirely divorced from the consciousness of performance and the necessary position of the listener that this inevitably entailed. There is much within Bach's own training and career to suggest that he was primarily a practical musician, one who composed (and of course improvised) from the perspective of performance. This is evident from his view – borrowed from Niedt – of figured bass as the fundament of music; thus performance and composition are by no means mutually exclusive. If it is valid to associate the German music of Bach's age with the practice and function of rhetoric, it would follow that he who is responsible for the invention, disposition and elaboration of an oration is equally responsible for its delivery as a persuasive performance. In the Lutheran tradition the principal role of music was to deliver a verbal text and effectively drive home its implications for the listener.

While there is much evidence that Baroque composers notated their compositions in the knowledge that good performers would continue the compositional process with spontaneous elaboration, it is my contention – and indeed that of Johann Adolph Scheibe (Bach's sternest contemporary critic) – that Bach included more of this so-called inessential ornamentation in his notation than virtually any other contemporary. However this apparently 'inessential' elaboration is often crucial to the elaboration of the basic musical 'invention'; indeed the line between musical idea and its elaboration and decoration is miraculously difficult to draw in the case of Bach's music. This is undoubtedly one of the factors which makes his music so durable and attractive to cultures which lay a premium on structural coherence and unity. It is also something which links the formal perspective of Bach with the rhetorical. A musical idea is reinforced, made more persuasive by the addition of musical ornaments, just as a verbal idea is strengthened by figures of speech. In Bach's case, it could be argued, his performing intentions are inescapable in any performance whatsoever. Any accurate performance at any time since Bach first notated the music is to some extent an historical performance; Bach, the performer and interpreter, is still 'alive' within the notation itself. Of course, we can never know how Bach and his colleagues actually performed, but it is fruitful (even 'authentic') to believe in one of the many performances that the notation might imply, rather than merely to regard the music as a fixed, eternal structure.

While it is impossible to determine whether the new forms of expression and insight facilitated by historical study have anything to do with what the original performers, builders and audiences experienced, there is no doubt that they can be genuine and authentic for us today, experiences which have value for their immediacy and inspiration. Nevertheless this line of thought also implies that such immediacy may soon wear thin – the novelty of the newly-discovered historical methods will, in the course of time, doubtless become ossified and commonplace. Here then, it is important that we come to terms with history as an ever-changing process: new factual discoveries subtly change our larger conceptions of the art of music and these changes of conception, in turn, inform us of new directions in which to research; moreover, our ideas as to which data and facts are important will themselves also change. Coupled with this internal circle of knowledge and experience are the external factors of our present time: changes in the conception and function of music, attitudes towards art, society and religion.

It soon becomes apparent that only certain historical elements are acceptable and useful in current practice. Moreover, however accurate our knowledge and precise our reconstructions, we can never experience directly the religious and cultural context of earlier ages. It is all very well to believe that a Bach chorale prelude creates edification and plumbs spiritual depths within the context of a modern religious service, but, on the other hand, the religious outlook of Bach's age could be almost detrimental to the case that his music should be preserved and used today. With belief in God came the belief in the intermediate authority of the aristocracy (semi-gods walking on earth, as it were), belief in certain forms of magic, mysticism and witchcraft. Nor was Bach's age one of religious uniformity and stability; while he almost certainly belonged to the orthodox, pre-Enlightenment establishment this can only superficially be related to the more formal of the systems of worship available today.

Thus there is no hard and fast rule as to which are the useable facts in matters of musical interpretation. If we are concerned only with the 'purely musical' factors – instrumental specifications, which finger to use where, for which trill – we are in danger of becoming sterile antiquarians. On the other hand, if we take too many of the wider historical factors into account – such as burning witches every time we perform Scheidt's *Tablatura nova*, in order to give some flavour of the age – our efforts will soon be thwarted by tiresome modern legalistic and moral conventions. Again, history is only of use if we keep alive our critical faculties, measuring traces of the past against our conception of the present and hopes for the future. History is a means towards modern musical experience, never the essence of that experience itself.

One of the great benefits – or curses – of our own age is that we exercise some degree of choice as to how we use and understand music of the past. If we seek music that represents unity and cohesion (certainly not foreign to Bach's own musical outlook), we may privilege those factors that add cohesion to the composition, those elements which, in performance, both interpret and add another layer to the structural edifice. If, on the other hand, we wish to experience again something of the impact of Bach's music as it was used in the society of his time, we might privilege the rhetorical implications, the various figures and devices within the music and their concomitant delineation in performance. Here we may be looking for a 'rough and ready' performance style which might seem diametrically opposed to the more refined styles of 'historical' performance today. Perhaps an even more desirable approach for us in our pluralistic age is to unite the structurally integrated style with the rhetorical, even to construct bridges, syntheses or 'productive conflicts' between them.

I was recently privileged to take part in a panel discussion on Bach and the organ with Peter Hurford and Peter Williams at the Cathedral Organists' 2000 Conference in Oxford. Much of the discussion centred on questions that have become quite commonplace in considerations of Bach interpretation. How should the dotting problems in the Eb Prelude, BWV 552 be handled? How much should one vary registration, especially in places marked *organo pleno?* But what was striking about the three panelists was that none of us was content to give hard and fast answers, however prescriptive we may have been in the past. Not only were we sceptical of whether we could be certain about any aspects of performance practice in Bach's time but we were also agreed that all historical information should be viewed critically and placed alongside other factors of our own performance culture. As Peter Hurford said, with the hindsight of his long and distinguished performing career, there is no point in sticking rigidly to a historical hypothesis (e.g. that the *Passacaglia* was played full organ without any respite) if this drove away the audience. After all, Bach and his contemporaries were just as – if not more – concerned with their audience as we are, given the role of music for preaching and edification; sometimes we might need to adjust the letter of practice in order to translate the original spirit into modern terms. Peter Williams, perhaps someone who has thought longest about Bach's organ works and their performance, stated that the more he had come to know, the more questions – rather than answers – he has found himself posing. Delegates expecting (or dreading) hard and fast answers to issues of Bach performance found that all we could suggest were further questions and even self-interrogation as to why we should want to know such things in the first place. A pessimist might suggest that we had lost confidence in how to interpret Bach using historical evidence, but an optimist might rather infer – as I do here – that the historical performance movement has come of age, and that historical inquiry opens up not only an infinite chain of questions but also possibilities of new forms of interpretation and expression. Moreover, our growing awareness of the basic cultural difference between our age and Bach's leads us to focus much more on our own motives and cultural preconceptions.

One final thought struck me about the conference: the host of British cathedral organists, all working extremely hard at what is often a daily grind of choral services, are virtually unique in the modern world in their maintaining of a tradition of pre-aesthetic music. In other words, a music that is performed to as high a standard as possible but in the service of an institution other than concert life and distinct from music as a form of entertainment or commodified culture (much as commodification might happen nowadays to support the choral foundations, in the form of popular CDs and broadcasts). The Anglican tradition is virtually the only throwback we have that parallels the way music must have functioned in Bach's time – something pursued in great thoroughness and excellence but seldom listened to for its own sake, something relating to larger religious and cultural traditions and something believed to have a form of religious significance in its own right. The very lack of a studied performance practice in the cathedral tradition must parallel Bach's own spontaneous approach to composition and performance: organs and choirs perform the job at hand rather than conforming to a specific historical or aesthetic ideal. Of course, cathedral organists should take on board any academic findings, historical discoveries and learn from the restoration and reconstruction of Baroque instruments, but only as a way of augmenting the incredible heritage that they have already inherited, as a way of developing and clarifying what they have been brought up to do. The chimera of a supposed 'musicological correctness' can only kill the tradition stone dead.

And finally, back to Bach 250 years after his death – how is he to be seen, heard and evaluated at the outset of the new century? Although most of us who work with Bach's music must share something of Adorno's view that this music possesses incomparable and timeless qualities, such an absolute view is increasingly difficult to hold of any composer within the increasingly broadening culture of music today. We will have to allow that Bach cannot hold as central or crucial a position in western culture as he did 50 years ago, however much we may wish this were not the case. Perhaps, on the other hand, it is surprising how well his music still works in an environment where virtually any music from the past is resurrected to enjoy equal democratic rights with that which has formed a pinnacle of the western canon. The historical performance movement is itself also part of a wider tendency for the styles of performance to splinter and multiply, and Bach, of all composers, seems to suffer the least for this. Indeed, now the concept of Bach on 'modern' instruments, particularly the piano, is itself enjoying a healthy revival. Despite the levelling dangers of plurality, the far more fluid and flexible ways of viewing and judging music today do allow us to replenish our appreciation of Bach in a manner that was perhaps not so possible at the last anniversary in 1950.

References

[1]   Paul Hindemith, *Johann Sebastian Bach* – a speech delivered on September 12, 1950 at the Bach commemoration of the city of Hamburg, Germany (New Haven, 1952), pp 16-19.
[2]   Theodor W Adorno, 'Bach defended against his devotees', *Prisms*, translated Samuel and Shierry Weber (Cambridge, Mass, 1981), p136.
[3]   *Ibid*, 145.

The Best of the Bunch
A personal view of some twentieth century landmarks

by
Stephen Bicknell

The chamber organ in the chapel of Frederiksborg Castle in Copenhagen is nearing the end of its fourth century of life. It is a remarkable tribute to the endless possibilities of organ building. Like a Fabergé egg in its intricacy and perfection, it marks the close of the career of the organ builder Esaias Compenius, friend of Michael Praetorius, and the probable collaborator in the *De Organographia* section of Praetorius's *Syntagma Musicum.* Its pipes – flues and reeds alike – are entirely of wood. It is not at all a typical organ of the early seventeenth century, but a one-off, a marvellous work of art in the form of a musical instrument. Its sound recalls three words used by Praetorius himself to describe the tonal novelties of his day: *frembder, sanffter, subtiler* (ætherial, subdued and subtle).

When an organ of such obvious quality and with such a remarkable pedigree survives unaltered down the ages, it is an easy matter to identify its maker as a great artist. There is a roll call of such organ builders whose names come to mind easily. From Hamburg Arp Schnitger and his son Frans Caspar; in Saxony Gottfried Silbermann, and in Alsace his brother Andreas and nephew Johann Andreas; from Paris the Clicquots, culminating in the great works of François-Henri Clicquot at the eve of the Revolution; in catholic southern Germany the masters of rococo organ building, Gabler, Riepp and Holzhay; in the nineteenth century the unmistakably pre-eminent Aristide Cavaillé-Coll.

Assessing whether the twentieth century has any names to add to this list is not such an easy task Recent history is so much more difficult to judge – which of us can tell whether an artist alive today is actually important to the plot of history or is just transiently interesting? The twentieth century was scarred by social, technical and economic upheaval. The world wars and a great depression changed the entire outlook of western culture.

Organ building entered the twentieth century in industrial guise, happy to wear the clothing of ingenuity and progress; it leaves the century in the humbler weeds of dedicated craftsmen breathing new life into an ancient tradition.

It has been too easy for those writing in the second half of the twentieth century to write off the achievements of the first half. Commentators on a whole range of subjects felt the need to distance themselves from the excesses of the late nineteenth century and from a generation who still believed that war was good sport. In our own field Norbert Dufourc and Peter Williams were amongst many commentators doubting the value of nineteenth century developments in organ building; Cecil Clutton and Ralph Downes could not quite be persuaded to join in the condemnation of things Victorian, but agreed in their dislike of everything Edwardian!

It is unfair to try and paint a picture of the early twentieth century using only a palette devised to suit a later taste. The landscape is rich and complex, and even in the great turmoil caused by the first World War and its aftermath, there was work of integrity and artistic quality to be found.

In Britain we look to the great works of Arthur and Harry Harrison as the first of the twentieth century landmarks. The extent to which their organs defined the expectations of an entire generation is beyond doubt. What is perhaps less obvious is the personal trouble they took to ensure consistent musical and technical quality across their entire output. In the period around 1900 there was a choice of methods to be adopted. Organs could be voiced entirely in the factory and then only regulated for power on site. If carried out with skill and care this method could be both commercially astute and musically sound – the great exponent of the 'fast' method was the house of Willis. The practice of Lewis represented the opposite pole, where stops in theory far less sociable and more risky (bold flue choruses, comparatively unstable low pressure reeds) were coaxed lovingly into a musically convincing result during long periods of balancing and finishing on site. Harrison & Harrison sought perfection, and the complementary skills of the two brothers brought finality respectively to splendidly efficient and durable mechanisms and to the painstaking on-site finishing of their instruments.

The Harrison recipe was based on a craft workshop, modest in size by the standards of the day, where the contribution of the individual was recognised and encouraged. There is evidence that the same level of artistic quality could be maintained in a more factory-like environment, and alongside the Harrisons I would cite the best work of Norman & Beard of Norwich in the period 1904 – 1916 as reaching a standard of excellence rarely encountered. This choice may come as a surprise: the Norwich works was on an impressive scale with space for three hundred men and its own railway siding; Herbert Norman formed an alliance with the maverick Robert Hope-Jones in 1902 and absorbed more influence from him than any other British builder; organs were turned out by the hundred and the pace of production alone would suggest that quality must have suffered.

Not so; though there was a long and complex chain of command between Herbert Norman and the teams of draughtsmen, voicers, organbuilders and site finishers, there was equally a well-defined system in place that ensured personal control of the final result and of every detail. This is revealed in organs of all sizes. The bread- and-butter organs, little tracker instruments for country churches, are not stock organs built to standard designs. They are all different from each other. Many survive in East Anglia, and they reveal the entire range of possibilities made possible by the intelligent use of a team of draughtsmen. Unusual configurations abound; each one is carefully tailored to its site, however awkward, and the need for compact layout is elegantly combined with good access. The mechanical actions are built to a high standard – Norman & Beard laid special stress on making their tracker organs easy and comfortable to play, at a time when most builders had eyes only for the convenient new tubular mechanisms.

In their larger flagship instruments, especially those for concert halls, Norman & Beard developed an advanced orchestral style and sophisticated pneumatic and electro-pneumatic mechanisms to go with it. Their masterpiece was the last organ built at the Norwich works, the giant four-manual for Johannesburg Town Hall. Completed in 1916 to a design by Alfred Hollins, this all-pneumatic instrument included no fewer than six manual departments, one being a floating Bombarde Organ with high pressure reeds and a grand Sesquialtera VI. It was tragically lost to view in a comprehensive rebuild in the 1970s. Very few of the larger Norman & Beard organs survive – in the neo-classical period they were unjustly despised and suffered untold indignities of alteration and replacement. Two notable exceptions are the magnificent four-manual of 1906 at Wellington Town Hall in New Zealand (demonstrated brilliantly by Christopher Herrick on a CD in his *Organ Fireworks* series) and the even more splendid instrument of 1912 in the Usher Hall, Edinburgh, silent for many years but now to be sympathetically restored. Like the organs of Harrison & Harrison, these instruments were most carefully finished on site. Though Herbert Norman could not possibly attend every installation himself, his detailed command structure meant that his skilled voicer-finishers were left in no doubt as to the extent of the responsibility they carried, and the results are beyond compare.

Wellington Town Hall, New Zealand; Norman & Beard 1906

Great Organ		Swell Organ		Choir Organ (enclosed)	
Double Open Diapason	16	Bourdon	16	Quintaton	8
Large Open Diapason	8	Diaphonic Diapason	8	Violoncello	8
Medium Open Diapason	8	Geigen Diapason	8	Echo Dulciana	8
Small Open Diapason	8	Rohr Flute	8	Viol d'Orchestre	8
Hohl Flute	8	Salicional	8	Voix celeste	8
Corno Flute	8	Unda Maris	8	Flauto Traverso	4
Principal	4	Principal	4	Zauber flute	4
Harmonic Flute	4	Lieblich Flute	4	Harmonic Piccolo	2
Twelfth	2⅔	Fifteenth	2	Schalmei	16
Fifteenth	2	Mixture	III	Orchestral Clarinet	8
Mixture	III	Contra Posaune	16	Orchestral Oboe	8
Trombone	16	Horn	8		
Tromba	8	Oboe	8	**Solo Organ (unenclosed)**	
Harmonic Clarion	4	Vox Humana	8	Harmonic Claribel	8
		Harmonic Clarion	4	Concert Flute	4

Bombard	16	Open Diapason Metal	(ext)	16	Contra Posaune	32
Tuba Mirabilis	8	Violone		16	Trombone (ext)	16
Tuba Clarion	4	Bourdon		16	Trumpet (ext)	8
		Echo Bass	(Sw)	16		
Pedal Organ		Octave Diapason	(ext)	8	Pneumatic action throughout	
Double Open Diapason	32	Principal	(ext)	8		
Open Diapason Wood	16	Flute Bass	(ext)	8		

If we admit that artistic excellence may have been compatible with the most advanced technical methods, then it seems only right to include the American builder E M Skinner among the century's great figures. I am not sure that many British players and listeners really understand how special a builder Skinner was. On this side of the Atlantic, news of his work came only though articles in the organ journals, and much of the description was coloured by the highly opinionated and dismissive views of Henry Willis III, who considered Skinner's tonal outlook to be overdependent on the ideas of Hope-Jones and lacking in 'ensemble' voices – the combination of loud mixtures and Willis-type chorus reeds that could be heard at Liverpool Anglican Cathedral and at Westminster Catholic Cathedral by the 1920s at least.

Skinner's reeds may have been less potent than those of Willis, and his schemes may have been balanced far more in favour of families of orchestral and imitative voices rendered expressive by total enclosure, but this was all in order to express a vision of tonal flexibility that remains captivatingly sophisticated and magical even after two generations of Organ Reform. In a Willis organ – indeed in most English instruments of the early twentieth century – the build-up from piano to fortissimo is handled by one route: the diapasons, upperwork and reeds of the Swell and Great organs are gradually brought together to provide a major crescendo. String stops, and the entire Choir and Solo organs are left out of the picture somewhat. In a Skinner organ the build-up can be accomplished via any one of a number of distinct tonal paths. One can start with strings alone, and add to the string tone at various levels of power until the larger ensembles appear only at the forte level – the decrescendo can then be made via the flutes. The flutes can then make an imperceptible metamorphosis to Oboe and then French Horn tone, before a crescendo is made to the Trombas and Tubas – and then back by any route one chooses whether to a soft diapason, Clarinet, Vox Humana or whatever. To make this system work there are compromises: to English ears the trebles and upperwork are rather underpowered and lacking in melodic strength, but this encourages the expressive use of the multiple swell boxes and makes the octave couplers more sociable in a wider range of combinations – including the tutti.

In Skinner's instruments the immense tonal flexibility is made available through mechanisms of unparalleled technical excellence and reliability. I am an admirer of good tracker organs, but that does not stop me from recognising that the speed, silence and repetition available from the Skinner chests (Pitman-type sliderless soundboards) is without compare, and that the development of an all-electric console with fully adjustable general and departmental pistons was an accomplished fact in the 1920s, when English companies were still struggling with the very concept of electricity. This may not entirely fit our view of organs today, but it is great stuff nevertheless. A magnificent unaltered survivor from Skinner's late period is opus 820 of 1931, at the Cathedral of the Holy Rosary, Toledo, Ohio.

Cathedral of the Holy Rosary, Toledo, Ohio, USA; E M Skinner, 1931

Great Organ				**Swell Organ (enclosed)**	
Double Diapason	16	Twelfth	$2\frac{2}{3}$	Melodia	16
First Diapason	8	Fifteenth	2	Diapason	8
Second Diapason	8	Chorus Mixture	IV	Salicional	8
Third Diapason	8	Harmonics	IV	Voix celeste	8
Viola*	8	Trumpet	16	Rohrflote	8
Harmonic Flute	8	Tromba	8	Flute Celeste II	8
Gedeckt*	8	Clarion	4	Echo Gamba	8
Erzahler	8	* = enclosed in Choir box		Octave	4
Octave	4			Flute triangulaire	4
Flute*	4			Flautino	2

Mixture	V	Flugel horn	8	Gamba	(Ch)	16
Waldhorn	16	Clarinet	8	Dulciana		16
Trumpet	8	Harp		Melodia	(Sw)	16
Oboe d'amore	8	Celesta		Bourdon		16
Vox Humana	8			Octave	(ext)	8
Clarion	4	**Solo Organ (enclosed)**		Cello	(ext)	8
		Gamba	8	Gedeckt	(ext)	8
Choir Organ (enclosed)		Gamba celeste	8	Stillgedeckt	(Sw)	8
Gamba	16	Flauto mirabilis	8	Super octave	(ext)	4
Diapason	8	Orchestral flute	4	Mixture		IV
Concert flute	8	Corno di bassetto	16	Fagotto	(Ch)	32
Gamba	8	Corno di bassetto	8	Trombone		16
Kleine Erzahler	8	English horn	8	Waldhorn	(Sw)	16
Kleine celeste	8	French horn	8	Fagotto	(Ch)	16
Gemshorn	4	Tuba mirabilis	8	Tromba	(ext)	8
Flute	4					
Nazard	$2\frac{2}{3}$	**Pedal organ**		Electro-pneumatic key and stop		
Piccolo	2	Major bass	32	action		
Carillon	III	Diapason	(ext) 16			
Fagotto	16	Metal diapason	(Gt) 16			

Whether there were any great builders in continental Europe in the early twentieth century I cannot be sure. Albert Schweitzer was just as uneasy. He found the large factory-built organs of Germany to be unimpressive – and presumably his judgement even covered the flagship instruments of Sauer, undoubtedly the pre-eminent German builder round 1900. Schweitzer turned first to France, singling out the small craft workshop of Cavaillé-Coll for special admiration – even though he encountered it in its final days after the great man's retirement and with Charles Mutin at the helm. He went further, and pronounced the great four-manual organ now in the Basilica of Sacré-Coeur in Paris as 'the ideal instrument for Bach'. But France lost its leading role in organ building at the beginning of the twentieth century: in 1905 the Church was disestablished, and the craft never recovered. To this day, France has been unable to enter a single name in the catalogue of great builders, despite the vital contribution of Gonzales in the 1930s and, more recently, the revival of small craft workshops engaged in restoration and the building of good neo-classical organs.

For some of his most important Bach recordings Schweitzer turned to England and the Harrison organ at All Hallows-by-the- Tower in London. It seems a surprising choice for a man who is regarded as the father of the classical revival, but surely the story here is to do with recognition of superlative quality. Harrison organs may have been romantic in character, but nowhere was the result more convincing.

All Hallows by-the-Tower, London; Harrison & Harrison 1928 (destroyed in 1941)

Great Organ		Voix Celeste	8	**Pedal Organ**		
Gross Geigen	16	Gemshorn	4	Double Open Diapason		32
Large Open Diapason	8	Mixture	III	Open Wood		16
Small Open Diapason	8	Double Trumpet	16	Violone	(Gt)	16
Hohl Flute	8	Trumpet	8	Sub Bass		16
Octave	4	Oboe	8	Octave Wood	(ext)	8
Octave Quint	$2\frac{2}{3}$	Clarion	4	Flute	(ext)	8
Super Octave	2			Trombone		16
Sesquialtera	III	**Choir Organ (enclosed)**				
Tromba	8	Contra Dulciana	16	pneumatic action		
Octave Tromba	4	Viol d'Orchestre	8			
		Wald Flute	8			
Swell Organ		Lieblich Flute	4			
Open Diapason	8	Piccolo	2			
Stopped Diapason	8	Clarinet	8			
Echo Gamba	8					

Nevertheless, with Schweitzer we reach a turning point, a signpost to what was to come in the second half of the twentieth century. Once the first world war was over, the emphasis was no longer on the inherited tradition of the nineteenth century, but on the exploration of radical new paths, sometimes described as a revival of ancient tradition, and sometimes moving towards the avowedly modern.

'Modern' is a funny word. We are accustomed to use it in reference to things that are recent: thus mobile phones, global warming, and sound-bites are all part of 'modern' life. Perhaps we need to use it with more caution, for in the twentieth century there was a Modern Movement that affected art, architecture, music and design – and that movement itself is now part of History. It doesn't matter whether your view of Modernism begins with Stravinsky, Schoenberg, Le Corbusier or the Bauhaus – these events are now in the distant past and are a matter for the historical record.

The Classical Revival in organ building – the Organ Reform Movement or *Orgelbewegang* – was also in its way part of Modernism. Yes, its first principle was the rediscovery of the past, but in that simple plan it invoked the spirit of William Morris and the pioneers of the Arts & Crafts movement, rejected the most advanced technical developments of the industrial age, ushered in an aesthetic in which austerity and absence of decoration were key elements, and introduced to organ building – in the revival of the *werkprinzip* – the idea that form should be dictated by function.

The tools of revolution were forged in the organ conferences of the 1920s and 1930s, at Hamburg, Freiburg, Amsterdam and Utrecht. Chief among the *sans-culottes* was Christhard Mahrenholz, who repeatedly challenged the commercial assumptions of the day, championing the artistic standards of 'old' organ building and decrying the many cheap expedients ('standard' pipe-scales, extension, reliance on trade supply houses) that characterised European organ building between the wars. It was not long before new tonal ideas were creeping into organs made in the big factories – new mutation stops even reached London by 1925 (in the Willis rebuild of the Anneessens organ at Farm Street catholic church, with the encouragement of Guy Weitz). But this was at first a very superficial makeover of existing practice and the great majority of instruments built in that difficult period offered more artifice than art. It took a couple of small builders with a completely fresh outlook to reintroduce the concept of craft quality to the organ.

These two were the Danish firms of Marcussen and Frobenius. The idea of high standards in design and craftsmanship was part of a wider movement in Scandinavia at the time. Modernism evolved in the far north as a continuation of a taste for restrained neo-classicism – it was not always revolutionary. Some decoration and 'prettiness' was permissible and, while modern materials and techniques might be used where appropriate there was an undimmed interest in woodworking and other traditional crafts. This view of modernism sat very well with renewed interest in older, 'classical' organs, and the encouragement of craftsmanship and tradition allowed the reintroduction of formal casework and all- mechanical key actions by the close of the 1930s.

For both firms the new style was in place by the eve of the second world war. Frobenius – the family were of German origin – tackled the restoration of the organ once in St Peter's Malmo, now in the Malmo museum, in 1941. Built in the early 1500s, enlarged with some pedal stops by Hans Brebos in 1572, Frobenius completed the picture with a new *rygpositiv* in a suitably matching manner. Meanwhile Marcussen, since 1920 under the direction of Sybrand Zachariessen, were building new organs with casework that reflected the excellence of Scandinavian cabinet-making. Their little choir organ of 1940 in the Gruntvigs Kirke, Copenhagen showed the level of quality and perfection they had already attained. The double case, both sections being fitted with folding doors, is traditional in form but entirely fresh and original in its interpretation: the specification is classical in inspiration and is intelligently adapted to the restrictions of the site, yet includes one or two modern touches:

Gruntvigs Kirke, Copenhagen, Denmark; choir organ, Marcussen 1940

Hovaedwaerk		Rygpositiv		Pedal			
Principal	8	Gedakt	8	Subbas		16	Mechanical key and stop action
Nathorn	8	Praestant	4	Bordun	(HV)	8	
Oktav	4	Rørfløte	4	Oktav	(HV)	4	
Quint	$2\frac{2}{3}$	Quintatøn	2	Dulcian		16	
Oktav	2	Scharf	II				
Mixtur	IV	Krummhorn	8				

The choir organ in the Grundtvigs Church, Copenhagen,
built by Marcussen in 1940.

Frobenius and Marcussen continued in the same vein of originality and excellence after the war. It is difficult to single out particular instruments from their joint work, but amongst the Frobenii one might mention the organ in St Jakob Copenhagen (3 manuals, 36 stops, 1953) and, closer to home, the peerless instrument at Queen's College Oxford (2 manuals, 22 stops, 1965). From the work of Marcussen, special mention might be given to the organ in the Nicolaikerk, Utrecht (3 manuals, 33 stops, 1956).

Gradually their philosophy began to spread. An Organ Reform outlook was already significant in the Netherlands in the 1930s, but it took the Frobenius-trained Dirk Flentrop to announce the new style at the level of quality already established in Denmark. As ever, connection with old organs was an important factor, and Flentrop's 1949 restoration of the 1725 F C Schnitger at Alkmaar was carefully executed without the invasive changes that characterised other similar work at the time. His new organs were as radical as any by his mentors, and at Doetchinem in 1952 he built his first fully-fledged modern classical instrument, a three manual organ with Hoofdwerk, Rugwerk, Boorstwerk and detached pedal towers.

The organ at Doetchinem, built by Flentrop in 1952.

Doetchinem, the Netherlands; Flentrop 1952

Hoofdwerk		Rugwerk		Boorstwerk		Pedaal	
Quintadeen	16	Holpijp	8	Eikenfluit	8	Prestant	16
Prestant	8	Quintadeen	8	Fluit	4	Octaaf	8
Roerfluit	8	Prestant	4	Prestant	2	Octaaf	4
Octaaf	4	Roerfluit	4	Gemshoorn	2	Nachthoorn	2
Ged. fluit	4	Sesquialter	II (treble)	Octaaf	1	Mixtur	IV
Nasard	2⅔	Octaaf	2	Cymbel	II	Bazuin	16
Octaaf	2	Quint	1⅓	Regaal	4	Schalmei	4
Mixtur	IV-VI	Scherp	I				
Trompet	8	Dulciaan	8				

Mechanical key and stop action

In Germany in the 1950s and 1960s a different kind of modernism prevailed, and it was one that sat less happily with the notion of the revival of tradition. Many companies were interested not simply in neo-classicism, but in a more futuristic plan based only loosely on classical principles. This led to the introduction of modern materials, new and unusual pipe forms, experimental off-unison mutations and aliquots, radical departures in form and layout, and an abiding interest in the novel for its own sake. Few builders managed to unite these disparate elements in a manner that has ensured both respect and longevity – some of the experiments were perilously close to the maverick ideas of Hope-Jones (only now turned on their head to emphasise every aspect of acute brilliance where Hope-Jones dealt mainly with the heavy and dull). The exception is again a builder who knew old organs and had respect for them: Rudolf von Beckerath of Hamburg. Von Beckerath never attained the levels of craft perfection that so distinguished his Danish contemporaries and his case designs were usually lumpy, sometimes crassly so, but the purity of his work is remarkable and his best organs have a rich boldness that makes an interesting contrast with the sharper-sounding organs of his competitors. Von Beckerath spent some time in the 1930s in France with Gonzales, inheriting along the way a set of shallot-making equipment that is alleged to have come from the Cavaillé-Coll workshop. The quality of his reeds ensured another distinguished and distinguishing element in his work.

One other builder deserves special notice, as having successfully combined Germanic modernism and radical new engineering solutions with a level of musical excellence that renders the results of more than ordinary quality: the Austrian company Rieger, headed by the brilliant engineer Josef con Glatter-Götz. There is very little classical about the best Rieger organs of the 1960s and 70s: many are based on a modern engineer's view of the organ as a constructivist sculpture floating in its surroundings. Some organs are asymmetrical, or hang ingeniously from hidden steelwork. The same engineering principles are applied to the mechanical actions, and Rieger have long been in the forefront of builders who make large and ambitious organs comfortably playable – always retaining mechanical manual couplers where their less conscientious competitors will happily concede a few rows of heavy-duty pulldown magnets. Glatter-Götz himself was as proud of the organ at Ratzeburg cathedral as of any other (4 manuals, 60 stops, 1978). The tonal scheme combines classical principles with an original eclecticism; the result, well known on recordings by Peter Hurford and others, is both startling and brilliant – perhaps the most convincing all-'modern' statement of the century.

The organ in Ratzeburg Cathedral, built by Rieger in 1978.

Ratzeburg Cathedral, Germany; Rieger 1978

Hauptwerk		Schwellwerk (enclosed)		Rückpositiv		Pedal	
Principal	16	Bordun	16	Principal	8	Principal	32
Octav	8	Holzprinzipal	8	Rohrflöte	8	Principal	16
Spitzflöte	8	Bleigedackt	8	Quintade	8	Subbass	16
Octav	4	Gamba	8	Octav	4	Octav	8
Nachthorn	4	Schwebung	8	Koppelflöte	4	Gedackt	8
Quinte	$2\frac{2}{3}$	Octav	4	Sesquialter	II	Octav	4
Superoctav	2	Viola	4	Gemshorn	2	Rohrpfeife	4
Mixtura major	I	Blockflöte	4	Quinte	$1\frac{1}{3}$	Rauschpfeife	VI
Mixtura minor	IV	Nassat	$2\frac{2}{3}$	Scharff	IV	Kontrafagott	32
Cornett V (from g)		Waldflöte	2	Rankett	16	Bombarde	16
Fagott	16	Terz	$1\frac{3}{5}$	Krummhorn	8	Posaune	8
Trompete	8	Sifflet	1	Zimbelstern		Schalmei	4
Spanisch trompete	8	Mixtur	VI				
Spanisch trompete	4	Dulzian	16	Brustwerk (enclosed)			
Glockenspiel		Oboe	8	Holzgedackt	8		
		Franz. trompete	4	Holzrohrflöte	4		
				Principal	2		
				Terzsepta	IV		
				Zimbel	II		
Mechanical action,				Regal	16		
electric stop action				Vox humana	8		

There are plenty of other famous builders who might be mentioned alongside von Beckerath and Rieger, building organs that appear to fit the modern mould in one way or another – some straightforward, some eclectic, some radical. However, in the juggling act between art and commerce that impinges so painfully on the craft of organ building there are many pitfalls that compromise quality and integrity. For example, there is a large group of modern builders who rely very heavily on trade supply houses for pipework, in particular buying reed stops ready voiced. The best of these suppliers, Giesecke and Killinger for example, certainly produce pipework that is technically refined, but the distance between their work and the final musical result on site is too great to ensure artistic excellence. To my ears at least builders who rely on subcontracted voicing fall short of the first rank, however competent they may be and however popular and successful they may have become both at home and overseas.

To follow the next twist in the narrow path of excellence, we have to return to builders whose work has been inspired by old organs. Some 'restoration' work in the later twentieth century was highly invasive. Marcussen's work at Haarlem in 1960 produced a fine result, but it involved a new wind system with schwimmer regulators, new key action, new upperwork, the lowering of wind pressures, the erasing of nicking on the flue pipes, and the revoicing of the reeds with new tongues. Ott's work at about the same time on Schnitger organs attempted to fit them to a preconceived neo-classical ideal, often ignoring the compelling evidence of original or former states, and again with the application of doctrinaire voicing techniques – open feet, no nicking, ultra-low pressures.

We know more about early organ-building now. Schnitger's pressures (for example) were not always low – between 75mm (3 inches) and 90mm (3.5 inches) was normal. Cut ups were not necessarily modest – in the smaller pipes of the mixtures a mouth height of between one-third and one-half the mouth width is not unusual. Various techniques- including sporadic nicking – were used to modify the speech transients of the pipes and bring them under artistic control. Reeds were often ponderous and heavy in tone. The result is perhaps darker and smoother than one might expect, given the sharp brilliance of some neo-classical organs supposed to have been inspired by the Hamburg school.

That new knowledge comes partly from organ builders and advisers who have approached the archaeology of early instruments in a more thorough and systematic manner, applying techniques from art conservation more familiar among harpsichord makers than organ builders. Two of these builders became especially prominent in the 1960s and 1970s.

My first is Jürgen Ahrend, in partnership with Gerhard Brunzema from 1954 to 1972, and continuing under his own name in Leer in Friesland to this day. Both builders had trained with Paul Ott, and their work in a small craft based organisation of less than ten people may have been a reaction to their previous experience. Work in the 1950s and 1960s centred round small organs of modern design and high craft standards, but was quickly joined by restorations of important earlier instruments, such as the 15th – 16th century survivor at Rysum (restored 1961) and the Müller at the Waalse Kerk Amsterdam (restored 1965). New organs were often modern in appearance, but followed old manufacturing practices with greater care than any other builder at the time. A fine example is the small three manual of 1970 at the Cantate Domino church in the north-west suburbs of Frankfurt. The plain asymmetrical design of this instrument is entirely contemporary, but its voice is timeless. Frankfurt is a city with many larger and newer organs in various styles – some specific, some eclectic. In a recent visit that included several of them, I could not help noticing how well this organ had stood its first decades of life and how its strong musical character transcended the apparently north-German inspiration of the scheme. This organ may have its roots in Freisland and the Hamburg style, but it still manages to provide the most convincing and musical *grand jeu* in Frankfurt!

The organ in the Cantate Domino Church, Frankfurt,
built by Ahrend & Brunzema in 1970.

Cantate Domino church, Frankfurt-Nordweststadt; Ahrend & Brunzema 1970

Hauptwerk		**Cornett**	V (from c')	Sesquialtera	II	Mixture	V
Bordun	16	Trompete	8	Scharff	IV	Posaune	16
Prinzipal	8			Krummhorn	8	Trompete	8
Spitzgedackt	8	**Ruckpositiv**				Clarine	4
Oktave	4	Gedackt	8	**Pedal**			
Koppelflöte	4	Prinzipal	4	Prinzipal	16	Mechanical key and
Quinte	$2\frac{2}{3}$	Rohrflöte	4	Subbass	16	stop action
Oktave	2	Waldflöte	2	Oktavbass	8	
Mixtur	IV	Spitzquinte	$1\frac{1}{3}$	Oktave	4	

Since 1970 Ahrend solo has become internationally famous for his protracted and dedicated restorations of the great works of Schnitger, among them St Cosmae Stade, Norden (Schnitger's home town), and the Jakobikirche Hamburg. These and other works have placed Ahrend way above his peers in terms of his understanding of old organs, and have set a new level of quality in the craft as a whole. That quality may be judged in his one British work, the small two-manual in the Reid Hall, Edinburgh, built on the advice of Dr Peter Williams.

My second historically-inspired builder is the Swiss firm of Metzler, based at Dietikon near Zürich. In the 1950s Oskar and Hansueli Metzler developed a close association with Poul-Gerhard Andersen of Marcussens, and in a number of important instruments they combined the new Danish style with meticulous Swiss craftsmanship. The organs in the Geneva Cathedral and the Grossmünster, Zürich are perhaps the best known of these collaborations. In 1960-1 Metzler were called on to restore the Johann Andreas Silbermann organ at Arlesheim; under the careful guidance of the consultant Heinz Köbel they treated the pipework with care and restored the winding system rather than replacing it with *schwimmer* regulators. Here began an important connection with early organs and, after 1963, the Dutch historian and conservationist Bernhardt Edskes joined as designer. The restoration of the little one-manual Schnitger at Nieuuw Scheemda in 1968 set new standards, and gradually a new style of organ building emerged which emulated the qualities of older work far more faithfully than before. Important examples can be found at the Stadtkirche in Frauenfeld (1968) and at the Grote Kerk in The Hague (1971, with a 32' front). The Metzler organ in Trinity College Cambridge (1976) is another fine example from this important period.

The organ in the Grote Kerk, The Hague, built by Metzler in 1971.

Jürgen Ahrend is alone amongst the classically-inspired builders I have mentioned so far in his continuing adherence to a single ideal, that of bringing alive the standards and assumptions of the distant past in organs that exist today, whether new or restored. All the others, to a greater or lesser extent, have suffered the cruel fate of becoming victims of their own success, and now build organs in the modern eclectic style. In one sense there is nothing at all wrong with that – the result is a lot of instruments that are generally useful and can, in one way or another, be relied upon to perform a wide range of repertoire. To what extent they do so convincingly would be another area to explore. I cannot help feeling that the new homogenised organs of the great European builders, the instruments that have been with us since the 1970s, are significantly less interesting than the sterling creations of the 1950s and 1960s – and I cannot help admitting to a certain sadness that many of them are now arriving in the British Isles on the basis of reputations formed thirty, forty and fifty years ago. There was a particular brilliance in the unpasteurised, unhomogenised, unskimmed organs of the early neo-classical period. In continental Europe, at least, that wonderful culture has been superseded by something that is to my ears more UHT.

In organ building there is both a Broad and a Narrow Way. Some of the Narrow Way has been tentatively sketched in this article. The next turn takes us across the Atlantic: in the last quarter of the twentieth century the greatest organ builders on the planet were to be found residing in North America.

G Donald Harrison, on the face of it a most gentlemanly and unassuming man, left England in 1927 to join E M Skinner. Henry Willis III thought he was sending him to give America a healthy dose of Willis principles. The owner of the Skinner company, Arthur Hudson Marks, needed more than that. Skinner was stubborn and not always careful with the company's money. Marks foresaw the need for a change in direction. Harrison himself kept his counsel, but gradually revealed in the early 1930s that his taste was for something new – a brighter, clearer style of organ building that has become known as 'American Classic'. There was a revolutionary spirit about Harrison's work for the Aeolian-Skinner company, but throughout his career it centred round pipes and tonal schemes and avoided issues of structure, placement and mechanism. Great works abounded – though so many organs were issued from the Aeolian-Skinner workshops that they were not all of the same class, and by the 1950s the quality began to go downhill. Harrison deserves a place in the hall of fame. His best instruments combine his memories of organs by Lewis with varied modern influences; the best bear his signature on the console label, indicating an occasion where he took personal responsibility for the musical result, inventing for himself the methods of on-site balancing and finishing that were so remote from his training in the house of Willis.

In the 1950s the American Classic was no longer quite enough. Its enlivened and invigorating tonal schemes were one thing, but the structure – and many artistic assumptions – were still based on the technical developments of the Skinner period. Walter Holtkamp challenged with organs that were more conspicuously modern, and even experimented with mechanical action, but in the post-war years eyes turned to Europe and to the latest neoclassical work, especially the organs of Flentrop. With wholehearted backing from younger players, especially the English emigré E Power Biggs, the first organs in the new manner arrived in America, one of the most notable being the 1958 three-manual Flentrop in the Busch-Reisinger Museum at Harvard. Biggs encouraged a whole generation to view organ music in terms of the old organs that inspired it. That generation then travelled to Europe to find out for themselves. What they found surprised them.

American organ builders bitten by the new 'bug' made their pilgrimages in the 1960s and 1970s and found the old organs deep in the controversy surrounding invasive post-war restorations. Where they found instruments that were little altered they heard sounds that were different from those that the little Flentrop had led them to expect: especially organs that were louder, fuller, darker and smoother than the modern imitations. For some of these builders – for example Charles Fisk, Fritz Noack and John Brombaugh the journey gradually became a mission to discover exactly how and why early organs sounded the way they did.

Noack voiced the concerns of others in the 1970s, wondering at the rattling aluminium actions and screeching low-pressure choruses of less-good neo-classical instruments. "Why this terrible waste of tin?", he wailed. Fisk delved deep into arcana of organbuilding craft, emerging with new revelations about the musical nature of 'live' wind from bellows rather than schwimmer regulators, and exploring the world of unequal temperament with enthusiasm. Organs of a new kind emerged in the United States, fit to challenge the recent imports.

Then, when John Brombaugh started organ building on his own in 1969 these thoughts coalesced into something more magical. His assumption seems to have been this: 'if we are to build organs that reflect the taste, skills and output of the old masters, then let us at least try to get it right!'. His early works appeared to stand at the point of departure offered by the new organs of Ahrend & Brunzema – old standards and a knowledge of old sounds combined with certain modern movement influences in design. By opus 16 in 1974 (Grace Episcopal Church, Ellensburg, Washington, 2 manuals, 11 stops) Brombaugh had gone several steps further. This instrument was based on careful surveys of old organs and their pipework, and though it was not a copy it represented a most important attempt to capture the glories of the past in greater depth than all previous efforts. The care taken is immediately evident in the casework, which is now enriched with mouldings, carvings, precious woods and gilding in exactly the rich manner that would have delighted our pre-industrial forebears. The quality is not simply a matter of bench work. Assiduous attention to detail and quality is carried through to the painstaking manufacture of pipes in archaic styles, and to their voicing on pressures not-so-very-low, and to the musical balance and finish.

The organ at Grace Episcopal Church, Ellensburg, Washington,
built by John Brombaugh in 1974.

Grace Episcopal Church, Ellensburg, Washington, USA; John Brombaugh 1974

Great Organ			**Brustwerk**	
Bourdon	16		Regal	8
Praestant I-II	8			
Holpijp	4	(bass & treble)	**Pedal**	
Octave	4	(bass & treble)	Subbass	16
Quinte	$2\frac{2}{3}$	(bass & treble)	Trumpet	8
Octave	2	(bass & treble)		
Tierce	$1\frac{3}{5}$	(bass & treble)	Mechanical key and stop action	
Mixture	II – IV			

Since the 1970s Brombaugh has gone on to build organs of many different sizes and kinds, though always based on the work of 16th and 17th century north European masters. Small organs include a fine instrument at Oberlin, Ohio with 'quarter tones' played by extra keys in the octave – a popular diversion for organ builders in the early 17th century and tried out by Father Smith at the Temple Church and at Durham Cathedral. Larger instruments include one or two with Swell divisions, ingeniously adapted to the Brombaugh aesthetic.

As well as an impressive opus list of his own, Brombaugh has inspired an entire school of craft organ building in North America. Several names are associated with this 'new' movement concerned with building 'old' organs – Paul Fritts, Ralph Richards and – perhaps pre-eminent among the Brombaugh inspired builders – George Taylor and John Boody. Taylor & Boody came to international notice in 1985 when they completed their organ for Holy Cross College, Worcester, Massachusetts – a magnificent four-manual recreation of the 16th century style of Hendrik Niehoff, and an instrument of stunning musical quality.

Holy Cross College, Worcester, Massachusetts, USA; Taylor & Boody 1985

Hauptwerk								**Pedal**		
Principal	16		Octave	4		Octave	4	Gross untersatz	(ext)	32
Octave	8		Rohrflöte	4		Spielflöte	4	Principal	(Hw)	16
Spillpfeife	8		Sesquialtera	II		Nasat	$2\frac{2}{3}$	Subbass		16
Quinte	(from c') $5\frac{1}{3}$		Octave	2		Gemshorn	2	Octave		8
Octave	4		Waldflöte	2		Tierce	$1\frac{3}{5}$	Octave		4
Tertia	(from c') $3\frac{1}{5}$		Sifflet	$1\frac{1}{3}$		Mixture	IV-V	Nachthorn		2
Quinte	$2\frac{2}{3}$		Scharff	V-VIII		Rauschende zimbel	III	Mixtur		V
Superoctave	2		Dulcian	16		Trompet	8	Posaune		16
Mixtur	VII-IX		Schalmey	8		Vox humana	8	Trompet		8
Trompet	16		Trichterregal	8				Trompet		4
Trompet	8		Zimbelstern			**Brustwerk**		Trompet		2
						Gedackt	8			
			Oberwerk			Blockflöte	4	Mechanical key and stop		
Ruckpositiv			Principal I-II	8		Octave	2	action		
Principal	8		Hohlflöte	8		Terzian	II			
Gedackt	8		Quintadena	8		Regal	8			

There is one strange element about the neo-classical organ builders I have mentioned so far – their taste, as reflected in their new organs, has gradually been retreating into the distant past of musical history. The first neo-classical organs of the 1950s seemed to point vaguely at the period round 1700; the best of those being built today drag us firmly back into the sixteenth century – before Bach and Buxtehude were even a twinkle in the celestial eye. This is just a coincidence: in an article that highlights the very best the century has to offer it is inevitable that the historically inspired builders take pride of place. But there have been significant attempts to explore other areas of the repertoire. The 18th century is beginning to receive more attention, with important restorations of organs in Saxony and Thuringia and some relevant copies – such as the lovely Noack/Wegscheider collaboration in the style of Z Hildebrandt in Houston, Texas. The romantic repertoire is also being provided for, though here the path of quality is far less consistently followed and while some attempts to recreate

19th century style have been successful there are plenty of others that simply do not meet basic standards. Notable essays in 19th century style include the lovely Ackermann & Lund organ in the Katarina Kyrka, Stockholm, built in 1975, generously provided with material for the French romantic repertoire, and tragically lost in a fire a few years ago. The best Cavaillé-Coll copy currently on the planet is undoubtedly the Fisk/Rosales collaboration at Rice University, Houston, Texas: this remarkable large three manual instrument moves far beyond the braying pseudo-French sounds that have plagued so many new organs in the 1980s and 1990s (sub-contracted reed voicing again partly to blame), and manages to recover some of the richness, grandeur and panache that Franck and Widor would have taken for granted. There are plenty of other 'French' organs around, many built in Germany and even now the Netherlands, as well as some coming from France itself. English builders have made their own contributions to this genre. Among them are some good and very good organs, but it takes a very special dedication and skill to enter fully into the spirit of another style: the leading examples only have been mentioned.

My survey of the world's best has not included any recent British builders. There is some remarkably good organ building in Britain today, especially from the workshops of Walker and Mander, but none of the more popular companies would be claiming to forge a new path – as Harrison's did after 1904. Their expertise now is mostly in the efficient production of all-purpose instruments. I would however like to pay passing tribute to two individuals: first to Ralph Downes who, though he was in a sense an amateur, became the finest organ-builder in Britain in the 1950s and whose organ at the Royal Festival Hall remains of great importance and interest; and, secondly, to William Drake, whose small output of new work has nevertheless struck a note of consistent craft quality and musical beauty.

What of the future? I believe the twentieth century closes on an exceptionally rosy picture. The preponderance – among high-quality 'art' organs at least – of instruments dedicated to the performance of 'early' music may raise several important questions, but the sheer quality of the results is beyond dispute. The best organs of the late twentieth century are of superlative quality, combining musical, architectural and craft elements in structures of considerable magnificence and beauty. In many respects organ building has brought a wonderful life to the hopes of men like William Morris, who sought – in the nineteenth century – a path that would restore the importance of craftsmanship in a world increasingly industrialised and commercial. I believe that Schweitzer's hopes are now fulfilled: an organ purchaser today is not obliged to take the off-the-shelf product of a commercially organised factory, but may choose to commission an individual work of art. That individuality – the power and character of an instrument different from its neighbours and contemporaries – is one of the great secrets of the craft. An organ that will play everything may be eminently satisfying, but the future of organ building and organ playing will continue to be charted by – and only by – dedicated pioneers.

The English Cathedral Organ in the Twentieth Century

by

Nicholas Thistlethwaite

History is seldom as neat and tidy as the historian might wish. As far as the English cathedral organ is concerned, the twentieth century began in 1896 with the completion of Robert Hope-Jones's electric organ for Worcester Cathedral. Whether one regards this remarkable instrument as the work of a visionary genius, or alternatively as one of 'the worst organs ever made by a careful, professional builder',[1] the Worcester organ offered a fair indication of the challenges which would engage the energies of cathedral organ builders in the twentieth century and anticipated many of the technical solutions they would adopt.

The Worcester story is well known.[2] Hope-Jones offered to combine the two Hill organs (1842, 1874) in the cathedral using the agency of electricity, enabling all sections of the instrument to be controlled from a single console. Fifty years earlier the need would not have arisen. However, the subsequent revival of cathedral life led to the introduction of nave services, frequently of a 'popular' nature. The existing organs were designed to accompany choirs. Some cathedrals therefore acquired an additional organ to accompany the congregational services, though few were as grand as the 51-stop instrument given by the Earl of Dudley to Worcester and placed in the south transept.

The problem was partly one of accommodation, partly one of control. Henry Willis had taken a major step towards solving these problems at St Paul's Cathedral (1872) where the division of the organ on either side of the choir increased the physical space for organ parts, and the application of a simple form of pneumatic action allowed the organist to control both halves from a single console. The organ, though, was still comparatively small (52 stops).

Willis tried a different approach at Canterbury in 1886 when he used an early form of electro-pneumatic action to connect the console, sited on a platform in the south choir aisle, to the soundboards in the triforium above. From a technical point of view the action was commendably successful (it survived until 1939) but the instrument cut little ice in the nave.

At Worcester, Hope-Jones used electricity to solve *both* the problem of accommodation (stowing a large organ away in different parts of the building) *and* the need to provide physically-separated sections to serve distinct functions in different parts of the cathedral but all controlled (the word is apposite) from a single console. The Great and Choir Organs occupied a case on the south side of the choir, the Swell Organ was on the north side, and the Solo Organ ('intended more as a Bombarde division, primarily for the accompaniment of singing in the nave')[3] and most of the Pedal Organ stood behind the Scott case in the transept. The console was placed in the easternmost bay of the north choir aisle. Relf Clark suggests that Hope-Jones thought of his instrument as a nave and chancel organ combined, the nave organ consisting of the transept section, together with the heavy-wind divisions of Great and Swell.[4] This may be so. No doubt organists enjoyed the novelty of being able to contrast divisions that were spatially and tonally distinct.

The Worcester organ is almost the first example of the application of electricity to enable whole divisions or individual registers to be placed apart from the main organ for musical effect. (Hill's Celestial Organ at Westminster Abbey, installed in 1895, slightly anticipates Hope-Jones.) It was to become a regular feature of twentieth-century schemes. Some buildings lent themselves to this treatment. Willis's reconstruction of the St Paul's Cathedral organ (1900) included the introduction of a chorus of tubas (16.8.4) in the north-east quarter gallery of the dome, and a 4-stop Altar Organ was placed over the north stalls to accompany Holy Communion. The organist seated at his console was able to produce sound at the east end of the choir, in the dome, or from the main organ on either side of the choir. Thirty years later, Henry Willis III added a powerful Trompette Militaire to the dome reeds and in 1949 a complete dome diapason chorus of Lewis pipework (16.8.8.4.4.II.V.III). Sumner commented that it was

> not to be thought of as an extension of the existing tonal appointments, but rather as a separate section for the purpose of accompanying a large congregation under the dome or in the nave. Of course, it can be used to give interesting antiphonal effects with other parts of the instrument...[5]

In other words, this spatial separation of the divisions was not only functional (congregational accompaniment), it also had musical possibilities (antiphonal effects).

The Mander rebuild of 1977 carried the same principle further. A new dome diapason chorus was provided, and the organ's westerly expansion reached its logical conclusion with the installation of three horizontal trumpets (16.8.4) and a 4-stop flue chorus in the gallery above the west door. Today, the Willis organ of 1872, renovated and modified, survives as the core of a 108-stop instrument, which has been adapted and extended throughout the twentieth century, taking account of changing needs, and exploiting the possibilities of electric action.

Westminster Abbey in 1913. The sliding stop-keys above the left jamb operated the Celestial Organ. The console dated from the Hill & Son reconstruction of 1908.

Photo: John Hunter

St Paul's Cathedral offers unique opportunities, architectural and acoustical, to which Liverpool Cathedral alone presents any serious challenge. The accommodation and control of Henry Willis III's 170-stop[6] Liverpool organ was only possible using electric action, although its placement on either side of the choir in the classic Willis manner was conventional. By 1939 the impending completion of the Central Space focused thoughts on the eventual shape of the organ, and the new console installed in 1940 provided for a 30-stop West End section (Great, Swell, Bombarde and Pedal), an accompanimental Central Space section (Swell, Choir and Pedal), and an 11-stop Corona section in the tower for 'aetherial and antiphonal effects'. The realisation of this scheme would have matched the spirit of Scott's Xanadu-like building wonderfully, but it was not to be. Only the Corona section was made but this perished in 1941 when Willis's Brixton works were bombed. Escalating costs led to the curtailment of Scott's plans, and today the only part of the organ that stands outside the two main chambers is the spectacular Trompette Militaire installed in the Corona gallery in 1998 by David Wells. It speaks on 40" wind pressure and would surely have met with the approval of Hope-Jones, whose own plans to install a Tuba Mirabilis on 100" wind pressure at Worcester remained unfulfilled.

Liverpool and St Paul's are exceptional buildings. In general, however, electric action was important to cathedral organ design for three reasons.

First, by doing away with the physical constraints of tracker action and (to a lesser extent) pneumatic tubing, it allowed organs to grow in size. The typical Willis cathedral organ was comparatively small – Salisbury (1876) had 55 stops, Truro (1887) had 45 stops, Lincoln (1898) had 58. Such instruments could be accommodated without too much difficulty in mediaeval buildings (though the Pedal pipes at Salisbury in the north transept remain an eyesore). The emergence in the first half of the twentieth century of a desire for more powerful organs with a greater dynamic and tonal range presented difficulties. The only way this could be satisfied was to build bigger organs. Swell boxes, large-scale pedal basses and expanded Solo divisions had to be squeezed in somewhere. Electrical transmission was the answer. It enabled one section of the organ to be detached from another – the Choir in the choir aisle at Chester (Hill 1910), the Great and Pedal in Southwell's nave triforium (Hill, Norman & Beard 1934), the Positive over the north choirstalls at Guildford (Rushworth & Dreaper

1961) – and allowed more to be packed into confined spaces in screens and behind choirstalls – as at Ripon (1913), Manchester (1933) and Durham (1970) Cathedrals, all by Harrison & Harrison. Given the architectural constraints, the increase in size which is so marked a feature of cathedral organ design during the twentieth century would have been impossible without the application of electricity.

It also permitted consoles to be sited away from the main body of the pipework so that the organist could hear both his instrument and the voices (of congregation and choir) more effectively. The removal of the console at Peterborough from a position just below the organ on the north side of the choir to a gallery on the south side (1931) must have been a revelation to the player, and similar moves at Hereford (1933), Winchester (1938) and Truro (1963) were equally significant. Guildford (1961), Coventry (1962) and Sheffield (1966) were new installations with detached consoles. The provision of a movable console at Blackburn (1969) took matters a stage further: now the cathedral organist, for centuries obscured from the gaze of the *hoi polloi* in

Chester Cathedral. The Hill console of 1910.

Photo: John Hunter

curtained lofts, became visible. There can be little doubt that the introduction of detached consoles made a contribution to the improvement in standards of accompaniment in English cathedrals during the twentieth century.

The third innovation made possible by electric action was equally important. At Worcester, Hope-Jones placed his Solo Organ with its Bombarde 16' and Orchestral Trumpet 8' in a prominent position behind the transept case, from whence they might be expected to give a lead to congregational singing. This became a preoccupation of twentieth-century builders: how to give a lead in buildings where the main organ was usually removed from the congregation.

Initially the provision of a powerful reed, located a little way from the main organ, was deemed sufficient. Harrison's 1908 Tuba at Ely was located in the north transept triforium from whence it spoke into the octagon, York's Tuba Mirabilis (1916) was intended to cajole nave congregations, and as late as 1965 Exeter acquired a Trompette Militaire concealed in the minstrels' gallery high above the nave. But the flexibility of electric action suggested other tempting possibilities. With the increasing use of cathedrals for great services from the 1950s onwards, and the consequent need for extra congregational support, the 'nave division' was conceived.

The earliest was also the most complete. At Bradford Cathedral in 1961, Hill, Norman & Beard reconstructed the 1904 Hill organ, and added a 13-stop Nave Organ, housed in a free-standing case, mounted on four pillars at the west end of the nave:

Manual		Wald Flute	2
Dolce bass	16	Quint Mixture	III-IV
Principal	8	Purcell Trumpet	8
Lieblich Gedeckt	8		
Salicional	8	**Pedal**	
Voix Celeste	8	Dolce bass	16
Octave	4	Gedeckt	16
Spitz Flute	4	Flute bass	8

The Purcell Trumpet was mounted horizontally at the top of Maufe's case, and the instrument had sufficient variety to be used as the sole accompaniment for congregational services.[7]

Mander adopted a different solution at Sheffield in 1970. Like Bradford, Sheffield Cathedral is a former parish church, and the adaptation of the building to cathedral purposes presented some difficulties. So a 'Nave Positive' was added to the main organ, mounted on a wall near the front of the nave. The stop list was more modest than Bradford's (8.8.4.4.2.1 1/3.1.II) and the department was intended to augment the main organ rather than stand alone.

Other divisions with a similar purpose followed: Canterbury (Mander 1980), housed in its own case in the north nave aisle, with a single Pedal stop, and playable from the main console on the screen; Chichester (Mander 1986), located in the nave triforium, and provided with its own console as well as an electrical connection to the main organ; Westminster Abbey (Harrison & Harrison 1987), a Bombarde Division in the triforium above the north case, with a diapason chorus, a cornet and three powerful reeds; Winchester (Harrison & Harrison 1988), a 9-stop Nave Organ, sited in the easternmost bay of the nave.

In each instance the organ-builder exploited the possibilities of electrical transmission to site a powerful chorus of flues or reeds where it could support congregational singing and provide an added dimension to the accompaniment of liturgy and ceremony. It is a twentieth-century solution to a nineteenth-century problem: where to site the organ once the choir screen has been swept away – the problem, in fact, which confronted Hope-Jones at Worcester in 1896.

Larger and more complicated organs necessitated an increase in accessories. Here, again, Worcester pointed the way. Hill's transept organ of 1874, with 51 stops, had 9 composition pedals and 8 couplers. Hope-Jones' new organ had 55 stops, 24 couplers, 26 'compound keys' in the key slips, 8 composition pedals, and a sforzando pedal. The compound composition keys were divided into three sections, providing a fixed combination, a pedal bass, and suitable couplers; several couplers worked on the 'double touch' principle that later became a common feature of cinema organ design.

Few of the distinctive complexities of Hope-Jones' console accessories were reproduced by other builders, but the increasingly orchestral approach to accompaniment together with the challenge of controlling unwieldy, multi-divisional instruments meant that console design would be a preoccupation of cathedral organists and organ-builders throughout the twentieth century, sometimes, it has to be said, to the exclusion of more fundamental musical considerations.

This is terrain in which it is sometimes difficult to distinguish the wood from the trees. In the earlier part of the twentieth century, the influence of Harrison & Harrison was salutary. A typical Harrison console would provide combination pistons[8] to each department, a small number (typically, one to each division) of adjustable pistons, reversible pistons or pedals to a handful of couplers and the pedal reed, and balanced swell pedals. The standard couplers, including a sparing use of octaves and sub-octaves, were augmented with 'unison off' couplers to departments with orchestral stops, and sometimes a coupler was provided to transfer the Great reeds to another keyboard (usually the Choir). The largest instruments might have a 'doubles off' foot piston and a set of couplers for combining manual and pedal pistons.

Other builders worked along similar lines. Willis organs of the mid-twentieth century tended to have more octave and sub-octave couplers, and also a greater number of reversible pistons (Hereford 1933), and this firm was one of the first to provide a bank of general pistons affecting the whole organ (St Paul's in 1925, and Westminster Cathedral in 1926, were equipped with four; Salisbury had eight in 1934).[9] At Norwich in 1942 Hill, Norman & Beard experimented

Photo: John Hunter

Hereford Cathedral. The Willis console of 1933, complete with general pistons, general crescendo pedal, swell shutter indicators 'and other convenient and helpful accessories… to make the control easy and flexible'.

with double touch combination pistons (the second touch brought on appropriate pedal stops – a recollection of Hope-Jones' compound combination keys?), and during the middle years of the century all builders devised their own mechanisms for the easy adjustment of piston settings,[10] and introduced general or departmental cancel pistons.

The introduction of solid-state technology in the 1960s provided the opportunity for a review of console accessories. Initially, builders used it to replace existing electro-mechanical systems, some of the earliest examples being New College, Oxford (Grant, Degens and Bradbeer, 1969), Gloucester Cathedral (Hill, Norman and Beard, 1970), and Worcester Cathedral (Harrison, 1972). Multi-level capture systems began to appear in the mid-1980s,[11] and sequencers and steppers in the 1990s (the St Paul's stepper, fitted by Mander in 1991, and the slightly later example at Westminster Abbey, installed by Harrison in 1994, must have been among the first). By the end of the twentieth century these devices had become an expected part of any console up-grading, and there is no denying that in a cathedral, with Organist, Sub Organist and Organ Scholar all performing regularly on the instrument, the provision of multi-channel combination systems is a convenience. Yet it has its dangers. At the end of the nineteenth century console gadgetry threatened to turn the cathedral organ into an orchestral 'one man band'; at the end of the twentieth century, the danger is that computer technology will obstruct the improvisatory and the spontaneous elements in the cathedral musician's art. It is different in the rather narrower musical sphere of the concert organist.

Photo: C R A Davies, courtesy of Harrison & Harrison.

Westminster Abbey. The Harrison & Harrison console,
following the addition of sequencers in 1994.

Throughout the twentieth century technology defined what was and was not possible for the cathedral organ. There were three distinct phases: the final applications of tubular-pneumatic action in the years up to *c*1920; the universal adoption of electro-pneumatic or electro-mechanical systems between then and 1975; the recovery and selective use of tracker action from 1975.

The design of organs was also, of course, affected by the changing role of cathedrals. Here, there were a number of factors. First, the use of cathedrals for major diocesan and other services increased dramatically in the course of the twentieth century. Secondly, liturgical reform – especially in the closing quarter of the century – encouraged the use of all parts of the building for processions, stations, baptismal renewal at the font, Communion administered from a nave altar. Thirdly, the choral repertoire grew and became more varied than it was a century before. Much later-twentieth century liturgical music makes novel demands on singers and organ.[12] Fourthly, cathedrals were more

Westminster Abbey in 1994. The console and north case.

extensively used for secular concerts. Fifthly, conservation (of historic organ cases, of historic fabric) became a major issue. All these factors were reflected in the evolution of cathedral organ design during the twentieth century, and their sometimes contradictory, and always challenging demands, explain why, by the end of the century, cathedral organs were less uniform in design than their predecessors a hundred years earlier.

Turning now to tonal design, it is possible to highlight a number of significant instruments from the last century.

The tonal extremes of Hope-Jones' Worcester organ were nowhere reproduced in their entirety, but some of his objectives and certain individual registers were imitated by progressive builders of the early-1900s. The ideal of massive diapason tone ('flooding' the building, is a favourite metaphor) complemented by weighty pedal basses and opaque but powerful chorus reeds met with approval. So, too, did orchestral strings of diminutive scale and the bright harmonic stops which represented the only upperwork on the Great and Swell at Worcester.

All these features appear in the work of Harrison & Harrison, the Durham organ-builders, who, with the firm of Henry Willis & Sons in turmoil, and with the Hill firm showing signs of exhaustion after three generations at the head of the profession, had edged into position as the leading cathedral organ-builders by 1914.[13] Harrison's reconstruction of the Ely Cathedral organ in 1908 has long been regarded as a landmark in English organ-building. There is truth in this: the specification represented the most complete expression of Arthur Harrison's (and George Dixon's) ideas at the time, and provided the basis for all Harrison's subsequent cathedral schemes. But Ely was incomplete (the Solo Organ was not installed until 1910, nor was it completed until 1914) and two significant cathedral rebuilds preceded it – Durham (1905) and Carlisle (1907). Durham, too, was incomplete; the Great, Swell and Solo reeds were revoiced with harmonic trebles, but it was not until 1935 that the other new pipework went in.[14] Nonetheless, the scheme was well on the way to expressing the tonal ideals which the later Ely work encapsulated. If Durham appears a touch less assured, it may be because Harrison was working with an instrument by Henry Willis (whom he admired) rather than, as at Ely, with an organ by Hill (whose work he and Dixon were united in disparaging).[15]

The Carlisle organ was also a Willis rebuild, but apart from a manual 32' and a mixture with the flattened 21st ('Harmonics') it displays all the features of Harrison's mature style.

Great Organ

Double Open Diapason	16
Large Open Diapason	8
Small Open Diapason	8
Stopped Diapason	8
Hohl-Flote	8
Principal	4
Wald-Flote	4
Twelfth	$2\frac{2}{3}$
Fifteenth	2
Sesquialtera (17.19.22)	III
Trombone	16
Tromba	8
Octave Tromba	4

Reeds on Solo
Choir to Great
Swell to Great
Solo to Great

Photo: John Hunter

Carlisle Cathedral, 1907. A typical early-twentieth century Harrison console.

Swell Organ (enclosed)

Lieblich Bordun	16
Open Diapason	8
Lieblich Gedeckt	8
Echo Gamba	8
Vox Angelica (c)	8
Octave	4
Lieblich Flote	4
Flautina	2
Mixture (12.19.22)	III
Double Trumpet	16
Trumpet	8
Oboe	8
Clarion	4
Orchestral Hautboy	8

Tremulant
Octave

Choir Organ

Double Salicional	16
Open Diapason	8
Claribel Flute	8
Viola da Gamba	8
Dulciana	8
Spitz-Flote	4
Flauto Traverso	4
Gemshorn	2
Cornopean	8

Swell to Choir
Solo to Choir

Solo Organ (enclosed)

Quintaten	16
Harmonic Flute	8
Concert Flute	4
Harmonic Piccolo	2
Viole d'Orchestre	8
Viole Celeste (F)	8
Viole Octaviante	4
Contra Fagotto	16
Clarinet	8
Vox Humana	8
Tuba (unenclosed)	8

Tremulant
Octave
Sub-octave
Unison off
Swell on Solo

Pedal Organ

Double Open Diapason	32
Open Diapason (extn)	16
Open Wood	16
Sub Bass (12 from Choir)	16
Violone	16
Octave Wood (extn)	8
Flute (extn)	8
Ophicleide	16
Fagotto (from Solo)	16
Posaune (extn)	8
Bassoon (enclosed)	8

Choir to Pedal
Great to Pedal
Swell to Pedal
Solo to Pedal

Combination Couplers
Great and Pedal combinations coupled
Pedal to Swell pistons

Accessories
4 combination pedals to Pedal
1 adjustable combination pedal to Pedal
3 combination pistons to Choir
4 combination pistons to Great
5 combination pistons to Swell
4 combination pistons to Solo
1 adjustable piston to each manual
2 reversible pistons (Sw to Gt, Gt to Ped)
1 reversible pedal (Gt to Ped)
1 pedal to each Tremulant
2 balanced swell pedals (Swell and Solo)

The use of extension for the Pedal ranks, the enclosure of pedal basses, the Great flutes (notably the triangular Wald Flote), the chorus of trombas, and the harmonic flutes, strings and orchestral reeds of the Solo (a completely new division) are typical of Harrison's cathedral work and feature in a long succession of organs over the next thirty years, among them Wells (1910), Gloucester (1920), Worcester (1925), Leicester (1930), Exeter (1932), and Manchester (1933). The series culminated in two instruments which are not strictly cathedral organs but have many affinities with them: King's College, Cambridge

(1934) and Westminster Abbey (1937). The King's organ was notable for its extensive provision of Pedal basses, the enclosure of the Great reeds, and the inclusion of small-scale mutations in the Choir; the Westminster Abbey organ was the ultimate in refinement – arguably the most complete expression of Arthur Harrison's tonal ideals. He died in November 1936 before it was complete.

Harrison had found a formula which satisfied English taste and the financial constraints of inter-war England, and he was wise enough not to depart from it. Notoriously conservative (this was, after all, a culture in which Vaughan Williams was regarded as avant-garde), musical taste approved of what now seems to some a rather repressed style of voicing – the musical equivalent of the famous English 'stiff upper lip'. Emotions were kept carefully in check and spontaneity was frowned upon.

The Willis firm, when it recovered (partially) from its tribulations, had a sporting shot at supplying both. Willis's organ for Westminster Cathedral (1922-32) possesses some of the drama and excitement that a Harrison organ of the period never quite achieves (due principally, no doubt, to the different treatment of the reeds) and the monumental Liverpool Cathedral organ (1926) had adventurous and romantic qualities – in *that* building – which justify treating Henry Willis III as one of the great builders of his generation. At Liverpool he rose to the challenge of creating a twentieth-century organ for an archetypally twentieth-century cathedral. One feels that his achievement would have astounded his grandfather.

Other firms made less of a mark. The century began with Norman & Beard's 5-manual organ for Norwich Cathedral (1900) – a largely conventional design apart from the 14-stop Echo Organ located in the choir triforium. Hill & Son enjoyed an Indian summer in the years before the First World War (Lichfield 1908, Chester and Manchester 1910) and J W Walker & Sons finally made it into the cathedral league with York (1903), Rochester (1905) and Bristol (1907). These were, however, instruments which represented the culmination of the Victorian era, rather than offering pointers to the future.

In due course, Hill, Norman & Beard had an opportunity to show how they would respond to the new fashion. Their reconstruction of the Peterborough Cathedral organ (1931) revealed that they had learnt from both Hope-Jones and Harrison. Southwell followed (1934) with its second (nave) console and dispersed arrangement, and then in 1942 they built an organ which made small but significant departures from the predominant style. This was at Norwich, where a fire had badly damaged the old Norman & Beard organ in 1938. The Pedal Organ of the reconstructed instrument had a complete flue chorus up to mixture and included no fewer than three 4' registers (admittedly, extensions). The Great was in two divisions, of which the 'major' division had a straightforward quint mixture rather than one with tierce or flattened 21st. The Choir also was in two sections; the unenclosed section was called Positive, and included a complete diapason chorus and two mutations. It would be wrong to read too much into this early attempt to re-establish the chorus structure of the organ, but these were straws in the wind which gave an indication of how development might proceed once more favourable circumstances prevailed.

It is a matter of history that the opening of the Royal Festival Hall organ in 1954 administered a sharp stimulus to the organ-building establishment in this country. Yet it was not immediately apparent in what ways the ethos of that instrument was relevant to cathedral organ design.

This did not, however, prevent it from influencing the aspirations of cathedral organists. Just as, in the early-1900s, progressive builders re-fashioned Victorian organs in their own image, so now, in the 1950s, 60s and 70s their successors attempted to do the same with organs inherited from the first half of the twentieth century. Amongst others, the organs at York (Walker 1960), Carlisle (Walker 1962), St Albans (Harrison 1962), Exeter (Harrison 1965), Durham (Harrison 1970), Southwell (HNB 1971), Wells (Harrison 1974), Ely (Harrison 1975), Canterbury (Mander 1980), Newcastle (1981), Westminster Abbey (Harrison 1982 and 1987), Winchester (Harrison 1988) and Rochester (1990 Mander) received what might now be called a 'makeover' and emerged, slightly dazed, in new guises. Inevitably, some schemes were more successful than others. Walker's reconstruction of York under the guidance of Dr Francis Jackson, and the characteristically thoroughgoing remodelling of St Albans by Harrison under the influence of Ralph Downes were unquestionably successful.

There were also a small number of new (or nearly new) organs. The philosophy governing the design of Harrison & Harrison's Coventry Cathedral organ (1962) was summed up as

> embracing what is valuable in all schools of organ building, all subservient to the main musical purpose. Transparency, colour and balance between choruses… these have been combined with the perfection of voicing and regulation for which English organ builders are famous.[16]

Photo: John Edis, courtesy of Harrison & Harrison.

Coventry Cathedral, 1962. The console in Harrison & Harrison's workshop.

More cryptically, the builders themselves noted,

> The builders' normal scaling has been followed, but experience gained in the building of the Royal Festival Hall instrument has not been ignored.[17]

A discreet but unmistakable disclaimer.

The Coventry organ remains one of the finest English cathedral organs of the period. Smaller, but equally adventurous, was Walker's new organ for Blackburn Cathedral (1969).

Great Organ		**Swell Organ**	
Quintaton	16	Rohrflöte	8
Principal	8	Viola da Gamba	8
Stopped Diapason	8	Celeste (G)	8
Octave	4	Principal	4
Rohrflute	4	Nasonflute	4
Nazard	$2\frac{2}{3}$	Nazard	$2\frac{2}{3}$
Blockflöte	2	Gemshorn	2
Tierce	$1\frac{3}{5}$	Octavin	1
Fourniture (15.19.22)	III	Mixture (12.19.22)	III
Plein Jeu (22.26.29)	III	Cymbale (29.33.36)	III
Trumpet	8	Fagot	16
		Trompette	8
Swell to Great		Cromhorne	8
Positive to Great		Clairon	4

Positive Organ			
Bourdon	8	Recorder	4
Prestant	4	Spitzflöte	2
Koppelflöte	4	Mixture (19.22.26.29)	IV
Principal	2	Serpent	32
Sesquialtera (12.17)	II	Posaune (extn)	16
Larigot	$1\frac{1}{3}$	Bombarde	8
Scharf (26.29.33)	III	Schalmei	4
Holzregal	16		
Imperial Trumpet	8	Great to Pedal	
		Swell to Pedal	
Swell to Positive (2)		Positive to Pedal	
		Gt & Ped combs coupled	

Pedal Organ		**Accessories**	
Contra Bass	32	6 thumb pistons to Positive	
Principal	16	7 thumb pistons to Great	
Subbass	16	8 thumb pistons to Swell	
Quintaton (Great)	16	7 toe pistons to Pedal	
Octave (extn)	8	4 general pistons	
Nachthorn	8	3 Tremulants (Positive, Swell Chancel,	
Fifteenth	4	Swell Transept)	

Visually and tonally, the Blackburn organ is an exciting instrument, entirely of its age, and more successful, many would say, than the slightly earlier Walker (1967) in the Metropolitan Cathedral, Liverpool.

Most interesting of all was the Gloucester organ of 1971, designed by Ralph Downes and built by Hill, Norman & Beard. Here, a principled consultant, progressive builders, and a selection of antiquarian material (both pipework and cases) made for a distinctive outcome. The organ was needed both to accompany the choral service in the choir and to lead large congregations in the nave. Its use at Three Choirs Festivals and for recitals had also to be considered. Downes developed a scheme for Great, Choir, Swell, Pedal and West Positive, attempting (as at the Festival Hall) to build each division around two choruses – principals and wide-scaled flutes. He chafed under the constraints of the old case, and was not averse to scandalising those he called (and it was not a compliment) 'antiquarians' by increasing the cut-ups of some of the old pipes.[18] He also gave great offence in some quarters by throwing out the 32' open wood (an 'irrelevancy') and discarding the Solo Organ.[19] The final result was an instrument of conspicuous integrity. Perhaps unsurprisingly, it has had no direct descendants.

By the 1970s questions were being asked about this wholesale re-modelling of organs which – though not necessarily to the taste of post-Festival Hall organists – had a musical character and coherence of their own. The reconstruction of the surviving Hill organs at Chester (1970) and Lichfield (1974) created unease in some quarters, and it is notable that from the mid-70s onwards a more conservative approach was taken to distinguished survivors (Peterborough 1981). Some attempts were made to reverse incongruous alterations (Southwark 1986) and at least one Edwardian cathedral organ received what was (almost) a straight restoration, pneumatic action included (Bristol 1988).

At the same time, a growing appreciation of mechanical action among teachers of the organ raised the further question of whether, with all the complex demands made on cathedral organs, and all the problems of location, it would ever be justifiable to revert to its use for a cathedral instrument. The rather different circumstances of the Roman Catholics made it easier for them to answer the question in the affirmative. Clifton Cathedral pioneered the way in 1972 with a 26-stop Rieger, followed by Northampton (1976) and St Chad's, Birmingham (1993) – the latter a substantial 3-manual organ by J W Walker & Sons Ltd housed in a sumptuous case in the west gallery. On the Anglican side of the fence, doubts persisted. Christ Church Cathedral, Oxford, acquired a mechanical-action Rieger in 1979, but Oxford's cathedral is atypical, and the indignities inflicted on the Father Smith case in order to accommodate the Swell were not encouraging.

So it was the reinstatement of the Chichester Cathedral organ (Mander 1986) that pioneered the successful return of tracker action to a mainstream Anglican cathedral. The 34-stop organ, containing pipework by Harris, Byfield, Knight, G P England, Gray & Davison, Hill and Hele had been out of use for some years following the failure of the pneumatic action. A scheme was developed, incorporating all the historic pipework, adding a small Solo Organ, and making other additions in keeping with the essentially nineteenth-century character of the organ. Tracker action was applied to key action and stops, although electric solenoids were provided so that the console could be equipped with pistons. The new nave organ, described above, is controlled by stop knobs below the music desk.

Three other (Anglican) cathedral organs were built during the 1990s with mechanical action. At Chelmsford (Mander 1994 and 1995) the main organ with 40 stops was sited in a west gallery, and the choir organ (24 stops) at the east end of the south aisle behind the choirstalls. The main organ's specification follows.

Great Organ

Bourdon	16
Open Diapason	8
Stopped Diapason	8
Gamba	8
Principal	4
Flute	4
Twelfth	$2\frac{2}{3}$
Fifteenth	2
Sesquialtera (17.19.22)	III
Mixture (22.26.29)	III
Posaune	8
Clarion	4
Cornet (mid C)	V

Swell to Great
Solo to Great
Choir to Great

Choir Organ

Stopped Diapason	8
Salicional	8
Principal	4
Flute	4
Flageolet	2
Mixture (19.22)	II-III
Cromorne	8

Swell to Choir

Combination couplers

Great & Pedal combs coupled
Generals on Swell comp. pedals
Full Organ

Accessories

8 thumb pistons to Great
8 thumb pistons to Swell
6 thumb pistons to Choir
8 general thumb pistons

Swell Organ

Stopped Diapason	8
Viola da Gamba	8
Vox Angelica (c)	8
Principal	4
Flauto Traverso	4
Mixture (17.19.22)	III
Fifteenth	2
Contra Fagotto	16
Trumpet	8
Hautboy	8
Vox Humana	8
Clarion	4

Solo Organ

Ophicleide	8

Pedal Organ

Open Diapason	16
Bourdon	16
Principal	8
Flute	8
Fifteenth	4
Bombarde	16
Trumpet	8

Great to Pedal
Swell to Pedal
Choir to Pedal
Choir Octave to Pedal
Solo to Pedal

8 composition pedals to Pedal
8 composition pedals to Swell/generals
1 piston to Ophicleide
8 reversible thumb pistons
3 reversible pedals
1 general cancel
2 Tremulants (Choir and Swell)
All combinations adjustable via multi-level capture system with 64 channels

Both the Chelmsford organs have tracker action to the keys and pedals, and electric action to the stops, and by means of a duplicate electric action the east end console also allows the player to use most of the west end organ. At Portsmouth Cathedral (Nicholson 1994) a new tracker instrument was built using pipework from an old Nicholson organ (formerly in Manchester Cathedral) and placed on the screen in the centre of the building. Shortly afterwards (1996) the same firm completed a new tracker organ inside the screen case at Southwell. Again, pipework from a Victorian organ (Nicholson 1868) was used as the basis for the tonal specification.

Photo: Courtesy of Mander Organs.

Chelmsford Cathedral. The console of the west end organ (1994) by N P Mander Ltd.

The reintroduction of mechanical action marked the reversal of a trend originating in the pneumatic and electric organs of the 1880s and 90s. Time will tell whether this proves to be the twentieth century's most significant legacy to the twenty-first century. The key to its success is the recognition that no single instrument can adequately serve the needs of the English cathedral – at least, in its Anglican manifestation. This is partly a matter of function (taking account of the far-reaching transformation of the cathedral's role during the twentieth century) and partly a consequence of architectural constraints. It makes sense to provide two organs, of which the principal instrument has tracker action and a well-proportioned tonal specification. The second organ may then be treated in a variety of ways: another tracker instrument to accompany the choir but with a console equipped to play sections of the main organ (Chelmsford), a comprehensive nave organ with its own console but also playable from the screen (Southwell), or a nave division, again with its own console and an electrical connection to the main instrument (Chichester). To that list one might add a free-standing tracker instrument in one of the long mediaeval naves found in shrine churches like Ely or Winchester, or two organs placed back to back on a central screen (as at Portsmouth). Curiously, this approach represents the recovery of a principle which was well understood by both the mediaevals and the Victorians, namely, that different liturgical spaces demand their own organs.

But if one legacy of the twentieth century is the re-invention of an old technology, the other is a new technology designed to assist the player in controlling (that word again) the resources of a complex musical instrument. Computer technology has enabled organ-builders to give organists a facility of control over large consoles only dreamed of by the concert organists of former generations. Those cathedral organists who have welcomed mechanical key action and disciplined tonal schemes have not been inclined to forego the advantages of electric stop and combination actions. In view of the diverse musical life of today's cathedrals this is hardly surprising. (But it has the unfortunate effect of encouraging parish church organists, whose liturgical requirements are rather different, to think that they have to have these facilities, too.)

It is to be hoped that the twenty-first century will see a move away from monster organs, poorly-sited, with sprawling tonal schemes, and a new willingness to match instruments to distinct liturgical spaces and tasks. Such an approach would have architectural as well as musical advantages. It would represent a final modification of the model inherited from Hope-Jones, exploiting (selectively) the technology that he championed, but rejecting his notion that an organ dispersed around the building (but playable from a single console) could adequately serve the needs of a great cathedral. It was his answer to the challenges of the 1890s, just as Hill's two organs of the 1870s answered the question for the previous generation. What, one wonders, will the answer be in 2050?

The author would like to record his thanks to Ian Bell, Geoffrey Morgan, John Norman and Mark Venning for kindly supplying information and correcting dates. However, the opinions expressed remain his own.

References

[1] Peter Williams, *A New History of the Organ* (London 1980), p 182.

[2] See, for instance: Relf Clark, 'An apparently controversial instrument', *BIOS Journal 17* (1993), pp 48-63; Stephen Bicknell, *The History of the English Organ* (Cambridge 1996), pp 291-7.

[3] Clark, op cit p 52.

[4] Idem.

[5] W L Sumner, 'The new diapason chorus in St Paul's Cathedral, London', *Organ* vol 30 (1950-1), pp 173-4.

[6] The 1926 console included a 'prepared for' Echo Organ of 22 stops which was never installed. See, W L Sumner, 'The Organ of Liverpool Cathedral', *Organ* vol 34, p 174.

[7] The Nave Organ was removed a few years ago when a pipeless instrument was installed.

[8] Or combination pedals, in the case of the Pedal Organ.

[9] Harrison & Harrison provided adjustable general pistons in some of their largest pre-war organs, for example, King's College, Cambridge (1934) and Westminster Abbey (1937) – respectively, two and one general piston.

[10] In Willis' Liverpool organ (1926) all the pistons were adjustable by means of a switchboard; by the 1930s his larger organs were equipped with a capture system and lock. By the early-1930s the larger Harrison consoles were fully-adjustable (e.g. King's College, Cambridge 1934).

[11] Mander provided an 8-level capture system at Canterbury in 1980. Harrison installed a dual memory capture system at Westminster Abbey in 1982, up-graded in 1987 and 1994. They employed multi-level systems with 8 memories (generals and divisionals) at Westminster Cathedral and Southwark (1984, 1986). Coventry acquired 8 divisional and 64 general memories in 1986. Westminster Abbey was eventually up-graded to 8 + 128 memories (1994) and Westminster Cathedral to 8 + 256 (1997). Information kindly supplied by Mark Venning.

[12] For example, the Tippet *Magnificat* expects a fanfare trumpet rather than a tuba.

[13] On the tribulations of Willis, and organ-building generally during the early-1900s, see, Bicknell, op cit pp 298-313.

[14] Richard Hird and James Lancelot, *Durham Cathedral Organs* (Durham 1991), pp 34-7, 52-4.

[15] Bicknell, op cit pp 298-9.

[16] David Lepine, *The music and organs of the cathedral and parish church of Saint Michael in Coventry* (Coventry 1962), p 9.

[17] Ibid p 13.

[18] Ralph Downes, *Baroque Tricks* (Oxford 1983), pp 206-7, 209-10.

[19] Ibid. p 204.

Heretical Thoughts
From a Neo-Orchestralist

by
Thomas Murray

An honest observer of today's cultural atmosphere must admit a discouraging fact – that many broadly cultured men and women find organ music unappealing. The instrument's association with the church in an age increasingly dismissive of organised religion has much to do with this, but what of the instrument itself? Does the general lover of music find the organ lacking in power? Certainly not. Wanting in grandeur? Hardly. Deficient in nuance and subtlety? – that "vocabulary" of expression common to other instrumental performance? More than likely. Devotees of symphonic, piano and chamber music find their preferred listening experiences rich in shading, suppleness, agility. The organ they find brittle, austere. Efforts to have more organ music heard on the radio are habitually met with rebuffs: "Oh . . . play something from an *organ* CD? Sorry. Whenever we put on an organ selection we are certain listeners will turn the dial."

During the century now past leading organists and those who write about organ design have claimed that the organ ought not to attempt an "orchestrally imitative" mode of performance, that pursuing such a path is alien to the fundamental nature of the instrument; but can we believe listeners or composers in the century ahead will give much notice to our chosen instrument if it cannot speak an expressive language common with the "mainstream"?

The aim of the present essay is to address this question in a general way, reviewing what was done in the twentieth century to enhance the expressive capability of the organ, encouraging a fresh look at the physical elements of the instrument with a view toward further advances in this direction and noting the recent work of one American firm with a reputation for exploring new possibilities. A brief account of the late twentieth-century revival in transcription playing and a few observations about attitudes toward the restoration of vintage Romantic symphonic organs will hopefully round out the picture.

Of the expressive tools inherited from the nineteenth century the swell enclosure is paramount. Blowing gently or forcefully into a pipe offers us no hope whatever in the quest for nuance because of the resulting distortion in pitch. The swell enclosure is therefore the proven means. Originally applied to short-compass departments of the *Echowerk* class, the swell enclosure soon embraced a much larger division of significant power and completeness. By the mid-twentieth century other divisions, three or more in large North American instruments, were enclosed, thereby offering kaleidoscopic shifts in colour as well as a smooth crescendo. These revolutionary expressive tools, in league with the versatility of electro-pneumatic registrational controls, became the agents for a mode of playing unimagined in earlier times. Some of those opposed to the trend later complained that it inspired no literature of stature, but the contributions of Vierne, Duruflé, Willan and Sowerby (all of whom embraced these expressive advances) hardly need defense today. Had the organ been stalled in its pre-Romantic state the 20th century might have given us nothing at all in the way of new music.

In time these advances were repudiated because of their association with bizarre tonal excesses. The revival of an abundant early repertoire made dynamic *crescendi* seem increasingly unimportant and, in the inexorable march of reactionary developments, the "neo-classical" builder tended to provide only a single swell enclosure, sometimes an ineffective one – by intent. Acknowledging the leaders of this trend and the more recent "historic instrument" movement need not be done here. The names are well known. They were and are the outstanding minds of their time, typically more charismatic and engaging than those whose lot it was to defend the *status quo*. Today the advocates of the "classic" tracker organ include many of the premiere players, organbuilders of stature, historians and consultants.

But is it not troubling that, for the present, the repertoire, modes of performance and styles of instrument are all so stubbornly rooted in the past? Even in the distant past. Naturally, our inherited riches can only come from the past. Yes, it is doubtless revealing to hear the earlier keyboard repertoire in Kirnberger, Valotti or quarter-comma meantone. True, a shallow suspended key action may have an effect on the playing of a *Tierce en taille.* But the frank realisation that we are, for all our riches, a tiny "minority interest" in the larger pool of music-lovers should be unsettling.

At this point we meet both a truism on one hand and a conundrum on the other. The truism is the constitutional human need for change. One need not look back very far to see its effects. In the North American organist's mid-twentieth century world the music of Bach and the composers surrounding him defined the "respectable" core of repertoire. From the Romantic period Franck, the Brahms *Chorale-Preludes* and Reger were admissible; Hindemith, Distler, Alain and Messiaen were perceived as being of enduring merit, as they have indeed proved to be. In contrast, Widor, Gigout and Karg-Elert were not taken seriously; Guilmant was utterly beneath notice. The Elgar *Sonata* might as well have been a sealed book and transcribed music was poison. Consider how our repertoire horizons differ today! The "respectable" core was not enough; we revisited our springs of repertoire and returned much the richer. Most importantly, the repertoire has grown with new works during the intervening years and the *corpus* of literature from other avenues of music which might be transcribed in an idiomatic and convincing way remains very large.

At this point we meet the conundrum – a familiar one: has the evolution of our instrument been fueled primarily by composers and performers who demand new development, or has the builder led the way by experimentation and invention? That query gives birth to related questions. What might come next? Who will lead? Some believe that, after the many stages of "classical" organ we have at last got it right with reproduced antiquity – the no-compromise, repertoire-specific instrument. Within academe this is currently argued with an air of authority and at times with an unbecoming *hauteur.* But could there be other futures? Might our highly nonstandardised instrument exist in a number of valid manifestations? Could the striving for greater expressivity, dormant for a time, be reawakened, and even be brought to its culmination, offering a new sort of instrument which could be a stimulant to the composer's imagination? The answer is implicit, and one North American builder's contributions toward that end, to be described later, are especially deserving of attention.

The chief accusation directed at those who advocate an orchestral approach to the organ is that of "mimicry". A proper organ, it is said, should never attempt to be a counterfeit orchestra. Let it be admitted at once that the organ cannot and need not simulate the symphony orchestra. Our Hautboy stops will never fool an oboist. But we have long known that the available variety of pipe forms produces a welcome variety of timbres. Ralph Kirkpatrick once opined that the "Baroque" organ with its Krummhorns, Blockflöten and Rancketts was "a frozen, pickled, Renaissance wind-band!" A wealth of colour contributes to a lively musical experience and there is no reason to think that the development of new voices, even today, is inherently inartistic. Does the discomfort come from giving the names of orchestral instruments to organ registers? Quite probably. Should we not think of them as what they are, the colours of our instrument?

The point to be recognised is this: though exotic timbres can be accessory to orchestrally-inspired playing at the organ they are not fundamental. The heart of expressive playing in the Romantic mode is the sensitive use of dynamic shading (provided by a swell enclosure) in perfect co-operation with rhythm (rubato, elasticity in tempo). In projecting a phrase with poetic feeling this marriage of techniques can be as satisfying when heard on a beautifully-voiced Diapason stop as when played on a specialised "imitative" register. Indeed, if a player cannot bring life to a phrase with a simple sound, the result will be no better on an alluring stop. To condemn the alluring sound as something meretricious, on the other hand, is to miss the point, for a thoughtfully- shaped phrase played with an alluring sound is the most winsome of all possibilities.

Describing the subtleties of musical interpretation in prose is far more difficult than describing technical and tonal developments in organbuilding; hence, this essay, like countless others before it, will inevitably cheat those facets of "orchestrally-inspired" organ playing which are best demonstrated at the console. In spite of my turning aside from performance issues at this juncture, one point deserves to be stressed: the concept of "orchestrally-inspired" playing must originate within the player. It is fostered initially by listening to other instrumentalists; it is made a reality only when the organist heeds

Ernest Martin Skinner (c 1925) poses with one of his French Horn pipes and the orchestral instrument. More than any other leader of his time, he sought to unite orchestrally-inspired colour with the traditional ensemble in Skinner organs. His adoption of Willis III mixture work beginning in 1924, a major step toward a return to classical chorus work in America, is sometimes overlooked. He saw no conflict between the "orchestral" and "classical" ideals and believed that both original organ literature and transcribed music were artistically valid. In his own words: "The Sermon on the Mount can be preached in any language".

the Biblical imperative: "Go thou and do likewise"!

Being able to "do likewise" requires a sympathetic organbuilder, who can provide instruments more amenable to music-making as it is done by other musicians. But as with performers, the current *Zeitgeist* in organ design seems largely one of fixation on the past. Why is this so? The visionaries in organ design a century ago could never be accused of failing to push their artistic horizon forward. It is with hesitancy that I use the words "forward" and "backward" as they are habitually employed (not least by clergy with an agenda for change) to mean "what I want" and "what I do not want". The point, however, is that the generation which created French Horns and multiplied swell boxes pressed their cause of greater colouristic and expressive potential into the future without knowing the result beforehand, yet confident that the result would be an artistic advance. Today, if someone should propose a truly new venture in organ design the response is likely to be: "the *literature* does not call for it!" What is meant, of course, is that the *literature of the past* does not call for it. Yet the evolved Romantic-eclectic organ is capable of a degree of versatility well beyond that which is explicitly required by the existing literature. (I would have written "the fully-evolved Romantic-eclectic organ" if it were not my premise that continued evolution is needed).

As in organ design, so in playing. Years of teaching have given oft-confirmed proof that too many of today's students have been told they must search a musical score for *written permission* to indulge in even the most modest expressive gestures. A crescendo, a ritard or the use of a particular colour is thought to be unfaithful to the composer unless written down! The result is too often an inhibited, passionless performance. Is it any wonder that, with such strictures, defined by "historic" instrument prototypes and codified registrational "recipes", some find themselves so attracted to improvisation and to transcription playing, where, at last, there is freedom to get the most out of a given instrument, where only a player's imagination and dexterity set the limits and where there is the promise of a fresh musical landscape to be seen?

Additionally, one sector of our profession attaches such great importance to 17th and 18th century music that it tends to define the "legitimate" organ as an "early" instrument. Though it is not my purpose to denounce this type of organ as being without value, it is a fact that such instruments are sometimes represented and sold to trusting clients as being more versatile than they can ever be. But enough. If the "virtual antiques" deserve a place under the sun, instruments that break new ground do as well. My selection of a specific North American firm known for breaking new ground is in no way intended to belittle the work of any other, but rather to invite attention to specific innovations developed for expanding the expressive powers of their instruments. No-one has a monopoly on the innovations described here, and, in any event, the field is wide open for new ideas.

Schoenstein & Co was established in San Francisco in 1877, bringing a tradition of organbuilding from Germany and helping to provide the first wave of church organs placed in California and the West. Felix Schoenstein's four sons received training both in their father's business and from apprenticeships with other builders. By 1977, however, the firm needed revitalisation and a clear artistic direction. Jack Bethards, San Francisco native, professional musician and well-informed *connoisseur* of organ design and history, saw the unique opportunity to pursue a long-cherished desire – to acquire an established firm and make the building of organs in the Romantic style his life's work. One of Bethards' early ventures in the design of new organs emerged from a minute study of Cavaillé-Coll's *orgues de choeur,* much admired for their fullness of tone and versatility. To become thoroughly equipped for this endeavour Bethards organised a study tour in 1985 in collaboration with Kurt Lueders for examining these hardy Cavaillé-Coll specimens as well as some of the lesser-known but undisturbed *grandes orgues* of moderate size. Steuart Goodwin, skilled voicer and finisher, David Broome, one of the world's acknowledged tonal designers and reed experts (trained at J W Walker) and pipe makers Robert Schopp and Fred Oyster of A R Schopp's & Sons participated in this tour by invitation. The measurements and data taken in this way have thus benefitted both Schoenstein's work and the work of important firms which procure pipework from Schopp. Following Cavaillé-Coll's precedent, Schoensteins have devised a formula for organs of 4 to 20 registers adaptable for church or *salon,* i.e. residence use. A number of these instruments have been built, but as we will see, Bethards' work has since followed a more personal path, all the while being nourished by later studies of Romantic organs in England and Germany.

Ever intrigued by the prospects for greater nuance, Bethards has introduced a number of developments which are uniquely associated with Schoenstein at the present time. One is double expression – the "box within a box". This plan is based on the strategy that the most quiet and the most powerful registers in a division gain in usefulness by having the greatest dynamic range possible. A second swell enclosure is built within a larger swell box, operable by a separate swell shoe if desired, usually containing a pair of muted strings and one or more powerful reeds. An example of this plan was carried out at St Paul's Church, K Street in Washington DC (heard to excellent advantage in solo playing and choral accompaniment on the Pro Organo CD *Show Yourselves Joyful),* where, in a Swell of 15 registers, the reed chorus (Posaune, Cornopean, Clarion), the more powerful of two mixtures and a quiet two-rank celeste are placed behind separate expression inside the main enclosure. Jeffrey Smith, organist-choirmaster of St Paul's, who played for two months on the Swell alone while the remainder of the instrument was installed, has often remarked on the extraordinarily smooth *crescendi* possible with the Diapason chorus, softer mixture and oboe in the main box, followed by the powerful doubly-enclosed voices. In practice, this disposition provides an aural effect similar to that of a well-planned two-manual instrument.

Though the high-visibility organs at St Paul's (1995-96, 51 speaking stops) and Schoenstein's *magnum opus* at First Plymouth Congregational Church in Lincoln, Nebraska (1997-98, 85 speaking stops) have predictably aroused most of the interest, it is in playing smaller organs that the value of double-enclosure is most useful. The two-manual (24 speaking stops) organ designed for the late Mark Buxton at Islington United Church (Toronto, Canada) provides an early instance of double-enclosure as well as a fine example of this builder's priorities.

At both Washington and Lincoln there is also a tremulant with variable speed. A balanced pedal commends itself as the ideal means for controlling such a feature and for this reason the player is given several options for the swell shoe customarily used for a register crescendo: it can be the register crescendo as anticipated, it can be assigned to operate one of the inner sets of expression shades or it can vary the pulse of the tremulant. Practice is needed before a player can be entirely confident of the result, but the combined effect of delicate dynamic shading and intentional control of vibrato is nothing less than startling, approaching as it does the expressivity of an instrument held in the hands and played with direct physical contact.

Though invention of new organ registers has been nearly nonexistent in the last half-century, one remarkable new voice has found its way into three new Schoenstein instruments. Taking special notice

Schoenstein's gallery organ (11 registers, 15 ranks) at First Plymouth Church Lincoln, Nebraska may be played from its own console or as a part of the main instrument. The most gentle register (Voix Sérénissime, two ranks) and the most powerful (Harmonic Trumpet) are placed behind double enclosure within the Swell. Schoenstein's casework here respects its art deco surroundings by avoiding profusion.

of the differences found in the registers of the traverse flute, with its Salicional-like low register (not a mystery really, considering the diameter and length of the orchestral instrument) Bethards developed a register ("Symphonic Flute" at Washington, "Boehm Flute" at Lincoln, voiced on 10" pressure in both cases) employing five different pipe structures through a compass of 61 notes: slotted metal pipes of narrow scale for the first 24 notes (not slotted from notes 25 through 34), where orchestral flutes have a reedy timbre, overblowing pipes for notes 35 through 42, double-mouth harmonic from notes 43 through 51 and double-harmonic, double-mouth for the highest range, where an intense piccolo is the result. This register responds especially well to the variable tremulant, even in the lowest octave, where the tone is reminiscent of the 'cello.

Traditional registers can also be combined in unusual ways. In addition to the unenclosed Tuba Magna at Lincoln the three doubly-enclosed Tubas (16' Ophicleide, 8' Tuba, 4' Tuba Clarion) may be drawn together at unison pitch under the Germanic designation *Tuben,* producing a sonority of impressive warmth. Another resource, provided very easily, is a spring-loaded toe-pedal which can engage the Solo to Great coupler (or other couplers and stops) for a momentary *sforzando* – a practical device for playing the opening measures of Guilmant's *Sonata I* and one that suggests all sorts of new uses, depending on the stops employed.

The appearance of multi-level combination controls, however, may be the single most inviting new development for players interested in an orchestrally-inspired mode of performance. This expanded potential for registrational refinement makes it possible to "play the stops as one can play the notes" as never before and has without doubt facilitated the revival of transcription playing. It also promises to encourage the growth of other, as yet unforseen, techniques.

For adjustable combinations I hold the strong conviction that the sequencers ("next" pistons) which have so completely invaded the new organ field in Europe are neither as secure nor as useful as a "range" feature, though this is now increasingly found in the UK. With this system a player finds the customary positioning of general and divisional combinations. There are multiple levels of memory and every combination on a given level does what one expects *unless* the player elects to give a piston a "range" beyond the section of the organ to which it normally belongs. Any divisional thumb or toe piston can then be made into a new general. Two noteworthy advantages for the "range" option are: (1) each piston produces *one predictable change* in the registration, not a different result when pressed at other times (as does a "next" piston), and (2) a piston capable of acting as a general combination is never more than an inch away from the player's hands. A sequencer, on the other hand, may be some distance away.

When confronting these new devices some players plead to "play it like I would normally". This has been anticipated, and all extraordinary features can be in "default" when the wind is turned on until called for. Ironically, reluctance to experiment with such new resources, seen at first as bothersome complications for the organist, is not unknown. Is it yet another symptom of our bondage to the past? The Blockwerk player, meeting with "stops" for the first time, might well have said: "They've ruined everything . . . it will never be the same!"

Mechanical action, whether straightforward or assisted, would probably do little to increase the usefulness of these developments. Doubly-enclosed chorus reeds require high pressures to be effective; in this respect a mechanical action tends to contradict the concept. It is essential to understand the equilibrium between the technique employed and the artistic objective, a principle well recognised by Schoensteins, whose actions are individual valve electro-pneumatic and very crisp in repetition. This choice reasserts the view of Ernest Skinner: "The modern organ, with its magnificent power and wealth of orchestral colour and perfection of mechanism, is made possible wholly through the disassociation of the touch and the wind pressure." In many ways Bethards is arguably the spiritual descendant of Skinner, in his artistic preferences, his persuasive advocacy and eagerness to pioneer. Why must aesthetic harmony and coherence be limited to centuries-old designs?

Unlike early twentieth century advocates of an orchestral ideal for the organ, however, we have learned too much to abandon the traditional ensemble. As emphasised earlier, colourism inspired by the orchestra is hardly unwelcome in organ music, but it is the moulding of sound, its inflection, which is essential to an orchestral concept. In answering the claim that the "symphonic" direction in organ design results in an imitative travesty, Bethards echoes the theme stated before: "It is a common misconception that the symphonic organ concentrates on celestes and solo stops, giving choruses short shrift… It is the musical expressive power of the symphonic medium we are after, not an imitation of the orchestra." The Diapason choruses in the Lincoln Schoenstein reveal the influence of Willis and Hill, yet one can see that there is the confidence to do things in an individual way. For one thing, the mixtures in both Great and Swell are designated *mezzo forte* and *forte,* while differing little in pitch. The Great also has a two-rank Cornet (Twelfth and Seventeenth of Principal scale) to give that slightly tart colouration familiar in a good Victorian chorus. The distinctive T C Lewis/Willis Lieblich Gedeckt, sadly a rarity in North America, has been copied precisely by Bethards from the Willis in St Dominic's Priory in London and can be found in much of Schoenstein's work.

One of the most invigorating aspects of all this is the emergence of a first-rank builder whose philosophy challenges the prevailing orthodoxy. Is the favourable reception elicited by Schoenstein's work an indication of how badly a change (an alternative, really) is needed? In North America as in Britain many of the illustrious assert that "only an organ with mechanical key action and stop controls can be a truly artistic instrument". The spirit of the day it may be, but is it just possible that this assertion has both the vitality of a fashion and its transience as well? I must confess an instinctive mistrust of claims to "the one right way" and would be suspicious of such a claim even if I knew nothing of the fine twentieth century Harrisons, Willises, Skinners and Casavants, all of which are stigmatised by this extravagant claim. It is especially surprising to find some academics, ostensibly the heirs to a liberality of thought, adopting a bias which ignores what might be learned, branding an entire branch of the art as undeserving of notice.

There are, however, the rustlings of independent thinking and a frank awareness that neither electro-pneumatic nor mechanical actions are all created equal, that the console of a large (and therefore tall) tracker instrument is likely to be in a wretched location for the player to hear, that electro-pneumatic mechanism makes the distinctive school of high-pressure voicing possible, and (to go to the core of the matter) that the degree of control over pipe-speech with a suspended action, though present, is by no means comparable with the attack and release possible with other instruments.

I find enjoyment in playing well-designed mechanical organs, especially those of moderate size. The touch of such an organ is distinctive and is most certainly different from other kinds of action. But the player is one person, the listeners (hopefully) many, and I do not delude myself by putting too much trust in what the fingers feel or thinking that the listener will sense such a large difference. Other facets of a performance are far more evident.

There is sure to be change; the human spirit demands it. It was therefore not entirely surprising to find a fresh interest in transcribing on the part of a new generation as the last century came to a close. In 1999, Editions Chantraine published Dvorak's *Symphony IX* ("From the New World") in an entirely new transcription by Stuart Forster, a young Australian whose playing of the piece on a superb E M Skinner organ is recorded on JAV CD #113. Forster, along with Ken Cowan, Erik Wm Suter and Bradley Welch are among those in their twenties who are exploring this avenue with noteworthy success. Of the preceding generation, Peter Conte, *titulaire* of the renowned Wanamaker Organ, follows in the path of his predecessor, the late Keith Chapman, in playing many transcribed works. Frederick Hohman, who has released numerous recordings on his own Pro Organo label, and Peter Sykes, whose recording of Holst's *The Planets* on a Raven CD quickly brought him acclaim, are two more players associated with this *genre*. Among British musicians, David Briggs and Thomas Trotter are well known in America for a repertoire enriched by their playing of transcriptions.

Happily, we hear less and less about the vintage Romantic-orchestral organ being categorically decadent, and the Organ Historical Society, which once concerned itself solely with antique tracker instruments, has led the way in recognising their value. Conservative restoration of these organs, though by no means the norm, is widely understood to be "taking the high road". There is palpable tension, however, between the ideal of a pure restoration (keeping all original console and combination equipment in use) and a renovation embracing the latest in registrational controls (which arguably carries forward the direction of the original design). The understanding of *direction is* crucial here. Where a First Open Diapason has been cast aside to make way for a Scharff, Trombas tranformed into Trompettes or swell shutters on the Choir banished to make a Positive, we are observing changes which negate the fundamental aesthetic of an instrument. Other alterations, such as expanding the registrational flexibility in a symphonic-style organ, may well *affirm* the direction pursued by the builders. It is clearly important to see this distinction.

For a preservationist restorer, the smallest component can be an icon; at the same time, new technology offers enormous musical advantages, especially when an instrument has many users. The question should perhaps be decided case-by-case, but with the question comes a related dilemma – is it better that we have an unaltered organ to teach us "how it was done back then" by Best and Lemare, or embrace new tools which more perfectly realise what they sought to achieve ? The performer must confront a similar question when approaching the published transcriptions of Best and Lemare – is there greater artistry in being faithful, first and last, to their versions or to the originals? One course enshrines a mode of playing from the past, making a "period piece". The other begins afresh – and quite possibly brings a finer result.

A survey of this subject would be incomplete without speaking of those American restoration specialists whose intimate knowledge of the orchestral organ has brought them an established reputation. Nelson Barden and Associates of Boston, renowned for their expertise with automatic player instruments, have created something truly unique in the Boston University Symphonic Organ, uniting instruments by Skinner and Aeolian with additional vintage pipework and Welte, Skinner and Aeolian automatic playing systems. This organ can also record and play through a state-of-the-art computer system and will soon be playable from a four-manual console. Barden's definitive publications on the career of Edwin H Lemare and his research into the Welte recordings of Lemare, Goss-Custard and other "orchestralists" became the catalyst for others, including Hohman and the present writer, to develop the playing techniques of that school some twenty years ago.

Edward Millington Stout of San Francisco is known for restoration work of the highest standard. The organs of Grace Cathedral and the Palace of the Legion of Honor, both four-manual Skinners, are in his care. The firm Czelusniak & Dugal has carried out an exemplary restoration of the early and large Skinner organ at Second Congregational Church in Holyoke, Massachusetts, as well as a sympathetic reconstruction of a yet earlier Skinner in the chapel of the same church, an organ which had previously suffered merciless "baroquification".

Of the firms hitherto known for new instruments, Schantz of Orrville, Ohio have recently made a departure in taking on two major renovation contracts: the Skinner organ in Severance Hall (home of the Cleveland Orchestra) and the very large Hill, Norman & Beard organ in the Town Hall at Melbourne, Australia.

Among the foremost in conservative restoration, with many completed projects to their credit, are Nicholas Thompson-Allen and Joseph Dzeda, who share curatorial responsibility for the organs at Yale University. The Thompson-Allen Company, established nearly fifty years ago by Aubrey Thompson-Allen from the Willis firm *via* Aeolian-Skinner, builds no new instruments, directing its attention solely to maintenance and restorations, some important examples being the Skinner and Aeolian-Skinner instruments at St Peter's Church in Morristown, New Jersey, St Luke's Church in Evanston, Illinois, St Paul's Church in Winston-Salem, North Carolina and St Peter's Church in Philadelphia. They will soon commence restoration of the Skinner organ in St Luke's Cathedral, Portland, Maine.

We are all fortunate that our instrument, found in a wide spectrum of manifestations, has survived perilous times and is still being made. We ought, and need, to make many more friends for it. As for those who already love the songs of Schubert, Wolf and Fauré, the operas of Mozart and Verdi, the glorious symphonic works of Elgar, the music of Stravinsky, Britten and Bernstein, but who believe our instrument fails to speak the same language – the kind of organ envisaged here is intended for them. And for composers, who also need to know that the organ can do far more than they realise.

Into the Twenty-third Century

by
John Norman

The organ was invented approximately 2,200 years ago, so it has just completed its twenty-second century. Will it make the small step, another 100 years, through to the start of the twenty-fourth ?

For the first eleven centuries of its life, the organ was a purely secular instrument. It was not till Georgius, a monk from Venice, returned from Byzantium (Constantinople), where organbuilding had survived the fall of the Roman Empire (just) that the church became interested, some 1,100 years ago. As a matter of fact the organs that he inspired were in some ways more primitive than those known to Nero and the ancient Romans. There was no stop action and the key action involved pulling out a slide to play a note and then pushing it back when you had finished with it!

Organs were taken up by the Benedictine monks and when music, written down, expanded to polyphony, a longer compass was needed and a proper key action was reinvented. We are fortunate that, in the fifteenth century, pictorial art had developed to the point where the Flemish artist Jan Van Eyck could paint a small organ quite accurately. Bigger organs, with bass pipes, required bigger pallets than could be accommodated in key-scale soundboards. Technical developments allowed the motion of the keys to be transmitted sideways and also allowed the bass pipes to be arranged alternately (organbuilders say 'in sides') so that a symmetrical organ case became possible.

From the triptych in Ghent Cathedral, by Jan Van Eyck, 1432.

Notre Dame de Valère, Sion, Switzerland, about 1400.
Drawing by Dr A G Hill

It is not always possible to know if experimentation by instrument makers or demands of composers came first. Certainly, in more recent centuries, Cristofori's pioneer pianos preceded any piano music and Cavaillé-Coll organs preceded the César Franck compositions which exploited them. On the other hand, intelligent instrument makers have always known which way the wind was blowing and done their best to anticipate the demands of the leading performers. Sometimes they go too far – as we shall see.

Secular Organs

Organs have always cost a great deal of money, so it is no surprise that in the medieval period, only the church was rich enough to afford large instruments. We must not forget, however, that the organ has always existed as a secular instrument. Intended for a more intimate environment, secular instruments have normally been much smaller and few pre-eighteenth-century examples survive. The little three-stop one-manual organ, dated 1602, now in Carisbrooke Castle, Isle of Wight, is the oldest in Britain. The compact two-manual 1612 Compenius instrument, built for the King of Prussia to dance to and now in Frederiksborg Castle, Denmark, can give a wonderful account of Tudor-period popular music.

When the Church of England fell into a bad way in the eighteenth century, many organbuilders made good the shortage of work by building chamber organs for the music rooms of the newly-rich. Mostly one-manual instruments, they formed a good part of the output of such builders as John Snetzler and Samuel Green. The cases were made as fine furniture; one Snetzler organ, somewhat altered but with a case designed by Robert Adam, was bought at auction in 1995 by the National Museum of Wales for £285,000. One wonders just how much these organs were actually used, however. The organ which Samuel Green made for Sandbeck Hall in 1790 showed hardly any wear on the key surfaces when it was restored for installation in Buckingham Palace Chapel in the early 1960s.

The next secular opportunity for organbuilders came with the nineteenth-century Town Halls. Their mission to bring music to the people, at a time when the symphony orchestra was in its infancy, led to the commissioning of such notable instruments as Birmingham Town Hall (Hill 1834), and StGeorge's Hall, Liverpool (Willis 1855), Leeds Town Hall (Gray & Davison 1859) and the Ulster Hall, Belfast (Hill 1862). These were followed by Concert Hall organs such as the Royal Albert Hall, London, (Willis 1871) These were (and are) large organs by any standards, grander even than cathedrals could afford or accommodate, despite their prosperity in the late nineteenth-century. Later instruments went overseas and the organs in Sydney Town Hall (Hill 1889), Cape Town City Hall (Norman & Beard 1904) and Wellington Town Hall (Norman & Beard 1904) still survive without significant alteration. The Town Hall organs were principally designed for the performance of orchestral transcriptions and I have a modern recording of the Sydney Town Hall organ accompanying *Amazing Grace* which sounds surprisingly convincing.

The secular organ also flourished in less gigantic form, made possible by nineteenth century technical developments. Tubular pneumatic action, controlled by perforated paper music, made possible the Gavioli showman's organ and all its successors, leading to the Belgian café organs of the 1930s. Although its high point is long past, manufacture continues on an occasional basis and newly-made folding paper music is still available. The showman's organ's smaller brother, the street organ, is still made in countries as far apart as Holland and Cuba. David Leach, in Huddersfield, has a continuing business in beautifully-made little portable instruments, some controlled by floppy disks.

It was but a small transition from the giant Victorian and Edwardian Town Hall instruments to the 50-stop four-manual built by Henry Willis III for the Elite Cinema, Nottingham, in 1920 (now in the Brangwyn Hall, Swansea). However, cinema owners (many of whom attended synagogue rather than church) took a strictly commercial attitude to their organs and the economy in space and cost offered by the Hope-Jones inspired Wurlitzer Unit organ led to a great outpouring of similar instruments by Compton, Christie (Hill Norman & Beard) and Conacher in the few short years from the mid-1920s to the spread of the talkies in the following decade.

Although the underlying technology (especially the prompt electro-pneumatic action) was transferable to church instruments, the musical objectives and voicing style were very different. The differences between the Theatre organ and the Church organ of the 1920s demonstrate an enduring feature of the instrument over many centuries. Like the 'Vicar of Bray' who kept changing his

Showman's organ by Gavioli.

allegiances but still retained his position, the organ has adapted over the centuries from accompanying Roman orgies to accompanying church choirs, from monody to polyphony, from Baroque music to Romantic music and from resonant churches to un-reverberant cinemas. No wonder the successful organbuilder has to be a multi-talented entrepreneur!

At the same time as 'classical music' seemed to be walking away from rhythm, the 1920s saw a great outpouring of popular music with a strong rhythmic basis, from Jazz to the Charleston. Henceforth the distinction has been not so much between church music and secular music as between 'classical music' and 'popular music'. The transistor radio, the cassette tape and the compact disc have now enabled us to be surrounded by reproduced music. Its mass availability has encouraged the spread of the percussion-based 'pop' style. Since 1930, the organ's monopoly of being the only way of making a loud musical noise without an army of performers has been whittled away by electronic amplification.

The theatre organ lives on in a modest way – a restored 20-rank Wurlitzer has recently been installed in Stockport Town Hall for people to dance to – but today's rock groups can produce far more decibels than any Wurlitzer ever could. However, even the 'pop' groups feel the need for a keyboard instrument to provide a sustained backing (dare we call it continuo?) and the electronic 'keyboards' commonly used for this purpose clearly have their roots in the 'one-man-orchestra' philosophy of the theatre organ. The advent of computer technology seems to be changing popular music yet again. The wheel of fashion turns so rapidly in this business that it is difficult to look too far ahead but we may well see instrumentalists replaced by computers in the new millennium, with only singers as 'live' musicians.

The Concert Hall

Despite all this talk of popular music, the real basis of organbuilding today is in our churches and in the concert hall. The revival of interest in seventeenth and eighteenth music in 'as written' form, not 'improved' by later re-orchestration, has led to a demand for small organs for continuo accompaniment. Around half a dozen such instruments have been made in each of the last thirty years, quite a considerable total. These little 'box organs', with the soundboard and pipes below the keys and the player looking over the instrument at the conductor, are derived from the 'bureau organ' designs which Snetzler brought over with him from South Germany in the 1740s. A typical box organ has a stop-list of

Box organ by Peter Collins

Stopped 8ft, Stopped 4ft, Principal 2ft and possibly a $1\frac{1}{3}$ft or a short-compass Sesquialtera. Although relatively portable, being designed to fit in the back of an estate car, such instruments lack weight relative to the sort of organ that Handel, say, would have expected to have in his orchestra pit. Two or three recent box organs have included an open Principal 4ft to help make good this deficiency. Although, if the player is to be able to look over the instrument, the Principal needs to run into a stopped bass for the lowest notes, this clearly adds a degree of gravitas to an otherwise lightweight instrument. Actually, Handel would have expected an Open Diapason 8ft as well, which presents a considerable spatial challenge, even without a full-length bass. Perhaps, before long, someone will accept this challenge?

At the other end of the concert scale, we have the large concert hall instrument. Here the outlook seems to be much more clouded. Much twentieth-century music demands very large (and very expensive) orchestral forces so, to help pay the bills, new concert halls are designed to seat as many people as possible. This leads to two problems. The first is the difficulty of making such halls sufficiently reverberant – a problem that has dogged the Royal Festival Hall ever since its inception – and the second is that such large halls demand very powerful organs to match. Despite the enormous strides which have been made in the design of mechanical key action in recent years, the limit that it places on wind pressures has caused problems for the designers of such organs. The 1982 Ralph Downes-designed Collins organ in the St David's Hall, Cardiff, uses mouth widths of more than one quarter the pipe diameter to get maximum output (at the expense of good speech). It just copes. The Marcussen organ in the Bridgwater Hall, Manchester, uses extensive duplication of ranks to the same end and, by repute, just fails to cope. My prediction is that if the concert hall organ is to survive, we just have to follow Father Willis's lead and use increased wind pressures (even if we don't follow Hope-Jones and Rudolph Wurlitzer all the way to twenty-inches). Will there will be further refinements of tracker action, perhaps controlling only smaller pipes, with all bass pipes operated by some form of pneumatic action? Alternatively, given that single-magnet all-electric actions have inherent response problems, someone may devise a multi-magnet solution, perhaps based on the recently restored action at Gloucester Cathedral, which will deliver enough of the qualities of tracker action to be acceptable to players.

The concert hall organ also faces two other challenges, one hopefully short-term, the other more serious. About eighty years ago concert pitch was 'finally' settled as A=439 Hz (C= 522). It crept up nevertheless and the official British Standard, promulgated just before the second war, was A=440 Hz (C=523.3). Orchestral pitch continued to creep upwards and, a few years ago, the British Standard was quietly dropped without any singers realising it. Now the Philharmonia plays at A=442, the Vienna Philharmonic at A=444 and one American orchestra is alleged to play at A=445. The reason quoted is that some string players think it gives them a bolder tone to impress the all-powerful recording companies. Whether or not one thinks this excuse is rubbish, it does pose a problem for the concert organ. Many continuo organs have transposing keyboards and, having no reeds and few large pipes, can be retuned for each concert. Re-tuning a concert organ, with many reeds and 16ft and 32ft pipes, is a long and expensive operation with a problematic outcome. Hopefully this silly business is but a passing fad.

The other problem faced by the concert organ is the dearth of new music being written for the instrument by composers with general reputations outside the organ loft. This is partly a matter for the music schools – the productive French school of composition that produced César Franck, Charles Marie Widor, Jehan Alain and Olivier Messiaen has never been replicated in this country. It is also partly a matter of patronage. Composers do not live on fresh air and need commissions. Who is to pay for them? Whilst this is a problem common to the whole world of 'serious' music, it seems particularly severe where organ music is concerned.

Cathedrals

The area where church music seems to be at its most flourishing is in our cathedrals. In contrast to church attendance nationally, cathedrals continue to attract as much or more support than hitherto. Even seven years ago the then Dean of St Paul's in London reported that he had counted 13 coach-loads of Japanese tourists *before* the 9.30am service on Sunday morning. As *In Tune with Heaven*, the report of the Archbishops' Commission on Church Music, said: "Visitors come, in some cases in their thousands, and cathedrals seek to help them to become pilgrims by a ministry developed to meet their needs. Music can have an important role in this ministry". The report also said: "There is no doubt that standards of singing and playing are much higher than they were fifty years ago". This improvement in standards has coincided with a public taste cultivated by the wide availability of recordings of the very best performers. There is a willingness to support live music where the performance and repertoire are of the highest quality, but a corresponding intolerance with the second-rate. The result has been that the public reputation of music in cathedrals has never been higher, shared with the Royal Peculiars and the top Oxford and Cambridge collegiate chapels. The reputation of the English choral tradition has a world-wide following. Its distinctive nature is widely admired and has been imitated, in organisation as well as in repertoire, in the old Commonwealth, the USA and now in Europe.

Even success has its problems! The growing use of our cathedrals, with its constant pressure on space, throws down several challenges for the organ. Historically, from the Commonwealth up to about 1850, cathedral organs were placed at the west end of the Choir, often on a screen where they could speak out clearly and directly to congregations seated solely in the Choir. Here they occupied the same relative position as in the parish churches as far as the daily choral services were concerned but did not attempt any serious provision for music west of the screen. The tone was fresh and direct and the longish reverberation could add warmth to the tone without leading to a rhythmic jumble. However, most of our cathedrals are effectively two or even three churches end to end. Even in the nineteenth

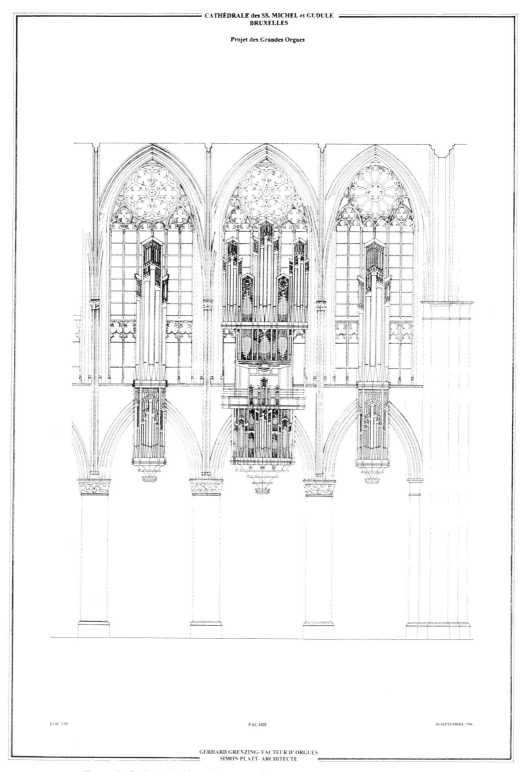

Brussels Cathedral, Nave Organ by Gerhard Grenzing, Barcelona, 2000.

century the popularity of nave services led to a need to provide appropriate organ support for congregational singing. Father Willis developed his high pressure reeds and increased the total power of the organ so that an instrument placed in the Choir could blast away sufficiently to lead a distant congregation in the nave. Willis thus avoided the expense of a second instrument and collected many commissions as a reward for his ingenuity – no fewer than 17 cathedrals.

However, high-pressure reeds have their limitations for present-day repertory, and as nave services get ever more popular and the use of cathedral naves for non-liturgical musical events continues to increase, cathedral chapters have tended to think again about organs in the nave. In some cathedrals attempts have been made to meet this requirement by small detached single-division sections of the main organ (Norwich, Hill Norman & Beard 1940; Canterbury, Mander 1980; and Chichester, Mander 1985). Similar divisions are now planned or under construction at Lichfield (Harrison) and Portsmouth (Nicholson). Heroic nave Trumpets have also been tried (Exeter, Harrison 1965 and St Paul's Cathedral, London, Mander 1977, the latter with a flue chorus).

As the situation often involves two very different sets of acoustical and musical requirements, there is a now trend towards two separate instruments (Chelmsford, Mander 1994; and Southwell, Wood 1992 and Nicholson 1996). A similar arrangement is planned for Sheffield Cathedral. The problem is one of space; not every cathedral has conveniently empty triforia like Southwell and Lichfield. The saga of the Worcester Nave organ is long and sad; the one thing that the present electronic proves is that such instruments are not the answer. It will require considerable courage but my prediction is that, taking our cue from the sixteenth century case at Chartres and following the modern examples in Cologne cathedral and in Brussels, we will see new nave organs hung boldly on the sides of cathedral naves.

Parish Churches
According to the managers of the National Pipe Organ Register, there are over 24,000 organs in Great Britain, the majority of which are in parish churches. How will they go forward to the new millennium? Here the picture is less rosy. Our parish churches are short of people, with declining numbers in many places, and they are short of money, thanks to quota increases well above the rate of inflation – increases driven partly by the past poor performance of the Church Commissioners' investments and partly by the cost of paying decent pensions to retired clergy. The results are a lack of funds for organs and organists and a consequent decline in the numbers of choirs. Statistics gathered by *The Organbuilder* suggest that the average organ is cleaned or restored only once in 44 years and either replaced or rebuilt with new action once in 154 years. One incumbent, interviewed recently, said he didn't think he could raise any money for the organ as he hadn't an organist. A brief trial of the instrument revealed why. There were several notes off on each manual. Which comes first, the chicken or the egg?

Another threat comes from a new iconoclasm amongst some evangelical clergy. This affects not just organs but almost any item of church building or furnishing. Like Cromwell's troops in the seventeenth century, the iconoclasts want to smash anything that reminds them of the old order. Out go the pews, out goes the organ ("we need the space for an interview room") and in comes a 'pop' group with loudspeakers and wires all over the floor and usually under-rehearsed instrumentalists. As a matter of fact even the instrumentalists are now under threat, with the availability of computerised MIDI file players and hundreds of hymns on CD or floppy disk. The hymns are mostly of American origin – *Jesus love's got under my skin* – and only the notes are recorded, not the sound, leaving the operator in control of both tempo and key, with potentially disastrous results. The protagonists of this order, like their historical predecessors, are often intolerant of any other point of view and think that their mind-set will eventually become universal. One can safely predict that this fashion will pass in due time but, as in the seventeenth century, probably not before considerable damage is done to our heritage.

Heritage considerations have come increasingly to the fore in the last fifty years. In mid-century the usual attitude to an old organ was to regard it as a mine of parts for a 'new' one, generally with a detached console. Now we have a greater respect for the importance of the original design of the organ and try to avoid diluting its character with *ad hoc* changes or additions. Organbuilders have become increasingly specialised in recent years and some firms now have a specific IBO accreditation for historic restoration. This involves the retention of original parts if possible and the use of similar materials to the original, avoiding, for example, the replacement of ivory key surfaces by plastic substitutes. There is one danger in all this; an over-emphasis on the importance of restoration can reduce the opportunities for new organs. We have to ensure that respect for the past does not the strangle the future of our art.

One change can be predicted. In other fields a full record of all work is an essential part of historic restoration and is usually a pre-condition of grants. Computers and word-processors make this much easier than before; and good record-keeping will surely become the norm with organs too.

Interestingly enough, computers and record-keeping are also helping to defend our heritage in another way. The National Pipe Organ Register (NPOR), held on a computer at Cambridge University, now has details of well over half the organs in the country. More important, the information is now available to all via the Internet. Just consult www.bios.org.uk/npor. The information is not always up to date as yet but the more people who use the NPOR and send in corrections where necessary the more accurate it will be. The Newman report to the Government on the churches' exemption from Listed Building legislation recommended that all denominational organ advisers compile a list of historic organs in their domain and that such instruments should be protected from removal until serious efforts have been made to find suitable new homes. Computers are very good at listing information and making it accessible; the NPOR represents a vital source of information to assist the listing of historic organs. Knowledge is power and one can forecast some battles ahead as the iconoclasts seek to side-step any restraint on their activities. One can also forecast that some evangelicals will want to opt out of the Faculty system, little realising that this would be jumping out of the frying pan into the fire, since it would be tantamount to handing over the management of two-thirds of our churches to the dead hand of English Heritage.

Electronics

Seventy years ago, electronic experimenters started making organ simulations, thinking that the organ was the easiest acoustic instrument to imitate. The earliest commercial instruments used electro-mechanical methods of generation; some makes were reliable, others not. The replacement of hot valves by transistors in the early 1960s improved reliability but it took the improvements in simulation in the 1980s, when digital technology replaced analogue technology, to make the instruments more acceptable.

We have now reached the situation where electronic instruments have taken over the "bottom of the market" and are the installation of choice where the calibre of music is considered unimportant and low first cost fundamental. In some ways this has done a service to real organbuilding. The low-grade organbuilders who would build you a cheap organ out of an assemblage of second-hand parts have largely disappeared and few will mourn their passing. All the successful organbuilders have moved upmarket and offer a quality of construction and finish far better than was usual fifty years ago. This trend seems likely to continue.

So far, and despite a few well-publicised exceptions, electronic instruments have failed to catch the high ground. Indeed in some ways they are backward looking. What real organbuilder now supplies consoles with stop tabs instead of knobs? But technology never stands still. What of the future? Certainly electronic components will continue to get cheaper. However, this may not be much help since they are already only a small part of the total cost of an instrument and there is not too much that can be done about the costs of cabinetwork which, in some cases, is already marginal in its quality and acceptability. Nor does anyone seem to be addressing the problems of the short replacement cycle that condemns the purchasers of electronic instruments to relatively frequent capital expenditure. However, one area of improvement may be the development of 'flat' loudspeakers, now on the horizon, that could liberate churches from the bulky and ugly loudspeaker boxes which blight many electronic installations.

The other possible advance is in the quality of simulation. However, unlike the transition from analogue to digital technology, no breakthroughs are imminent and the major problems which the electronic makers face are the 'one-size-fits-all' stop lists and the low standards of installation and tonal finishing which afflict all but a very few. Perhaps an instrument which seeks only to copy will never win wide respect; the opportunity is rather for an enterprising maker to develop a new sound that no other instrument can offer and which composers feel they cannot do without. The synthesiser has achieved this in some popular music but failed elsewhere. If it happens in church music we shall all have to watch out.

Organ Builders

A hundred years ago, most successful organbuilders were relatively large concerns. You had to be big to afford a steam engine to drive the power tools to cut and finish wood. The J C Bishop firm went bust in 1880 because it wasn't mechanised. It is different today; portable electric tools now allow some small firms to be efficient manufacturers, computers help them to keep the accounts and the internet helps to publicise their work. Some successful organbuilders employ only three to six people, although they cannot handle the biggest instruments.

This trend has been helped by the emergence of specialist suppliers. There have always been specialist metal pipe makers and no organbuilder has made his own electrical parts since about 1960. But now you can buy tracker action and electrical parts from UK-based specialists who are major world suppliers. There are specialist case designers, specialist reed voicers, specialist CAD designers and even a specialist site foreman. The client can have the benefit of an accredited specialist consultant, too. The difficulty with a proliferation of small firms is that it becomes more difficult for someone coming in to the craft to get an all-round training. This problem will have to be addressed. The legacy of good people brought into organbuilding by Maurice Forsyth-Grant may well outlive the legacy of his instruments.

After a big fall in the 1970s, employment in British organbuilding has remained steady in recent years at around 450 people. Of course many organbuilders restrict themselves purely to restoration and to tuning and this probably accounts for more than half the work today. However, around twenty organbuilding firms make at least one new instrument in any given year and although there have been some high profile instruments imported from Euroland, about 20% of the new organs made here are exported, not only to the USA but also to Japan and Scandinavia. Indeed, we are now in the situation where many of the best new British organs cannot be seen in Britain.

So what do we see organ builders doing in the next century? We can expect an increasing emphasis on conservation and restoration in our parish churches, but opportunities for distinguished work in our cathedrals. Increasing wealth means that musicians can now afford their own house organs instead of relying on a piano with a pedal attachment and construction of such instruments is a growth area. One characteristic which the organ has, not shared by piano-makers or orchestral instrument makers, is the direct contact between players and makers, since the organbuilder is not insulated from his customers by dealers. It is still a very personal business with direct feedback of changing musical tastes, so if we can be confident of one thing, it is of continuing change.

Organ Mechanism – Key Action

The past century has seen a whirlwind of change in organ mechanism. Key action in new instruments has gone from tracker to tubular pneumatic to electro-pneumatic (or electric) and back to tracker again. Even the technology of tracker actions has changed; from wood-based at the beginning of the century to metal-based components in the 1970s and 80s and now back to wood again.

In 1982 almost exactly 75% of new organs made in this country had tracker key action; in 1998 it was 92%. Knowledge of the techniques involved in making a manageably light key action, unknown in the nineteenth century, is now nearly universal, though there are still considerable differences between makers. One of the unresolved debates is over the relative merits of bushed and un-bushed actions. Bushed actions interpose leather or felt in the various holes of action components through which metal parts pass in order to stop any rattling noises when the action is played. Un-bushed actions (universal before the nineteenth century) use direct metal-to-metal contact. It is a matter of priorities. Bushed actions are quieter but un-bushed actions are crisper, with less friction and less unwanted 'give'. The availability of specialist parts made to a very high standard of accuracy, with minimal bushing, has narrowed this debate. One can hope that in the future, still better parts will give us the best of both worlds – both crisp and silent – thus ending the debate.

Another debate, more nearly resolved, concerns the method of keeping the action taut and in good adjustment. Victorian actions used a lead-weighted 'thumper' above the manual keys, providing constant tension but variable depth of key movement. This method could not be used on the pedal keyboard which was left un-tensioned, leading to a characteristic rattle. Modern tracker actions mostly use a fixed key travel and tension the actions, both manual and pedal, with a square or backfall frame which can move on a pivot. This is held either by a spring (with a damper to stop it moving quickly under a heavy chord) or by "dummy trackers" which cancel out any movement of the organ frame. Most builders seem now to be moving to the latter system.

The conventional British tracker action uses a key with a pivot in the middle, with the back of the key connected to a pivot (a 'backfall') to reverse the direction of pull. The conventional French action is 'suspended', with the key pivoted at the back and the action connected in front of the pivot so no backfall is required, though the key itself may need to be longer. In the 1980s there was a big debate over the relative merits of the two systems, the suspended system claiming to be more direct, with lower inertia. In truth, there is not much in it and organbuilders are moving towards a pragmatic approach, using whichever system happens to suit the layout of the particular instrument in hand. A trend which one hopes will progress further is a change in the design process, starting from the feel of the key and then working back to the soundboard, instead of the other way round. Computers have come to our aid here. Many leading organbuilders have been using CAD (Computer-Aided Design) for several years instead of pencil and paper. It seems only a matter of time before this becomes universal for anyone making new instruments.

Although tracker action predominates for new organs, and seems likely to continue to do so, existing tubular and electric action organs are often unsuited for conversion to tracker. There is thus a continuing need for electric or electro-pneumatic actions, also for second consoles for otherwise tracker instruments, as recently at Christchurch Priory. 'Solid-state' coupling actions, using transistors and diodes, were introduced around 1970 and have been joined by computer-controlled scanning systems which need only a small co-axial cable to connect them to the console. These have proved reliable, although one wonders whether, when they do eventually go wrong, there will be anyone around who knows how they work.

There was a hope in the 1960s that simple all-electric actions would prove more durable than conventional electro-pneumatic mechanism. This has not proved to be the case and single magnet actions have mostly been found unresponsive through fundamental limitations in magnet design. However pioneer multiple magnet actions were made as long as 30 years ago and proved exceptionally responsive. It seems possible that, combined with contact-less magnetic key sensors which can detect the speed of movement of the key, it would now be possible to make an all-electric action which is just as responsive as tracker. That still leaves the 'feel of the key' problem to be solved, but surely this will not prove to be beyond the wit of man in the coming century.

Consoles

Players have wished for simple methods of changing the stops quickly ever since the invention of the 'shifting movement' in the eighteenth century. These have become ever more sophisticated over the years and there seems little reason why the process should stop now. This is related to the size of instrument of course. In the 1960s one often came across the silliness of five thumb pistons being provided to control a four-stop Choir organ; in current practice only simple mechanical stop-action and combination facilities are normally provided for instruments smaller than about 18 stops. Above this size, electric stop-actions and pistons quickly adjustable by setter piston (once prohibitively expensive) are now commonplace. Electronic solid state memories enable each player to have his own private piston settings and general pistons are now provided on many instruments. The only limit to their number seems to be the restricted space between the keys.

The electro-pneumatic machines formerly used to move the sliders, which tend to need fairly frequent re-leathering, have been replaced by large solenoids. These are quite rapid enough for stop-action and, in nearly forty years experience, have proved very reliable. There has also been a trend to replace worn pneumatic piston action with electric solenoids behind the knobs. This has not always been an advance; the new mechanism often only moved the knobs about 5/8 inch (15mm), so you couldn't see clearly which knobs were in and which were out. Fortunately organbuilders can now buy solenoid mechanisms that move the knobs a full inch. Even so, a couple of recent restorations have shown that, properly refurbished, pneumatic operation of the knobs can still be very satisfactory.

Like many console details, the appearance of the stop-knobs seems very much a matter of fashion. The fat solid ivory knobs used by Hill and by Willis a hundred years ago are things of the past. Wooden knobs with mock-ivory inserts have become the general rule, ivory substitutes being more acceptable here than they are on the keys, where the feel of the surface is so important. Recent work has continued the British tradition of sumptuously-finished consoles including, in the best work, the more recent return to hand-finished lettering on the knobs. The 1960s fashion for white engraving on black knobs is not yet dead, but seems destined to go soon; the lettering becomes difficult to read in dim light or when the knob becomes dirty. As to the layout of the knobs, the recent fashion for terraced jambs, Cavaillé-Coll style, is excellent when you need to see over the console (better than stop-keys) but a pointless complication otherwise.

Both organbuilders and players have been divided over the relative merits of toe pedals and toe pistons for many years. Do not expect an early resolution of either this debate or the one over the design of pedalboards, straight versus radiating and concave versus flat.

The latest technical development is the sequencer, which, in effect, allows you to step through a series of general pistons by repeatedly pressing the same piston. At a recent recital the performer only pressed one piston the whole evening, but he pressed it 200 times! Another player likens the liberating effect of a sequencer to that obtained by playing from memory instead of from the score. One's whole practice and performance time can be devoted to music instead of trying to decide where a hand can be spared for this that or the other. Furthermore, memory is now so cheap that you can store the sequencer set-up for a given piece permanently so, next time you play it, the registration is all ready for you. At Southwell Minster the system has the capability to store up to 4,995 combinations for the whole organ. An alternative system in increasingly common use is the 'stepper', by which means the general pistons are sequentially accessed through a single 'advance' piston thumb and/or toe. The costs of this sort of thing are still dropping so one can predict that such facilities will soon become normal for any substantial instrument.

Raising the Wind

"Sine me nihil" it said on the stop-knob. "What's that", I said. "Have you forgotten your Latin", he said, "It means 'Nothing without me' – in other words, drawing the knob turns the blower on." These days we all take the electric blower for granted.

Medieval organs had levers to raise 'feeder' bellows which then dropped under their own weight to supply the wind. The 1862 Schulze at Doncaster originally had such a system but, in the previous century, the popularity of chamber organs led to the development of a more space-saving arrangement, with a rectangular reservoir bellows to store the wind, fed by feeder bellows placed underneath. The reservoir bellows stores wind between the pulses of air delivered by the feeders and, when demand is light, gives the human blower a chance to rest.

The bellows has to deliver a nearly constant pressure, as even a small variation will upset the tuning of treble pipes. Eighteenth-century organ builders minimised variations by making the feeder bellows wedge-shaped and designing them to drop below the horizontal when empty. Nineteenth-century builders preferred rectangular bellows since they have double the storage capacity for the same size. Capacity was also increased by giving the bellows a long vertical movement, keeping the pressure constant by providing a double set of ribs, one folding in and the other folding outwards, neatly cancelling out their effect on the pressure. This 'double-rise' reservoir bellows became the standard in Victorian organs.

The invention of the fan blower changed everything. The output from the blower is regulated by a control valve which automatically shuts the outlet from the blower when the bellows is full. If the blower is large enough to support full organ, the sole function of the bellows is to operate this valve. In practice, wind flows out of the bellows in fits and starts; staccato chords in the left hand will cause particularly sharp changes. A moving column of air has inertia, which takes energy to start and stop, causing a drop in the pressure when the chord is first held and a surge when it is released. This can show itself as either a slow wave (perhaps twice or three times a second) or as a faster dither, depending on the dimensions of the bellows and wind-trunks. Our ears are choosy – we like a slow wave, like a well-tuned Celeste, but we find a fast dither deeply unattractive. J C Bishop invented the 'concussion bellows' in 1826 to reduce wind surges and slow them. The 1988 Kenneth Jones organ in Emmanuel College Chapel, Cambridge, provides cut-outs to the concussions, controlled from a stop-knob, so that the player can choose what level of unsteadiness he prefers.

In the early 20th century, many organbuilders changed from double-rise bellows to single-rise. A reasonably quick-acting valve will allow so little movement that any change in pressure will not be noticeable. However, such a bellows must be made large enough or the 'flexibility' in the wind supply that results from the inertia of the air in the wind-trunk will be too rapid to be musical. This is why Harrison & Harrison remained faithful to double-rise reservoirs when everyone else abandoned them. Nevertheless, organs are often seen as consuming valuable space so there is considerable pressure to make them as compact as possible. The ultimate is to do away with the bellows altogether. This is possible if the fan of the electric blower is so designed that a constant pressure is generated no matter how much wind is used. In practice, this means making the blower rather inefficient. This does not matter too much in a very small organ and constant-pressure blowers have become almost standard in box organs.

On larger instruments the next most compact arrangement is to build a diaphragm-type bellows into the underside of each soundboard. These devices are generally known by their German name of 'Schwimmer' bellows, though 'Regulator' is a more accurate term since all the device has to do is to operate the control valve, there being no need to actually store any wind; the fan blower delivers it in a continuous stream. The weakness of the schwimmer bellows is that the wind is just *too* perfect, just *too* steady, so some builders have gone back to the wedge (diagonal) bellows of the eighteenth century, citing a modest pressure variation as a positive advantage. The pressure does vary slightly from full to empty when raised by hand or foot and allowed to fall as a feeder bellows. However, attempts to combine feeder bellows with electric blowing have not met with wide success and, if a wedge bellows is used merely to work a blower control valve, it will move so little between silence and full organ that the pressure variation becomes purely theoretical and the wedge construction a waste of space.

So what now is the general practice for new organs? Organ builders are divided. Some normally fit schwimmers so that instruments can be made as compact as possible, enabling them to stand in good positions without being physically over-intrusive. Others swear by conventional bellows of one kind or another, pointing to their long life, to the less rigid tone and the ability to specify the beauty of a Dom Bédos-type tremulant. This looks like a battle set to continue into the 21st century. If you can spare the space for conventional bellows, they are probably best. If you cannot spare the space, at least there is an alternative.

The latest innovation is a device which automatically slows down the blower when you are not playing, reducing electricity consumption and noise, and speeds it up again when you hit a large chord, all without any moving parts. As it can then run the blower rather faster than normal the device can also rescue a blower that is slightly undersized. It could become almost a standard fitting.

Organ Cases
With distinguished exceptions, architects have not usually been very successful as organ case designers. Organ cases nevertheless still tend to follow architectural fashion. After all, the organ is normally the largest piece of furniture in a building. It was natural therefore that in the seventeenth and eighteenth centuries that case designs followed the fashion for classically inspired Baroque and Rococo furniture, tempered by the realities of accommodating bass pipes on display. The nineteenth century Gothic revival led to a search for truly Gothic originals, of which few survived, so many organs were designed to look like giant versions of the Van Eyck portative. This was later simplified to a 'fence' of zinc bass pipes standing on top of simple panelling. Following on the famous dictums of Father Willis, many musicians grudged expenditure of money on cases, arguing that the money was better spent on extra stops. This poverty-stricken approach often condemned ugly organs to out-of-the-way locations.

When architectural modernism arrived, with its emphasis on function and honesty, Walter Holtkamp devised a system with treble pipes on display in the front of the organ and basses behind. This style was never as popular here as in its native America, though one of the larger examples is the American-influenced three-manual instrument in the Mormon Hyde Park Chapel, Kensington, London, (Hill Norman & Beard 1961). Another way of expressing the layout of the organ honestly is to follow the *werkprinzip* and show the layout of the organ in the design of the case. Height and space restrictions make a full Hamburg-style case impossible in the majority of instruments in this country but J W Walker, Hill Norman & Beard, Peter Collins, Grant Degens and Bradbeer and many others built organs with full tone-cabinet style cases. Many were somewhat 'brutalist' in style, without applied decoration, relying on their overall form for visual effect.

As the brutalist tide has receded, designers have been able to incorporate more decoration into their cases. David Graebe's monumental pair of organ cases in Lancing College Chapel (J W Walker

Hyde Park Chapel, Kensington, neo-Holtkamp layout, Hill Norman & Beard 1961.

and Frobenius organs 1986) led the way in the use of high-quality carving. Several recent instruments have used Italianate case designs to provide simple decoration but the new William Drake organ in the chapel of the Houses of Parliament is a realisation of a highly-ornate Victorian Gothic design by Pugin. A recent Mander instrument has even been made in Chinese style. As yet, however, no-one has attempted to pick up the current architectural theme of metal, glass and tented roofs!

With modern woodworking machinery the quality of cabinetwork has risen to rival even some of the best eighteenth century instruments; virtually all new organs now have decent cases of one style or another. Several free-lance designers now compete for organbuilders' business and it can be argued that the state of organ case design is healthier than it has been for centuries. Subtly, one wonders if it is all a response to the electronics. If you have a real organ, flaunt it! Certainly the provision of a decent case has enabled several recent instruments to be placed in prominent positions which might not have been tenable had they been less good looking. This trend seems set to continue.

Chamber organ, Washington DC,
Mander Organs, 1999.

Tonal Design

There is always a tension between the younger organbuilders who are all for the latest trends in tonal design and the older ones who want to stick to a style with which they are familiar. Thus, at the beginning of the 20th century, Arthur Harrison and Norman & Beard were both influenced by Hope-Jones and by George Dixon, the critic, whereas Hill and Willis, on the other hand, were both considered old hat. Sometimes, of course, this looking forward goes to extremes such as in the quite extraordinarily foundational 1929 four-manual Hill Norman & Beard in Melbourne Town Hall, Australia, complete with 32ft Diaphone on 20-inch wind, during 2000 being rebuilt and augmented by Shantz of America. Some forty years later, Grant Degens & Bradbeer went to the extreme in the other direction in the neo-Baroque instrument at New College, Oxford. This organ, like several of Maurice Forsyth-Grant's creations, has already undergone tonal modification.

The mainstream has, of course, moved more cautiously. Norwich (Hill Norman & Beard 1940), with its unenclosed Choir organ in a chair case, was probably the first cathedral organ to start to move away from the Dixon influence, although the Continental *orgelbewegung* had, at that time, largely passed this country by. The Royal Festival Hall organ (Harrison & Harrison, with Ralph Downes, 1954) gave everyone a big shock but spawned no direct copies. Nevertheless both Walter Goodey at J W Walker and Mark Fairhead at Hill Norman & Beard were both influenced by recordings of the Schnitger organ at Steinkirchen and tried their hands at neo-Baroque voicing.

This style started with musicians' complaints that the standard Harrison cathedral organ, with its smooth and almost hesitant speech, was unsuitable for Bach. Most of the argument was about one feature of the restored Schnitger organs: the explosive, if uneven, attack of the pipes when starting their note. The debate opened up a detail of voicing technique, the practice of 'nicking', a series of light cuts made by the voicer in the edge of the languid and the lower lip of the pipe-mouth. A pipe without nicks will speak quickly and explosively, with a pronounced 'spit' before it settles down to the correct note. Nicking controls the spit and, if heavy, slows up the speech and curtails the upper harmonics. In neo-Baroque voicing the nicking is omitted and the foot of the pipe is left wide open so that it can fill with wind very quickly. The power of the pipe is regulated by pressing the bottom lip and closing up the flue. From about 1950 both Walker's and Hill's started to voice Choir-Positives without nicks. Later, Grant, Degens and Bradbeer applied this technique to whole instruments which became well- known for their aggressive choruses.

One can see the progression. Firstly a nominal following of one facet of the *Orgelbewegung* – the unenclosed third manual with a proper chorus structure, then the interest in pipe speech and the implementation of open-foot voicing without nicking. For a while however, it went no further, organists seeking the eclectic organ and regarding a neo-Baroque Positive division as an effect, not as part of the whole structure of the instrument. Nevertheless some felt that we should go further and copy precisely the construction of the instruments of eighteenth-century Hanseatic Germany. One of the most influential instruments has been the organ in the chapel of Queen's College, Oxford, made by Frobenius in 1965. This has separate tone-cabinets for each department and both stop and key action are mechanical. Following the Queen's College instrument, adoption of the principles of the Hanseatic organ gradually spread, including not only the tonal design and voicing but also the use of tone-cabinets and, from about 1970, tracker key-action.

At this point many leading musicians pronounced the British organ dead and pressed for Hamburg-style instruments with *werkprinzip* layout, tracker action and aggressive neo-Baroque voicing. Some distinguished instruments were imported. There were those who maintained that the organ of early eighteenth-century Hanseatic north Germany was the high point of the design of the instrument, that all subsequent development had been decadent and that therefore organ design should remain static, copying historic models as accurately as possible. It hasn't happened. We have now passed on from these instruments which, looking back, now seem rather brash. The lack of dynamic flexibility is the problem, leading to the re-introduction of mild string stops and of Swell divisions instead of high-pitched Brustwerks. Gradually most organbuilders have abandoned voicing without nicks and returned to regulating pipes at the foot. Apart from anything else, experience showed that the natural 'spring' of the pipe-metal often caused flue-regulated pipes to go out of adjustment.

As might be expected, the present situation has led to differences of opinion. On the one side we have our church musicians, in the van of a movement to recognise the validity of late 19th-century

British and French organs as vehicles for the repertoire. This line of thought follows from the continuing popularity of the English tradition of cathedral and collegiate choirs and their music. On the other side, there are concert players who still hanker for basically neo-Baroque organs and this is still leading to some high profile imported instruments.

Gradually, however, opinion has changed. There have been attempts to copy the organs of Cavaillé-Coll, with varying success. We have learned to value what we have, both from the 19th century in the work of Hill, Willis and others, and from the fragmentary remains of 18th century work. Whether building in a style inspired by the nineteenth century masters or looking back a further century (and there are genuine differences of style between builders), most British organbuilders today voice in the style of Bridge, England, Hill or Gray & Davison, producing good choruses without spit and rounded but still quite 'open' reeds. Stop-lists increasingly recognise that the origins of the second manual were from an enclosed miniature Great organ rather than from an enclosed Positive or Brustwerk and that such divisions are particularly good for the vast body of British choral music. Examples of these changes in style are shown in the accompanying table.

The Changing Face of the Second Manual 1740-2000

St Helen's Church, Bishopsgate, London
Griffin 1743
Swell

Open Diapason	8
Stopt Diapason	8
Cornet	V
Trumpet	8
Clarion	4

A short-compass division placed above and behind and behind the Great organ. A rival proposal by Jordan, not accepted, had an Hautboy in place of the Clarion, which would have been more usual.

The Chapel, Ashridge
Elliot 1818
Swell

Open Diapason	8
Stopped Diapason	8
Principal	4
Hautboy	8

A short-compass division placed behind the Great organ, at a higher level.

Blandford Forum, Parish Church
Hill 1876 (remainder of organ by England 1794)
Swell

Bourdon	16
Open Diapason	8
Stopped Diapason	8
Principal	4
Mixture	III
Oboe	8
Trumpet	8

A classic nineteenth-century full-compass English Swell with a flue Double. Placed behind the Great organ.

Holy Trinity, Lyonsdown, New Barnet
Walker 1900
Swell

Bourdon	16
Open Diapason	8
Stopped Diapason	8
Echo Gamba	8
Voix Celeste	8
Principal	4
Mixture	II
Oboe	8
Horn	8

A turn-of-the-century example including two narrow-scale string stops.

Queen's College Chapel, Oxford
Frobenius 1965
Brustpositive

Gedeckt	8
Principal	4
Rohrflute	4
Gemshorn	2
Quint	$1\frac{1}{3}$
Scharff	III
Cromorne	8

Based on a 4ft Principal, this department is placed below the Great organ, just above the console. Note fractional-length reed stop.

Hucknall Parish Church, Notts.
(Now in Sedbergh School Chapel)
Church 1976
Swell

Stopped Diapason	8
Gamba	8
Principal	4
Nason Flute	4
Octave	2
Quint	$1\frac{1}{3}$
Sharp Mixture	III
Dulcian	8
Shawm	4

Placed just above the console in the Brustwerk position with folding doors, not conventional Swell shutters. Note re-introduction of a mild string stop.

Mill Hill School Chapel
Mander 1985
Swell

Chimney Flute	8
Viola da Gamba	8
Principal	4
Stopped Flute	4
Gemshorn	2
Larigot	$1\frac{1}{3}$
Mixture	III
Hautboy	8

Placed immediately above the Great organ with conventional shutters. Note re-introduction of a full-length reed.

Oakham Parish Church
Tickell 1995
Swell

Chimney Flute	8
Salicional	8
Voix Celeste	8
Principal	4
Flute	4
Gemshorn	2
Mixture	III
Cremona	16
Hautboy	8

For lack of height, placed behind but slightly higher than the Great organ. Note introduction of a Celeste and of a 16ft reed.

Westbourne Parish Church
Tickell 2001
Swell

Open Diapason	8
Chimney Flute	8
Salicional	8
Voix Celeste	8
Principal	4
Flageolet	2
Sesquialtera	III
Cremona	16
Hautboy	8

This division will be placed below the Great organ, the console being slightly detached. Note re-introduction of the Open Diapason and replacement of a sharp quint mixture by a more moderately-pitched Tierce mixture.

One issue which has attracted little attention so far is that of tuning methods. The organ is particularly sensitive to the tuning because its sound does not die away like that of keyboard instruments that are plucked or struck. The problem is that Equal Temperament produces equally bad (sharp) thirds in every key. If your registration includes a Tierce or a Mixture with a third-sounding interval in it, a chord with a third in it will cause a clash between the third-sounding pipe of the lower note of the chord (tuned true) and the unison-sounding pipe of the upper note, tempered by about a seventh of a semitone.

Mild unequal tunings such as Young's or Vallotti improve the thirds in the more popular keys such as F,C,G and D at the expense of the less popular keys such as F# and C# major. These tunings, now adopted by several organbuilders, make Sesquialtera stops more versatile and seem to have caused no restriction of the repertoire in practice, one player recommending unequal tuning for Messiaen! We will see more use of them.

Musical fashion is more like a spiral than a pendulum. When fashion swings back it never goes quite to the same place. We may go back to organs of a previous period – inspired by the music that was written for those instruments – but the true artist never makes an exact copy – he always puts in something of his own as well. The trend is towards a greater interest in the variety of tone colour characteristic of some nineteenth century organs without abandoning the use of lighter wind-pressures, of reasonably complete choruses, of tracker key-action and the placement of organs with good cases in decently open positions. The challenge for the twenty-first century AD (the twenty-third century of the organ) is to provide instruments which can perform a wide range of music with integrity without themselves having their character diluted by compromise.

Lancing College Chapel, J W Walker, 1986.
Case designed by David Graebe

A Visit to the World's Largest Pipe Organ, with Some Impressions, Views and Opinions

by
Patrick Burns

Few enthusiasts for the pipe organ will be unaware that the largest pipe organ ever built is installed in the Convention Hall in Atlantic City, New Jersey, USA. By co-incidence the world's largest fully operational pipe organ is but sixty miles away in the city of Philadelphia installed in what was formerly the John Wanamaker store now renamed Taylor & Lord. The huge resources of this instrument are almost all working, through the dedicated efforts of its enthusiastic curator Peter Van der Spek. It is therefore understandable that this should be regarded as the largest organ in the world. The major difference, however, is that the Wanamaker organ has almost trebled in size from the time of its installation due to the fact that the Wanamaker store had a staff of at least thirty in its own organ building department so enabling the organ to grow to the size that it is today.

The Atlantic City Auditorium organ is a different story altogether. This was and still is the largest single installation of a complete instrument built at one time. But why so large? It is necessary at this point to consider the Auditorium itself.

The length of the hall is approximately 150 metres (500 feet); 88 metres wide (350 feet); 43 metres high (138 feet) and with a volume of 15,500,000 cubic feet. You could build a thirteen storey building in the centre of the auditorium before it would touch the ceiling! The building is so large that it has been possible to fly a helicopter inside!! On completion it must have been one of the largest enclosed spaces on earth. This then sets the scene for the home of the largest organ in the world.

But how large? If we consider that the largest instruments in this country are the Royal Albert Hall in London and the Anglican Cathedral in Liverpool with approximately ten thousand pipes each, and observe that this instrument contains nearly thirty three thousand pipes, we can then begin to grasp just how enormous it is. Here in a single room clear of any obstructions can be seated 41,000 people!

This then was the situation facing the designer of the organ, Senator Emerson Richards. A few words about this remarkable man. A native of Atlantic City, from a wealthy and privileged background and a member of the state Senate, he was a man whose status could be used with considerable influence. I think of him as the world's luckiest organ enthusiast! He had already master-minded the design of a huge 5-manual organ of over 100 ranks for the Atlantic City High School auditorium. This organ no longer exists in its original home but is largely intact in store in Arizona. Senator Emerson Richards' great passion in life was the pipe organ. His wealth enabled him to indulge his passion and he had a number of installations in varying sizes in his Atlantic City home – the last installation being of approximately 100 ranks. His wealth also enabled him to travel – he met some of the world's greatest organists and was aware of the different styles of organ building particularly in Europe. His knowledge of organ building techniques was limitless and more than one organ builder regarded him as the most talented (amateur) organ builder they had ever encountered. It is not difficult to imagine therefore that the authorities in Atlantic City were quite happy to go along with Emerson Richards' ambitious if not unique plans for the design of this great organ. Who could therefore blame him for indulging his great passion?

As one enters the Auditorium (that is from the opposite end to the stage) those coming to see the organ might wonder where it is. The pipework is in fact hidden from view in eight separate organ chambers. One also instinctively looks for the console. Due to the great size of the building this is so far away on the right hand of the stage that it appears to be the size of a postage stamp – this is a BIG building! Clearly the prime question for Emerson Richards together with the hall authorities was how to provide sufficient organ tone to fill such a huge building. No orchestra could project sufficient sound from the stage, and electrical amplification available in the 1920s could have done little to enhance it. It is therefore not difficult to imagine that Richards' scheme of heroic proportions was the only way of providing music in the hall.

The organ console is contained in a large circular cubicle with huge removable doors. Once these are removed the player sits within the cubicle but because of the size of the console and the door openings one nevertheless feels quite exposed to the auditorium. I found the appearance of the console in the first instance to be breathtaking – perhaps because it was the realisation of a long held dream. Clearly the organ world will have its own views about the appearance of the console – I have heard it described as being grotesque – that is one opinion! I consider it to be an ergonomic masterpiece. The fact that one can reach any one of its stop keys which are arranged in a spherical fashion corresponding to the natural arc of the organist's arm displays the outstanding talent of its designer. There are fifteen horizontal rows of stop keys. The higher rows have their faces on an almost vertical plane so that they can be easily read and as the rows of stop keys graduate downwards the face of the stop keys are inclined almost to the horizontal.

The seven manuals are arranged as follows. (1) Choir: 85 notes – 7 octaves; (2) Great: 85 notes – 7 octaves; (3) Swell: 73 notes – 6 octaves; the remaining 4 keyboards i.e. Solo, Fanfare, Echo and Bombard are all 61 notes – 5 octaves. Incidentally the famous 7th manual does not control its own division of pipework but is simply a coupler manual for the Gallery organs.

The entire console action is all electric – certainly quite an achievement for the late 1920s. The Wanamaker console is electro-pneumatic and many American organbuilders including Wurlitzer still controlled their stopkeys with electro-pneumatic actions. It was once boasted that the use of the General Cancel piston here resulted in barely a 1-volt drop in voltage. This seems almost impossible for a console of this size – they were in fact cheating a little bit because if a stop key was already in the 'OFF' position it would not draw any current through the General Cancel piston but it was nevertheless very clever technology for the period. The electro-mechanical stopkeys themselves are mounted on a cast aluminium chassis that would appear to be a one-off project. It seems to me that the builders of this instrument set themselves the very highest standards of organ building engineering.

The console contains 1,235 stopkeys; there are 168 thumb pistons and 37 toe pistons; six balanced expression pedals controlling 13 swell boxes and one master crescendo pedal. Incidentally while operating some of the swell pedals it is possible for one swell pedal to open the shutters on one division while simultaneously closing the shutters of another division. There are 18 tremulant controls and it is possible to adjust the speed of each tremulant from additional controls on the console. Again clever technology for the period.

The stopkeys control 587 flue stops, 265 reeds, 35 melodic percussions, 46 non-melodic percussions, 164 couplers and 138 swell box selectives. It is possible for the organ technician to gain access to this huge amount of equipment in comparative ease. It is indeed impressive to survey from inside the console the fifteen rows each side of the stopkey units together with the associated wiring which ultimately exceeds the girth of a man's arm and is beautifully laid out in a neat and tidy fashion. An unusual feature to the eyes of a British organ builder but at one time an almost standard procedure by American builders is the fact that the entire coupling of this huge instrument is accomplished by a mechanism which is incorporated into the extended length of the key frames. The couplers are operated by solenoids on the edge of the key frame. When operated they pull the contacts for that entire keyboard into contact with the individual contact of the keys. The cleverness of this mechanism is the fact that it is driven by the movement of the key under the influence of the organist's fingers and therefore does not require an independently powered movement for each key.

This then is the master console, but originally there was a second mobile console containing five manuals connected by a 150 foot cable that enabled it to be moved around on the stage. This console has now been disconnected but fortunately has survived and is on display in the entrance foyer of the hall. It controlled all 449 ranks but from only half as many stopkeys. It is nevertheless an impressive piece of work with its nine banks of stopkeys either side of the manuals.

So who was responsible for all this magnificent work? The company chosen was Midmer Losh of Merrick, Long Island, New York. Hardly one of America's best known or indeed biggest organ building companies. The name Midmer Losh is derived from two individuals, the first of whom was Reuben Midmer who emigrated from England to the USA in 1840. He worked for a couple of organ builders in the New York area, going into business for himself in 1860. He was also joined by his son Reed Midmer. Eventually this company was bought in 1920 by Charles Seibert Losh; for me this man is the hero of

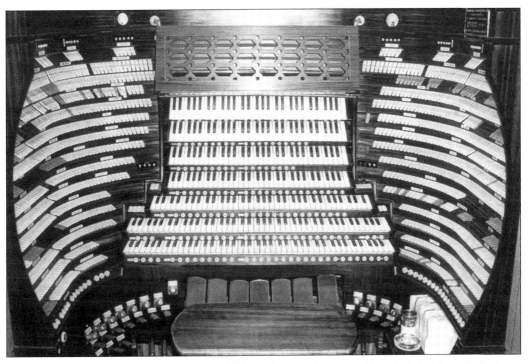

Note how the Stop key faces are always visible to the organist irrespective of what rail you look at. Note also the unusual 85-note keyboards to Choir and Great divisions.

The left hand Stop panel contains all the controls for the Pedal, Swell, Fanfare, String and Gallery organs.

Rear view of the seven manual keyboards

Rear view of stop rail keys

this enormous project. Seibert Losh grew up in Hagerstown, Maryland, one-time home of the world's largest organ building company, M P Moller, who went out of business in 1992. Seibert Losh eventually became the eastern sales manager for this company in New York and was regarded as a crackerjack salesman. He had all sorts of weird and wonderful ideas about organ building including the use of the 85 note keyboard, the idea being that it would enable organists to play the pedal part at the bass end of the keyboard.

Seibert Losh was soon joined by his brother George whose degree in mechanical engineering probably accounts for some of the general excellence of their work. Under the dynamic leadership of Seibert Losh they were able to obtain additional factory buildings including one over three storeys high and 100 feet long. An additional stroke of luck for the Losh brothers was the fact that the Welte company went out of business. Welte had just completed a modern factory in New York city with over $175,000 worth of machinery and equipment. The Losh brothers bought this from the receiver and operated it in addition to their considerable premises elsewhere.

The letting of the contract was apparently quite difficult – one might imagine that any number of the great American organ building companies would rush, for reasons of prestige, to get the job. NOT SO. For further details one should read the forthcoming book by Stephen Smith which covers this matter extensively. Certainly Ernest Skinner, one of America's premier organ builders, was not interested. One reason for this was that Emerson Richards drew up very detailed requirements for the estimate.

Senator Richards was extremely well versed in the esoterics of organ building. He also had considerable knowledge of the legal profession. This allowed him to express his requirements, views and opinions using his legal experience to get what he wanted. He knew exactly what he did want and he got it! Bids for the project went out in 1928; three firms but not Midmer Losh submitted bids. All of these were above the sum set aside for the project which was $300,000. One firm who went for the job was Kimball of Chicago. Welte also tried and Senator Emerson Richards also invited Henry Willis III who politely turned it down refusing to work to somebody else's specification. Bids were sent out again and of the three companies that were involved, Midmer Losh was the lowest at $347,200. It is known that Midmer Losh eventually ran into financial problems with Emerson Richards seeking additional funding. It is likely that the entire project cost in the region of $500,000. It has been suggested that the reluctance of some of the builders to get involved in the project was because of the use of 100 inch pressures that ultimately proved to be a unique feature of this instrument.

Construction started in May, 1929 and took nearly four years to complete. It has been suggested that at times there were up to 80 men working in the hall where certainly the largest organ pipes ever made, the 64 foot Diaphone, plus the 32's, were all actually constructed. This brings us to the subject of the unique pipework.

Let us start with the 64 foot diaphonic Dulzian. It is constructed of 3 inch thick timber. The resonator at the base is 10 inches square becoming over 2 foot square at its open end. The vibrating tongue is 31 inches long, 3 inches wide, 7/16ths inches thick and weighs 14 pounds. This tongue vibrates at 8.17 cycles per second. The pedal organ also contains the largest and heaviest open 32 foot metal ever made. Bottom C is $38\frac{1}{2}$ feet long; 24 inches in diameter and is made of zinc at 5/16th inches thickness. Bottom C weighs 2,200 pounds. This rank is voiced on 20 inches of wind using double languids. Such was the weight and thickness of these pipes it was not possible to construct them using the traditional methods of the organ pipe maker but due to the ingenuity of Midmer Losh they were made by a smoke stack rolling machine used for the production of chimneys on river boats. These must be the largest smokeless flues in the world!

There are nine full length 32 foot ranks and eight reeds voiced on 50 inches of wind plus a further four at the unique pressure of 100 inches. The sound of some of these fabulous reeds has to be heard to be believed. An unusual but necessary requirement is that many of these reed pipes are held down in their holes by large springs. Midmer Losh took no chances.

Other unusual features are the 32 foot Contra Trombone pipes in the Fanfare division. These huge wooden pipes lie down horizontally on the steel girders that make up the roof construction. The rank is approximately 90 feet above the main floor and voiced on a pressure of 35 inches of wind. There can be few organs in the world that can boast a Fanfare 32 foot Pedal Trombone firing its tone directly out into the building from a horizontal position.

Looking up the length of the mighty 64ft Diaphone.

Wind regulators for the right main chamber's Pedal, Great and Solo departments.

In the same division there is a 7 rank Stentor Mixture voiced on 35 inch wind. These pipes used the double languid device allowing them to produce enormous power. The inventor of the double languid is Vincent Willis, uncle of Henry Willis III, and in this instance were voiced by Harry Vincent Willis who was a cousin of Henry Willis III. Harry Willis, Vincent's son, did much of the voicing and tonal finishing of the organ.

Also in the Fanfare division is a 4 foot Major Clarion; its pipes are mounted horizontally pointing directly at the ceiling grill. There is also a Gamba Tuba which apparently is incredibly powerful. Actually this is an open wood rank of flared construction.

The Fanfare division is halfway down the building with the pipework accommodated in the ceiling void. On the opposite side of the building at the same height is the Echo division. This section contains 27 ranks voiced on 15 and 25 inch pressures. It had the effect of sounding like the full Swell of a normal church organ despite the fact it was labelled Echo!

The layout of the organ is a little complex but if we stand in the middle of the hall and look at the enormous stage there are huge chambers left and right. The left chamber contains pipework of the Swell, the Swell Choir, unenclosed Choir and String one division. It also contains pedal ranks including the aforementioned 32 foot Open Metal. The chamber to the right of the stage contains the Great, the Great Solo flues, the Great solo reeds, the Solo and the Percussion. It also includes a huge pedal division containing the 64 foot Diaphone and other 32's. These two chambers face and project their sound down the length of the hall. Immediately in front of both these chambers are two additional chambers at the height of the gallery. These speak across the width of the hall. The one on the left contains the Choir; the one on the right the Brass Chorus and String two. Halfway down the hall as previously mentioned in the roof space on the left is the Fanfare Division and the third String division. Below this at gallery level is the gallery Diapason Chorus and the Orchestral section. On the right hand side, in the roof location, is the Echo. Below this at gallery level are the Gallery reeds and flutes.

There are 20 divisions, 130 ranks of Mixtures and 84 Reeds. As an organ tuner I am frequently asked to nip in and tune the reeds. I have worked out that at Atlantic City, allowing at least $4\frac{1}{2}$ hours to visit every chamber, it would probably take 24 hours working non stop to tune all the reeds!

A complete tonal analysis, division by division, is beyond the scope of this article. I can only suggest that you read Stephen Smith's book, soon to be published, which covers the specification completely.

Although this is a personal view I would like to comment on the Great 8ft Diapasons. There are 10 of these, one is voiced on 4 inches, 3 at 10 inches, 3 at 15 inches, 1 at 20 inches and 2 at 30 inches. Admittedly this is a mere fraction of the instrument but we cannot deny the importance of the major diapason ensemble. While I have heard the instrument described as grotesque, hideous and a freak, and no one could deny that it does not have its problems, I was totally unprepared for what I heard from the Great Diapason Chorus. There are better people than I who have the talent for describing different tone colours and sounds. I can only say this. If the Dome Diapason Chorus at St Paul's Cathedral is described as "golden rain" then this immense chorus from Atlantic City is "silver and sparkling rain". Considering that with one exception not one of these ranks is voiced on less than 10 inches of wind I think that these American organ builders and voicers were true masters of their craft; while some ranks have immense drive and definition others are quite mild and delicate but it all gels into a magnificent musical sound. Add the Great Reeds and the enormous pedal reeds down to 64 foot pitch and for me you are hearing the most awesome organ sound on the face of the earth. How can the humble organ builder create such a magnificent, stirring and dramatic sound such as this? It is at times like this that I feel we underestimate the pipe organ. I regard this instrument as the eighth wonder of the world.

Obviously an instrument of this size requires a tremendous amount of wind. There are 8 blowers with a combined total of 605 horse-power. The most interesting and yet disappointingly small to look at is the blower that provides the 100 inch pressure. This runs at 3,500 revs per minute and has machined aluminium blades revolving in a machine cast iron casing with a mere 32nd inch clearance. This is in fact a booster blower and takes its supply direct from the output of one of the larger blowers. It feeds the 100 inch pressure stops via a 12 inch galvanized wind line with a total length of approximately 450 feet. This enables wind to be delivered at a relatively cool temperature to the pipework. Interestingly, there are no wind regulators or bellows located within the blowing plants. Wind is fed at static wind pressure to all the individual pressure wind regulators which are not actually accommodated under or near the wind chests and soundboards.

The huge-scale Contra Tibia Clausa 32ft (stopped).

The Major Clarion (50 inches wind pressure)

These are, in fact, accommodated almost entirely outside the chambers then ducted through to the instrument. The wind regulators are described as being diaphragmatic. In other words they are not the bellows type of device but a form of sprung floating panel.

The soundboards or wind chests are, of course, electro pneumatic and most of them operate on the pitman stop control system. The pitman soundboard at one time was almost universally used in America by all the leading builders and is still employed by some today. The term pitman describes only the stop mechanism – it has nothing to do with the actual pipe valve which in this case is attached to a rocking lever with a pneumatic purse or pouch being the operating device. The pitman stop device is merely a 2-way shifting device which operates at the speed of the key mechanism and also permits the valve chambers to contain pipe pressure wind all the time, balancing the pressure on the note pneumatics thus extending their life span. Observations indicate that apart from a few repairs the leatherwork dates from the original installation.

All the electrical primaries in the instrument are triggered by chest magnets. As an organ tuner one of the most amazing sights for me were the relay rooms of which there are eight. These rooms, which are in fact long corridors, contain all the note switching from the console. This is operated by an electro-pneumatic device and the room itself is pressurised from the blower. As previously stated, the couplers are controlled from the keyboards. These relay rooms under wind pressure deal entirely with the note information from the keyboard directing it to the appropriate wind chest. In his wisdom, Emerson Richards would not permit the organ builders to place more than eight stops on any soundboard. This keeps the attack and repetition lightningly fast. Consider the Great organ with 63 ranks of pipes – you would need seven soundboards to accommodate the pipework with each soundboard requiring its own key relay mechanism. This is ALL controlled from within the relay room. Hold just one note and you will see the pneumatic motor, with its contact wipers attached, operating. This one note device is approximately one foot long. When you stand and survey the magnitude and complexity of just one of the eight relay rooms you become aware of what an enormous undertaking this project was. What impressed me is that for servicing you just walk into the room, have the wind put on and are able to stand and service all the delicate contact mechanisms without removing a single panel or faceboard. This is one of the most intelligent and glorious bits of organ building I have ever encountered. Incidentally the outside walls of these rooms are protected by steel hoops that prevent the outer walls of the relay room blowing to bits under the influence of wind pressure!

From an organ building point of view there are a number of ingenious and sensible features in this instrument. Perhaps this was the influence of George Losh, the engineer. One of the most remarkable features is the accommodation of the immense 64 foot Diaphone pipes that rise vertically through four levels of organ building! These pipes do not actually stand on their chest as in conventional organ building – Midmer Losh's idea is clever. The chest containing wind and mechanism is actually at head height where the magnets and primaries are easily serviced. Wind is then fed through the bottom of this chest into individual note boxes that reach the floor. These contain the Diaphone spring and valve. Access to these is quick and simple through an inspection panel. The impulse from the valve box is then fed through to the base of the resonator which, of course, does stand on the floor. These then rise vertically behind and out of the way of the actual wind chest.

I should like to bring my article to an end with some general views and opinions. Was it too big? Yes, probably. It is interesting to note that William H Barnes, one time well known American architect, was named as the alternative consultant in case something happened to Richards. He always maintained that two separate 50 rank instruments along the lines of that which Kimball installed in the ballroom which is adjacent to the auditorium, would have been sufficient. But could anybody have envisaged how large an organ would have to be to fill a building of some seven acres and 15,500,000 cubic feet? – a building which is equipped with a public address system with an amplification power of 28 times the natural tone. The organ, of course, had to have adequate volume without amplification. The law that the intensity of sound is inversely proportional to the square of the distance cannot be violated. This auditorium called for a volume and intensity of tone never before required. Remember some parts of the organ are 325 feet away from the console. It was a brave, bold and imaginative scheme. It was a one-off; it had never been done before. I personally believe it elevated the art and craft of organ building to a level never achieved before or since. I take my hat off to the Losh brothers and Richards.

One of the eight relay rooms. This room is pressurised from the wind system and contains the note switching contacts and relays, which are one of the most intelligent pieces of organ building design to be encountered anywhere in the world. There are thousands of wires and contacts all easily accessible to the organ technician.

On a rather sad note Richards and Seibert Losh fell out. Clearly Losh had serious disagreements with Richards. He actually complained to the Mayor of the city about Richards' philosophies. Richards was not having any of this and because of his status and authority he had orders barring Losh from the Convention hall. This was enforced by the Convention hall guards. Losh was so despondent he left the company and so was denied seeing and hearing this great masterpiece completed. Within three years, at the age of only 53, he had died of pneumonia.

Acknowledgements

There are a number of people whom I wish to thank for helping me prepare this article.

First and foremost my secretary and assistant Ms Dorothy Hearn; Mr Dennis McGuirk, one time curator of the organ who retired in December 1998; Mr Stephen Smith who is completing what will certainly be the definitive book covering every aspect of this instrument, and the Editor of the *IAO Millennium Book* for giving me the opportunity to write this article.

Organ Statistics – from a booklet entitled *World's Largest Organ in World's Largest Auditorium*

A total of 225,000 board feet of timber was used in its construction.

The metal pipes are made of combinations of tin, lead, zinc, and brass, according to the tone desired.

Weight of the organ is approximately 150 tons.

Wind supplied by the eight large blowers, varying from 40 to 60 H.P. each, total 36,400 cubic feet per minute at various pressures from $3\frac{1}{2}$-inch to 100-inch wind pressure.

There are 455 ranks of pipes, the number in each rank varying from 32 in the pedal to 61 to 121 on the manuals. There are 14 percussions including chimes, harp, marimba, xylophone and grand piano.

So great a number of stops demanded the inventing of a special electrical mechanism for controlling them, such as remote controls, combination actions, relay controls and pneumatic actions. With the acquired skill of 100 pipe organ technicians, it took four years to build and complete this gigantic project.

Aside from the keyboards in the console, there are 12 portable auxiliary keyboards, attached by electric cables, and placed in the different parts of the organ. These keyboards are used for tuning, voicing and maintenance work.

The electric wiring that connects the console with the relay rooms and pipe chests would circle the earth at the equator five and a half times, 137,500 miles of wire.

The swell shutters are made of aluminium – an original idea in organ building.

Most of the large pipes were fabricated in Convention Hall.

If you were to take a complete tour of the organ it would require four-and-a-half hours of time.

The organ's 30 tremolos are adjustable to various speeds by the organist.

The cost of the main organ in 1929, was slightly over $400,000, but at today's prices it could scarcely be built for $10,000,000. Many of the large wood pipes had to be fabricated in a special shop on the site. The main chests are supported on steel beams and a steel frame.

Emerson Richards, Organ Architect wrote of this instrument:

"The Auditorium Organ is a "straight" not a "unit" organ in design. All departments have a complete ensemble with the normal harmonic development usually found in a straight organ. In addition some of the departments have been augmented by adding unit voices of a character that do not affect the ensemble. Thus in addition to the straight Great there are a number of enclosed unit ranks of an complementary nature called Great-Solo. These voices can be played from their own stop keys on either the Great or Solo manual. There is also a similar section between The Swell and Choir. In the following stop list these units are listed with the Great and Swell and are not repeated with the Solo and Choir since they are identical. The Pedal has a complete ensemble from 64' to mixtures and in addition has the usual extensions and manual borrows."

This shows the outside of the relay room – note the steel hoops preventing the outside walls of the relay room blowing out under the influence of the pressure in the relay room.

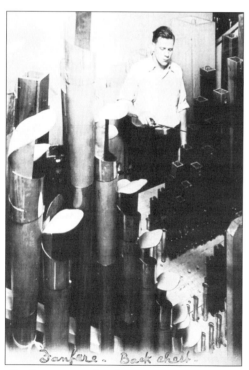

Fanfare organ – Gamba Tuba made from wood

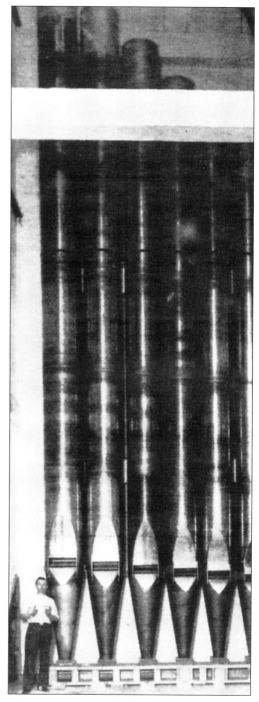

Here are the pipes of the lower half octave of the pedal metal Diapason 32ft. The low C pipe is 38 feet, 6 inches long, 24 inches wide, made of cold rolled zinc, 5/16 inches thick and weighs over one ton. It is by no means the largest pipe in the organ but even it had to be assembled in the chamber.

Register List
By *Stephen D. Smith, President of the Atlantic City Convention Hall Organ Society, Inc.*

Within the available space, it is only possible to give brief details of what *The Guinness Book of World Records* calls 'this heroic instrument'. Nevertheless, what follows is undoubtedly one of the most accurate and complete register lists of the seven-manual console to appear in print, even though two duplexed departments have been omitted. Couplers are shown in italics and mixture ranks which can be played independently of their compositions are indicated by 'Dup'. 'Ext' denotes a register extended from a stop on the same department and the origin of duplexed registers is indicated by the following key: PR=Pedal Right, PL=Pedal Left, Ch=Choir, Gt=Great, GS=Great-Solo, Sw=Swell, SC=Swell-Choir, So=Solo, Fa=Fanfare, Ec=Echo, G1=Gallery I, G2=Gallery II, G3=Gallery III, G4=Gallery IV, S1=String I, S2=String II, Per=Percussion. PF=Prepared For (certain Pedal mixtures only, all of which were to be obtained by duplexing from manual ranks). Construction materials: b=brass, c=copper, t=tin, spm=spotted metal, m=metal, stm=stopped metal, w=wood, stw=stopped wood, pm=papier-mâché (Echo organ Bassoon only). Materials and wind pressures are not shown for extended or duplexed registers: see the parent stops from which these are derived for details (this is done by referring to the voice numbers shown to the left of each register's name). Extension is employed widely among the Pedal, Great-Solo, and Swell-Choir departments but, even so, 218 (69%) of the 314 voices (449 ranks) are straight. Any of the 13 swell boxes may be switched onto any of the six swell pedals and 'reverse action' (whereby the swell box opens when the swell pedal is tilted backwards and vice versa) is available for String II, String I, Swell-Choir, and both Great-Solo divisions.

Pedal Right
Right Stage Chamber
11 voices, 11 ranks, 903 pipes

17	Diaphone *Ext*	64
21	Sub Principal *Gt*	32
1	Contra Tibia *Ext*	32
1	Quint Tibia *Ext*	21-1/3
2	Diaphone Phonon *Unit 50" w*	16
22	Diapason *Gt*	16
4	Principal *Unit 30" w-m*	16
21	Diapason *Gt*	16
82	Geigen Principal *GS*	16
3	Tibia Major *Unit 30" w*	16
1	Grand Bourdon *Unit 20" stw*	16
59	Major Flute *So*	16
81	Wald Flute *GS*	16
83	Tibia Clausa *GS*	16
5	Viol *Unit 30" m*	16
6	Gross Tierce *Unit 20" m*	12-4/5
2	Quint Diaphone *Ext*	10-2/3
1	Quint Tibia *Ext*	10-2/3
3	Quint Tibia *Ext*	10-2/3
4	Quint Principal *Ext*	10-2/3
83	Quint Minor *GS*	10-2/3
7	Septieme *Unit 20" m*	9-1/7
4	Octave Principal *Ext*	8
22	Octave Major *Gt*	8
85	Octave Diapason *GS*	8
82	Octave Geigen *GS*	8
87	Gross Gemshorn *GS*	8
3	Tibia Major *Ext*	8
1	Tibia Clausa *Ext*	8
86	Doppel Gedeckt *GS*	8
5	Viol Octave *Ext*	8
6	Gross Tierce *Ext*	6-2/5
3	Quint Tibia *Ext*	5-1/3
4	Quint Principal *Ext*	5-1/3
1	Quint Tibia *Ext*	5-1/3
7	Gross Septieme *Ext*	4-4/7
4	Super Octave *Ext*	4
85	Super Octave *GS*	4
3	15th Tibia *Ext*	4
1	15th Flute *Ext*	4
5	15th Viol *Ext*	4
6	17th Tierce *Ext*	3-1/5
1	19th Flute *Ext*	2-2/3
3	19th Tibia Major *Ext*	2-2/3
5	19th Viol *Ext*	2-2/3
7	21st Septieme *Ext*	2-2/7
4	22nd Tibia *Ext*	2
81	22nd Flageolet *GS*	2
6	24th *Ext*	1-3/5
3	26th Tibia *Ext*	1-1/3
7	28th *Ext*	1-1/7
1	29th Flute *Ext*	1
	Mixture *PF*	XI
	Reed Mixture *PF*	V
17	Dulzian *Ext*	64
17	Contra Dulzquint *Ext*	42-2/3
8	Contra Bombardon *Ext*	32
17	Contra Dulzian *Ext*	32
17	Quint Dulzian *Ext*	21-1/3
9	Grand Ophicleide *Unit 100" m*	16
73	Tuba Magna *So*	16
8	Bombardon *Unit 35" m*	16
74	Trumpet Profunda *So*	16
17	Dulzian *Unit 35" w-m*	16
10	Trumpet *Unit 20" m*	16
96	Saxophone *GS*	16
100	Krummhorn *GS*	16
95	Oboe Horn *GS*	16
97	English Horn *GS*	16
98	French Horn *GS*	16
99	Vox Baryton *GS*	16
8	Quint Bombard *Ext*	10-2/3
17	Quint Dulzian *Ext*	10-2/3
9	Ophicleide *Ext*	8
8	Octave Bombardon *Ext*	8
17	Octave Dulzian *Ext*	8
78	Bugle *So*	8
10	Octave Trumpet *Ext*	8
100	Octave Krummhorn *GS*	8
99	Vox Baryton *GS*	8
10	Quint Trumpet *Ext*	5-1/3
8	Quint Bombardon *Ext*	5-1/3
17	15th Dulzian *Ext*	4
10	15th Trumpet *Ext*	4

Pedal Left
Left Stage Chamber
10 voices, 16 ranks, 955 pipes

11	Diaphone *Ext*	32
12	Diapason *Ext*	32
11	Diaphone *Unit 50" w*	16
320	Major Diapason *20" w*	16
13	Diaphonic Diapason *Unit 35" m*	16
12	Diapason *Unit 20" m*	16
117	Diapason *Sw*	16
15	Tibia Clausa *Unit 20" stw*	16
147	Doppel Gedeckt *SC*	16
311	Stopped Diapason *SC*	16
14	Bass Viol *Unit 20" w*	16
254	Bass Viol *S1*	16
131	Bass Gamba *Sw*	16
148	Cone Gamba *Sw*	16
12	Quint Diapason *Ext*	10-2/3
311	Stopped Quint *SC*	10-2/3
148	Cone Quint *SC*	10-2/3
11	Octave Diaphone *Ext*	8
13	Octave Diapason *Ext*	8
12	Octave Phonon *Ext*	8
15	Gross Flute *Ext*	8
149	Clarabella *SC*	8
152	Octave Gemshorn *SC*	8
14	Cello *Ext*	8
155	10th *SC*	6-2/5
156	12th *SC*	5-1/3
157	14th *SC*	4-4/7
11	15th *Ext*	4
12	15th *Ext*	4

152	15th Gemshorn *SC*	4
15	15th Flute *Ext*	4
155	17th *SC*	3-1/5
156	19th *SC*	2-2/3
157	21st *SC*	2-2/7
152	22nd Gemshorn *SC*	2
12	22nd *Ext*	2
15	22nd *Ext*	2
15	29th *Ext*	1
16	Stentor Sesquialtera *20" m*	VII
	8-12-15-17-19-21-22	
	Grave Mixture *PF*	VI
18	Contra Bombard *Ext*	32
19	Fagotto *Ext*	32
20	Major Posaune *Unit 50" m*	16
18	Bombard *Unit 50" w-m*	16
138	Trumpet *Sw*	16
142	Horn *Sw*	16
161	Bass Clarinet *SC*	16
19	Fagotto *Unit 20" m*	16
160	Oboe *SC*	16
162	Vox Humana *SC*	16
20	Major Posaune *Ext*	8
18	Octave Bombard *Ext*	8
161	Octave Clarinet *SC*	8
19	Octave Fagotto *Ext*	8
160	Octave Oboe *SC*	8
19	12th Horn *Ext*	5-1/3
18	15th Bombard *Ext*	4
160	15th Oboe *SC*	4
19	15th Horn *Ext*	4
19	19th Horn *Ext*	2-2/3
19	22nd Fagotto *Ext*	2

Pedal Right Gallery

298	Contra Violone *Ec*	32
233	Diaphone *G1*	16
242	Flute Maggiore *G2*	16
220	Bourdon *Ec*	16
214	Flute Spire *Ec*	16
266	Contra Bass *S2*	16
298	Contra Viol *Ec*	16
265	Double Bass *S2*	16
267	Contra Viol *S2*	16
213	Contra Gamba *Ec*	16
220	Flute Quint *Ec*	10-2/3
214	Cone Flute *Ec*	8
298	Viol *Ec*	8
298	Viol *Ec*	4
235	Trumpet Sonora *G1*	16
231	Tuba d'Amour *Ec*	16
227	Chalumeau *Ec*	16
226	Contra Bassoon *Ec*	16
230	Vox Baryton *Ec*	16
226	Bassoon *Ec*	8

Pedal Left Gallery

236	Grand Diapason *G3*	16
171	Dulciana *Ch*	16
197	Major Flauto *Fa*	16
176	Double Melodia *Ch*	16
176	Flute Melodia *Ch*	8
299	Contra Trombone *Fa*	32
205	Posaune *Fa*	16
206	Bombardon *Fa*	16
299	Trombone *Fa*	16
188	Trombone *Ch*	16
249	Saxophone *G4*	16

209	Tromba Quint *Fa*	10-2/3
299	Trombone *Fa*	8
188	Tromba *Ch*	8
210	Tromba Tierce *Fa*	6-2/5
209	Tromba Quint *Fa*	5-1/3
210	17th Tromba *Fa*	3-1/5

Pedal

Pedal Divide

Choir to Pedal		8, 4
Great to Pedal		8, 4
Swell to Pedal		8, 4
Solo to Pedal		8, 4
Fanfare to Pedal		8, 4
Echo to Pedal		8
Gallery I, II, III, IV to Pedal		
Brass Chorus to Pedal		
String I, II, III to Pedal		

Pedal Percussion
Right Stage Chamber

K	Persian Cymbal *Per*		
J	Persian Cymbal *Per*		
I	Chinese Gong Roll *Per*	Roll, Strike	
H	Cymbal *Per*		
FG	Snare Drums Roll *Per*		
E	Snare Drum Roll *Per*		
D	Bass Drum *Per*	Roll, Strike	
C	Bass Drum *Per*	Roll, Strike	
C	Bass Drum *Per*	Roll, Strike	
B	Contra Drum FF *Per*	Strike	
B	Contra Drum FF, MP *Per*	Roll	
B	Contra Drum *Per*	Strike	
A	Piano *Left Centre Chamber*	16, 8	
108	Chimes *GS*	8	

Pedal 2nd Touch

17	Diaphone *PR*	64
11	Diaphone *PL*	32
13	Diaphone *PL*	16
3	Tibia Major *PR*	16
5	Contra Viol *PR*	16
3	Tibia Major *PR*	8
5	Viol *PR*	8
3	Tibia *PR*	4
5	Viola *PR*	4
17	Dulzian *PR*	64
18	Contra Bombard *PL*	32
8	Contra Bombardon *PR*	32
9	Ophicleide *PR*	16
20	Posaune *PL*	16
18	Bombard *PR*	16
8	Bombardon *PR*	16
9	Octave Ophicleide *PR*	8
20	Posaune *PL*	8
8	Bombardon *PR*	8
17	Dulzian *PR*	8
18	Bombard *PL*	4
17	Dulzian *PR*	4
108	Chimes *GS*	8
H	Cymbal *Per*	
JK	Cymbal Persian *Per*	
FG	Snare Drums *Per*	Roll
E	Snare Drums *Per*	Roll, Strike
D	Bass Drum *Per*	Strike
C	Bass Drum *Per*	Roll, Strike
B	Contra Drum *Per*	Roll, Strike
Fanfare to Pedal		

Gallery I, III to Pedal		
Brass Chorus to Pedal		
String I, II to Pedal		

Unenclosed Choir (Manual I)
Left Stage Chamber
6 voices, 9 ranks, 657 pipes, 3.5" wind

165	Quintaton	16
166	Diapason	8
167	Holz Flute	8
168	Octave	4
169	Fifteenth	2
170	Quint Rausch 12-15	II
170	Scharf Mixture 19-22	II

Choir (Manual I) Enclosed
Left Forward Chamber
29 voices, 37 ranks, 2792 pipes
10" wind unless otherwise stated

176	Contra Melodia *Ext*	16
171	Contra Dulciana *Ext*	16
172	Diapason *m*	8
173	Diapason *m*	8
184	Gemshorn *m*	8
185	Gemshorn Celeste *m*	8
171	Dulciana *Unit m*	8
174	Dulciana Celeste *m*	8
177	Philomela *w*	8
176	Melodia *Unit w*	8
178	Concert Flute *w*	8
179	Unda Maris *w*	8
308	Nachthorn *stm*	8
186	Viola Pomposa *m*	8
187	Viola Celeste *m*	8
310	Voix Celeste (2 rks) *t*	8
171	Dulzquint *Ext*	5-1/3
309	Fugara *m*	4
175	Dolce *Unit m*	4
180	Flute Spindle *m*	4
181	Flute Overte *m*	4
176	12th Melodia *Ext*	2-2/3
175	12th Dulzard *Ext*	2-2/3
182	15th Flageolet *m*	2
176	15th Melodia *Ext*	2
175	15th Dulcett *Ext*	2
175	19th Dulce *Ext*	1-1/3
175	22nd Dulcinett *Ext*	1
196	Acuta 19-22-24-26-29-31 *m*	VI
183	Flute Mixture 15-17-19 *m*	III
188	Contra Tromba *Unit 20" m*	16
189	Tromba Real *20" m*	8
190	Brass Cornet *20" b*	8
191	French Horn *m*	8
192	Clarinet *m*	8
193	Bassett Horn *m*	8
194	Cor Anglais *m*	8
195	Kinura *m*	8
188	Tromba Clarion *Ext*	4
Choir to Choir		16, 4
Great to Choir		8
Swell to Choir		8, 4
Solo to Choir		8, 4
Fanfare to Choir		8
Echo to Choir		8
Gallery I, II, III, IV to Choir		
Brass Chorus to Choir		
String I, II, III to Choir		

Choir-Swell (Manual I)
This department is duplicated, stopkey-for-stopkey, from the Swell-Choir with each register being available on the Choir manual regardless of whether or not it is in use on the Swell manual. The following registers are also playable from the Choir-Swell.

108	Chimes *GS*	8
E	Snare Drum *Per*	Roll, Tap
FG	Snare Drums *Per*	Roll, Tap
O	Wood Block *Per*	
M	Castinets *Per*	
N	Triangle *Per*	
P	Tom Tom *Per*	

Grand Choir (Manual I)
Duplexed from Pedal Left

11	Diaphone	16
11	*Diaphone Melody*	16
11	Diaphone	8
12	Diapason	8
13	Diaphonic Diapason	8
15	Tibia Clausa	8
14	Viol	8
18	Bombard	16
19	Fagotto	16
20	Posaune	8
18	Bombard	8
18	*Bombard Melody*	4
19	Chalumeau	8
19	Octave Oboe	4
	Grand Choir On	

Choir 2nd Touch (Manual I)
Duplexed from String II

265	Double Bass	16
266	Contra Bass	16
267	Contra Viol	16
265	Viola	8
267	Viol Cello	8
266	Viol Cello	8
266	Viol Cello	4
267	Viol Cello	4
	Fanfare to Choir	
	Gallery I to Choir	
	String I, II to Choir	

Great (Manual II)
Right Stage Chamber
38 voices, 63 ranks, 4647 pipes

21	Sub Principal *Unit 20″ w-m*	32
22	Double Diapason I *Unit 20″ w-m*	16
23	Double Diapason II *15″ m*	16
24	Double Diapason III *10″ m*	16
25	Sub Quint *15″ m*	10-2/3
21	Prin Principal *Ext*	8
26	Diapason I *30″ m*	8
27	Diapason II *30″ m*	8
28	Diapason III *20″ m*	8
29	Diapason IV *15″ m*	8
30	Diapason V *15″ m*	8
31	Diapason VI *15″ m*	8
32	Diapason VII *10″ m*	8
33	Diapason VIII *10″ m*	8
34	Diapason IX *10″ m*	8
35	Diapason X *4″ spm*	8
53	Harmonic Flute *15″ m*	8
54	Flute Overte *15″ m*	8

36	Quint *20″ m*	5-1/3
37	Octave I *20″ m*	4
38	Octave II *20″ m*	4
39	Octave III *15″ m*	4
22	Diapason Octave *Ext*	4
40	Octave IV *10″ m*	4
41	Octave V *10″ spm*	4
55	Harmonic Flute *15″ m*	4
42	Gross Tierce *15″ m*	3-1/5
43	12th Major *20″ m*	2-2/3
44	15th I *20″ m*	2
45	15th II *15″ m*	2
46	15th III *10″ m*	2
21	Super Principal *Ext*	2
47	Rausch Quint 5-8 *30″ m*	II
48	Rausch Quint 12-15 *30″ m*	II
49	Grand Cornet *20″ m*	XI
	Sub quint-1-5-8-10-12-14-15-17-19-22	
50	Major Sesquialtera 10-15-17-19-22 *20″ m*	V
52	Furniture 17-22-26-29-33-36 *15″ m*	VI
51	Schulze Mixture 15-19-22-26-29 *4″ spm*	V
49	Scharf Mixture 17-19-22 *Dup*	III
51	Doublette 22-26 *Dup*	II
56	Trumpet *30″ m*	16
57	Harmonic Trumpet *30″ m*	8
58	Harmonic Clarion *30″ m*	4
E	Snare Drum *Per*	Roll, Tap
FG	Snare Drums *Per*	Roll, Tap
N	Triangle *Per*	
L	Tambourine *Per*	
M	Castinets *Per*	
O	Wood Block *Per*	Roll, Stroke
P	Tom Tom *Per*	
108	Chimes 2nd Touch *GS*	8
EFG	Muffled Drums 2nd Touch *Per*	
	Choir to Great	16, 8, 4
	Swell to Great	16, 8, 4
	Solo to Great	8, 4
	Fanfare to Great	8, 4
	Echo to Great	16, 8, 4
	Gallery I, II, III, IV to Great	
	Brass Chorus to Great	
	String I, II, III to Great	

Great-Solo (Manual II) Enclosed
Right Stage Chamber
25 voices, 25 ranks, 2124 pipes, 15″ wind

108	Chimes *Unenclosed*	8
107	Harp *Unenclosed*	8, 4
94	Xylophone *Unenclosed*	4, 2
	Organ Division	
81	Wald Flute *Ext*	16
83	Tibia Clausa *Ext*	16
82	Contra Geigen *Ext*	16
81	Wald Quint *Ext*	10-2/3
83	Quint Tibia *Ext*	10-2/3
84	Diapason Phonon *Unit m*	8
85	Horn Diapason *Unit m*	8
82	Geigen Principal *Unit m*	8
87	Gemshorn *Unit m*	8
88	Gemshorn Celeste *Unit m*	8
81	Wald Flute *Unit w*	8
83	Tibia Clausa *Unit stw*	8
86	Doppel Gedeckt *Unit w*	8
89	Viola d'Gamba *Unit t*	8
90	Vox Celeste *Unit t*	8
91	Terz Gemshorn *Unit m*	6-2/5
81	Wald Quint *Ext*	5-1/3

92	5th Gemshorn *Unit m*	5-1/3
93	7th *Unit m*	4-4/7
84	Octave Phonon *Ext*	4
85	Octave *Ext*	4
82	Octave Principal *Ext*	4
87	Gemshorn *Ext*	4
88	Gemshorn Celeste *Ext*	4
81	Wald Flute *Ext*	4
83	Stopped Flute *Ext*	4
86	Doppel Flute *Ext*	4
89	Viola *Ext*	4
90	Viola Celeste *Ext*	4
88	10th Gemshorn *Ext*	3-1/5
91	10th *Ext*	3-1/5
81	12th Flute *Ext*	2-2/3
83	12th Minor *Ext*	2-2/3
92	12th *Ext*	2-2/3
93	14th *Ext*	2-2/7
85	15th *Ext*	2
82	15th Geigen *Ext*	2
87	15th Gemshorn *Ext*	2
81	15th Piccolo *Ext*	2
88	17th Gemshorn *Ext*	1-3/5
91	17th *Ext*	1-3/5
92	19th *Ext*	1-1/3
93	21st *Ext*	1-1/7
87	22nd *Ext*	1
91	24th *Ext*	4/5
92	26th *Ext*	2/3
93	29th *Ext*	1/2
87	36th *Ext*	1/4
	Orchestral Division	
95	Oboe Horn *Ext*	16
100	Krummhorn *Ext*	16
96	Saxophone *Ext*	16
97	English Horn *Ext*	16
98	French Horn *Ext*	16
99	Vox Baryton *Unit m*	16
95	Oboe *Unit m*	8
101	Clarinet *m*	8
100	Krummhorn *Unit m*	8
102	Orchestral Saxophone *m*	8
96	Saxophone *Unit m*	8
97	English Horn *Unit m*	8
103	Orchestral Oboe *m*	8
98	French Horn *Unit*	8
106	Kinura *m*	8
105	Vox Humana *Unit*	8
99	Vox Humana *Ext*	8
95	Octave Horn *Ext*	4
100	Krummhorn *Ext*	4
96	Saxophone *Ext*	4
97	English Horn *Ext*	4
98	French Horn *Ext*	4
105	Vox Humana *Ext*	4
64	Flute 12th *stw*	2-2/3
	(Formerly on Solo Organ)	

Grand Great (Manual II)
Duplexed mainly from Pedal Right

4	Principal	8
1	Tibia Clausa	8
3	Tibia Major	8
3	*Tibia Melody*	4
5	Viol	8
5	*Viol Melody*	4
21	Octave Gt	4
4	Super Octave	2

17	Dulzian	32
8	Trombone	16
8	*Trombone Melody*	8
9	Ophicleide	8
10	Trumpet	8
10	Clarion Clarion	4
10	*Clarion Melody*	4
	Grand Great On	

Great 2nd Touch (Manual II)

254	Viol Phonon *S1*	8
265	Viol Cello *S2*	8
266	Viol *S2*	8
267	Viol *S2*	8
	Solo to Great	8, 4
	Fanfare to Great	8
	Gallery I to Great	
	Brass Chorus to Great	
	String I, II to Great	

Swell (Manual III) Enclosed
Left Stage Chamber
36 voices, 55 ranks, 4456 pipes
15" wind unless otherwise stated

117	Double Diapason *Unit m*	16
131	Contra Gamba *Unit m*	16
118	Diapason *m*	8
119	Diapason *m*	8
120	Wald Horn *m*	8
124	Tibia Plena *w*	8
125	Hohl Flute *w*	8
126	Gross Gedeckt *stw*	8
127	Harmonic Flute *m*	8
312	Harmonic Flute Celeste *m*	8
135	Gamba *m*	8
136	Gamba Celeste *m*	8
132	Violin *t*	8
133	Viol Celeste I (2 rks) *t*	8
134	Viol Celeste 2 (2 rks) *t*	8
128	Ocarina *m*	4
121	Octave *m*	4
117	Octave *Ext*	4
129	Traverse Flute *w*	4
313	Silver Flute *spm*	4
131	Salicet *Ext*	4
137	Gambette *m*	4
122	15th *m*	2
130	Orchestral Piccolo *w*	2
146	Plein Jeu 15-19-22-26-29-33-36 *spm*	VII
317	Cymbal 12-15-17-19-21-22-24-26 *spm*	VIII
123	Furniture 15-19-22-26-29 *spm*	V
138	Double Trumpet *Unit 30" m*	16
142	Double Horn *Unit m*	16
139	Harmonic Trumpet *30" m*	8
140	Field Trumpet *30" m*	8
143	Posaune *m*	8
144	Cornopean *m*	8
314	Muted Trumpet *m*	8
145	Flugel Horn *m*	8
315	Krummhorn *m*	8
316	Vox Humana *m*	8
141	Trumpet Clarion *30" m*	4
138	Trumpet Clarion *Ext*	4
142	Octave Horn *Ext*	4
	Swell to Swell	16, 4
	Choir to Swell	16, 8, 4
	Solo to Swell	16, 8, 4
	Fanfare to Swell	8, 4

	Echo to Swell	16, 8, 4
	Gallery I, II, III, IV to Swell	
	Brass Chorus to Swell	
	String I, II, III to Swell	

Swell-Choir (Manual III) Enclosed
Left Stage Chamber
17 voices, 17 ranks, 1542 pipes
15" wind unless ottherwise stated

147	Gross Gedeckt *Ext*	16
311	Stopped Diapason *Ext*	16
148	Cone Gamba *Ext*	16
152	Gemshorn *Unit m*	8
153	Gemshorn Celeste *Unit m*	8
154	Gemshorn Celeste *Unit m*	8
147	Doppel Gedeckt *Unit stw*	8
150	Doppel Spitz Flute *Unit 10" w*	8
149	Clarabella *Unit w*	8
311	Stopped Diapason *Unit stw*	8
148	Muted Gamba *Unit m*	8
155	3rd *Unit 10" m*	6-2/5
156	5th Major *Unit 10" m*	5-1/3
148	Quint Gamba *Ext*	5-1/3
153	Quint Gemshorn *Ext*	5-1/3
157	7th *Unit 10" m*	4-4/7
152	Octave Gemshorn *Ext*	4
150	Spitz Flute *Ext*	4
149	Claribel Flute *Ext*	4
147	Doppel Flute *Ext*	4
311	Stopped Flute *Ext*	4
151	Zauber Flute *Unit stw*	4
148	Cone Flute *Ext*	4
158	9th *Unit 10" m*	3-5/9
155	10th Major *Ext*	3-1/5
154	10th Gemshorn *Ext*	3-1/5
159	11th *Unit 10" m*	2-10/11
153	12th Gemshorn *Ext*	2-2/3
156	12th *Ext*	2-2/3
149	12th Flute *Ext*	2-2/3
311	12th Stopped Flute *Ext*	2-2/3
157	14th *Ext*	2-2/7
152	15th Gemshorn *Ext*	2
147	15th Gedeckt *Ext*	2
151	Magic Flute *Ext*	2
158	16th *Ext*	1-7/9
155	17th Major *Ext*	1-3/5
154	17th Gemshorn *Ext*	1-3/5
159	18th *Ext*	1-5/11
156	19th Major *Ext*	1-1/3
153	19th Gemshorn *Ext*	1-1/3
159	21st *Ext*	1-1/7
152	22nd *Ext*	1
151	22nd Zauber *Ext*	1
158	23rd *Ext*	8/9
155	24th *Ext*	4/5
159	25th *Ext*	8/11
156	26th *Ext*	2/3
152	29th *Ext*	1/2
156	33rd *Ext*	1/3
152	36th *Ext*	1/4
19	Fagotto *PL*	32
160	Contra Oboe *Ext*	16
161	Bass Clarinet *Ext*	16
162	Bass Vox Humana *Ext*	16
160	Oboe *Unit m*	8
161	Clarinet *Unit m*	8
162	Vox Humana *Unit m*	8
160	Octave Oboe *Ext*	4

161	Octave Clarinet *Ext*	4
162	Vox Humana *Ext*	4
163	Marimba Harp Repeat, Stroke	8, 4
164	Glockenspiel Single, Repeat	4
164	Glockenspiel Single	2

Solo (Manual IV) Enclosed
Right Stage Chamber
22 voices, 33 ranks, 2085 pipes

59	Major Flute *Ext*	16
59	Quint Flute *Ext*	10-2/3
71	Stentor Diapason *30" m*	8
79	Diapason *Dup*	8
60	Tibia Rex *30" m*	8
59	Major Flute *Unit 30" w*	8
61	Hohl Flute *20" w*	8
62	Flute Overte *20" m*	8
66	Cello Pomposa *20" m*	8
67	Cello Celeste *20" m*	8
68	Violin *20" m*	8
69	Violin Celeste *20" m*	8
59	Quint Flute *Ext*	5-1/3
72	Stentor Octave *30" m*	4
79	Octave *Dup*	4
63	Wald Flute *30" m*	4
59	Major Flute *Ext*	4
70	Viola Pomposa *20" m*	4
65	Harmonic Piccolo *20" w*	2
79	Grand Chorus *m*	IX
	1-5-8-12-15-19-22-26-29	
80	Carillon 17-19-21-24 *30" m*	IV
73	Tuba Magna *Ext*	16
74	Trumpet Profunda *Ext*	16
74	Quint Trumpet *Ext*	10-2/3
75	Tuba Imperial *100"*	8
73	Tuba Magna *Unit 50" w-m*	8
78	Bugle *50" b*	8
76	Trumpet Royal *30" m*	8
74	Trumpet Profunda *Unit 30" m*	8
77	English Horn *30" m*	8
104	French Horn *20" m*	8
	(Formerly on Great-Solo)	
73	Magna 5th *Ext*	5-1/3
73	Tuba Clarion *Ext*	4
74	Trumpet Clarion *Ext*	4
	Solo to Solo	16, 4
	Choir to Solo	8
	Great to Solo	8
	Fanfare to Solo	8, 4
	Echo to Solo	8
	Gallery I, II, III, IV to Solo	
	Brass Chorus to Solo	
	String I, II, III to Solo	

Solo-Great (Manual IV)
This department is duplicated, stopkey-for-stopkey, from the Great-Solo with each register being available on the Solo manual regardless of whether or not it is in use on the Great manual.

Fanfare (Manual V) Enclosed
Left Upper Chamber
21 voices, 36 ranks, 2364 pipes

197	Major Flute *Unit 20" w*	16
212	Stentor Diapason *Dup*	8
199	Stentorphone *20" m*	8
198	Stentor Flute *35" w*	8
200	Pileata Magna *20" stw*	8

304 Gamba Tuba *20" w* ...8
305 Gamba Tuba Celeste *20" w* ...8
212 Stentor Octave *Dup* ...4
197 Major Flute *Ext* ...8
201 Flute Octaviante *20" m* ...4
306 Gamba Clarion *20" w* ...4
202 12th Recorder *20" m* ...2-2/3
203 15th Fife *20" m* ...2
212 Stentor Mixture 1-5-8-12-15-19-22 *35" m* VII
204 Cymbal 19-22-26-29-33 *20" m* ...V
307 Harmonic Mixture *20" m* ...VI
205 Contra Posaune *Ext* ...16
206 Contra Bombardon *Ext* ...16
299 Contra Trombone *Ext* ...16
209 Tromba Quint *Unit 20" m* ...10-2/3
207 Harmonic Tuba *Unit 50" m* ...8
207 *Tuba Melody* ...4
208 Ophicleide *50" m* ...8
205 Posaune *Unit 50" m* ...8
206 Bombardon *Unit 35" m* ...8
209 Tromba *Ext* ...8
299 Trombone *Unit 35" w-m* ...8
210 Tromba Tierce *Unit 20" m* ...6-2/5
209 5th Tromba *Ext* ...5-1/3
299 5th Trombone *Ext* ...5-1/3
207 Harmonic Clarion *Ext* ...4
211 Major Clarion *50" m* ...4
205 Octave Posaune *Ext* ...4
206 Clarion *Ext* ...4
299 Trombone Clarion *Ext* ...4
210 10th Tromba *Ext* ...3-1/5
209 12th Tromba *Ext* ...2-2/3
206 15th Clarine *Ext* ...2
   Choir to Fanfare ...16, 8, 4
   Great to Fanfare ...8
   Swell to Fanfare ...16, 8, 4
   Solo to Fanfare ...8
   Echo to Fanfare ...8
   Gallery I, II, III, IV to Fanfare
   String I, II, III to Fanfare

Echo (Manual VI) Enclosed
Right Upper Chamber
22 voices, 27 ranks, 1896 pipes
15" wind unless otherwise stated
298 Contra Violone *Ext* ...16
213 Contra Gamba *Ext* ...16
214 Contra Spire Flute *Ext* ...16
215 Diapason *m* ...8
219 Wald Horn *m* ...8
220 Clarabella *Unit stw-w* ...8
214 Spire Flute *Unit m* ...8
216 Spitz Flute *m* ...8
217 Flute Celeste I *m* ...8
218 Flute Celeste II *Unit m* ...8
222 Flute Sylvestre *m* ...8
223 Flute Celeste *m* ...8
221 Tibia Mollis *stm* ...8
298 Violone *Unit 25" w-m* ...8
319 Violone Celeste *25" m* ...8
213 Gamba *Unit m* ...8
220 Open Flute *Ext* ...4
224 Rohr Flute *stm* ...4
214 Cone Flute *Ext* ...4
298 Viol *Ext* ...4
213 Viol Gamba *Ext* ...4
218 10th Spitz *Ext* ...3-1/5
220 12th Flute *Ext* ...2-2/3

214 12th Spire *Ext* ...2-2/3
220 15th Flute *Ext* ...2
214 15th Spire *Ext* ...2
218 17th Spitz *Ext* ...1-3/5
214 19th Spire *Ext* ...1-1/3
214 22nd Spire *Ext* ...1
225 Mixture Aetheria 15-17-19-22-26-29 *m* ..VI
231 Tuba d'Amour *Ext* ...16
226 Contra Bassoon *Ext* ...16
227 Chalumeau *Ext* ...16
230 Vox Humana *Ext* ...16
231 Tuba d'Amour *Unit 25" w* ...8
228 Trumpet Minor *m* ...8
227 Clarinet *Unit m* ...8
229 Cor d'Amour *m* ...8
226 Bassoon *Unit pm* ...8
303 Vox Humana I *m* ...8
230 Vox Humana II *Unit m* ...8
227 Octave Clarinet *Ext* ...4
231 Tuba d'Amour *Ext* ...4
226 Octave Bassoon *Ext* ...4
230 Vox Humana *Ext* ...4
232 Chimes ...8
   Echo to Echo ...16, 4
   Choir to Echo ...8
   Great to Echo ...8
   Solo to Echo ...8
   Fanfare to Echo ...8
   Gallery I, II, III, IV to Echo
   String I, II, III to Echo

Gallery I (Floating)
Right Centre Chamber
4 voices, 10 ranks, 754 pipes
233 Contra Diaphone *Unit 25" w-m* ...16
233 Diaphone *Ext* ...8
318 Diapason *Dup* ...8
318 Octave *Dup* ...4
318 Mixture Mirabilis 1-5-8-12-15-19-22 *25" m* VII
235 Trumpet Mirabilis *Unit 100"* ...16
235 *Trumpet Melody* ...16
234 Tuba Maxima *Unit 100"* ...8
235 Trumpet Imperial *Ext* ...8
234 Clarion Mirabilis *Ext* ...4
234 *Clarion Melody* ...4
235 Clarion Real *Ext* ...4
   Gallery I to Bombard (Manual VII)

Gallery II (Floating) Enclosed
Right Centre Chamber
7 voices, 9 ranks, 621 pipes, 25" wind
242 Flute Maggiore *Unit stw* ...16
243 Jubal Flute *w* ...8
243 *Flute Melody* ...4
244 Harmonic Flute *m* ...8
242 Flute Melodic *Ext* ...4
245 Harmonic Flute *m* ...4
246 Harmonic 12th *m* ...2-2/3
247 Harmonic Piccolo *m* ...2
248 Harmonic Mixture 17-19-22 *m* ...III
   Gallery II to Gallery II ...16, 4
   Gallery II to Bombard (Manual VII)

Gallery III (Floating)
Left Centre Chamber
6 voices, 9 ranks, 681 pipes, 20" wind
236 Contra Diapason *Unit m* ...16
237 Diapason I *m* ...8

238 Diapason II *m* ...8
239 Octave I *m* ...4
236 Octave II *Ext* ...4
240 Fifteenth *m* ...2
241 Mixture 12-15-19-22 *m* ...IV
A Grand Piano ...16, 8, 4
   Gallery III to Bombard (Manual VII)

Gallery IV (Floating) Enclosed
Left Centre Chamber
8 voices, 8 ranks, 596 pipes, 25" wind
249 Contra Saxophone *Ext* ...16
300 Brass Trumpet *b* ...8
302 Egyptian Horn *b&c* ...8
301 Euphone *b* ...8
253 Major Clarinet *m* ...8
250 Major Oboe *m* ...8
251 Musette Mirabilis *m* ...8
252 Cor d'Orchestre *m* ...8
249 Saxophone *Unit b* ...8
249 Octave Saxophone *Ext* ...4
   Gallery IV to Gallery IV ...16, 4
   Gallery IV to Bombard (Manual VII)

Brass Chorus Enclosed
Right Forward Chamber
8 voices, 10 ranks, 730 pipes
109 Trombone 25" *m* ...16
110 Trombone 25" *m* ...8
111 Tromba 25" *m* ...8
112 Tromba Quint 20" *m* ...5-1/3
113 Trombone 25" *m* ...4
114 Tromba 12th 20" *m* ...2-2/3
115 Trombone 15th 25" *m* ...2
116 Tierce Mixture 10-17-22 20" *m* ...III

String I (Floating) Enclosed
Left Stage Chamber
11 voices, 20 ranks, 1436 pipes, 25" wind
254 Contra Basso *Unit m* ...16
255 Cello *m* ...8
256 Cello Celeste (2 rks) *m* ...8
257 Cello Celeste (2 rks) *spm* ...8
258 Violins (2 rks) *t* ...8
259 Violins (2 rks) *t* ...8
260 Violins (2 rks) *t* ...8
261 Violins (2 rks) *t* ...8
262 Secundo Violins (2 rks) *spm* ...8
263 Secundo Violins (2 rks) *spm* ...8
254 Octave Viola *Ext* ...4
264 Secundo Violins (2 rks) *t* ...4
   String I to String I ...16, 4
   String I Melody ...16, 4
   String I Pizzicato
   String I Separation (Unison Off)

String II (Floating) Enclosed
Right Forward Chamber
24 voices, 36 ranks, 2658 pipes, 15" wind
265 Double Bass *Unit m* ...16
266 Contra Bass *Unit w* ...16
267 Contra Viol *Unit m* ...16
268 Viola Diapason *m* ...8
269 Violincello *w* ...8
270 Cello Phonon *m* ...8
271 Cello *m* ...8
272 Cello Celeste (2 rks) *m* ...8
273 Viola Phonon *m* ...8

274 Viola Celeste (2 rks) *m* ...8
275 Viol Phonon *m* ...8
276 Viol Violin *t* ...8
277 Viol Celeste I (2 rks) *m* ...8
278 Viol Celeste II (2 rks) *t* ...8
279 Viol Celeste III (2 rks) *m* ...8
280 Viol Celeste IV (2 rks) *t* ...8
281 Viol Celeste V (2 rks) *m* ...8
284 Viol Principal *m* ...4
282 Violin (2 rks) *m* ...4
283 Viola (2 rks) *m* ...4
265 Octave Cello I *Ext* ...4
266 Octave Cello II *Ext* ...4
267 Octave Violin *Ext* ...4
287 Quint Flute *Ext* ...5-1/3
287 Stopped Flute *Unit stw* ...4
288 Flute 12th *stw* ...2-2/3

287 Piccolo *Ext* ...2
285 String Mixture 10-15-17-19-22 *m* ...V
286 Tromba d'Amour *m* ...8
   String II to String II ...16, 4
   String II Melody ...16, 4
   String II Pizzicato
   String II Separation (Unison Off)

String III (Floating) Enclosed in Fanfare
Left Upper Chamber
9 voices, 17 ranks, 1217 pipes, 15" wind
289 Cello Celeste I (2 rks) *t/m* ...8
290 Cello Celeste II (2 rks) *m* ...8
291 Viola Celeste (2 rks) *m* ...8
292 Viol Celeste I (2 rks) *m* ...8
293 Viol Celeste II (2 rks) *t* ...8
294 Viol Celeste III (2 rks) *m* ...8

295 Viol Celeste IV (2 rks) *w/m* ...8
296 Viol Celeste V (2 rks) *t* ...8
297 Cor Anglais *m* ...8
   String III to String III ...16, 4
A Grand Piano *Left Centre Chamber* ..16, 8, 4

Tremolos: Master, Unenclosed Choir, Choir, Choir Philomela, Great Tibia, Great-Solo (Organ), Great-Solo (Orchestral), Swell, Swell-Choir, Swell-Choir Vox Humana, Solo 20', Fanfare, Fanfare Pileata Magna, Echo, Gallery IV, String I, String II, String III

Mixture Compositions

Pedal

Stentor Sesquialtera (VII)

$8'$	$5\frac{1}{3}'$	$4'$	$3\frac{1}{5}'$	$2\frac{2}{3}'$	$2\frac{2}{7}'$	$2'$

Great Organ

Rausch Quint I (II)

$5\frac{1}{3}'$	$4'$

Rausch Quint II (II)

$2\frac{2}{3}'$	$2'$

Grand Cornet (X)[1]

$8'$	$5\frac{1}{3}'$	$4'$	$3\frac{1}{5}'$	$2\frac{2}{3}'$	$2\frac{2}{7}'$	$2'$	$1\frac{3}{5}'$	$1\frac{1}{3}'$	$1'$

Sesquialtera (V)

C1	$3\frac{1}{5}'$	$2'$	$1\frac{3}{5}'$	$1\frac{1}{3}'$	$1'$
F#2	$4'$	$3\frac{1}{5}'$	$2'$	$1\frac{3}{5}'$	$1\frac{1}{3}'$
C#4	$5\frac{1}{3}'$	$4'$	$3\frac{1}{5}'$	$2'$	$1\frac{3}{5}'$
F#5	$8'$	$5\frac{1}{3}'$	$4'$	$3\frac{1}{5}'$	$2'$

Mixture (V)[2]

C1	$2\frac{2}{3}'$	$2'$	$1\frac{1}{3}'$	$1'$	$\frac{2}{3}'$
F2	$4'$	$2\frac{2}{3}'$	$2'$	$1\frac{1}{3}'$	$1'$
C#4	$5\frac{1}{3}'$	$4'$	$2\frac{2}{3}'$	$2'$	$1\frac{1}{3}'$
C#5	$8'$	$5\frac{1}{3}'$	$4'$	$2\frac{2}{3}'$	$2'$

Fourniture (VI)

C1	$1\frac{3}{5}'$	$1'$	$\frac{2}{3}'$	$\frac{1}{2}'$	$\frac{1}{3}'$	$\frac{1}{4}'$
C2	$2'$	$1\frac{3}{5}'$	$1'$	$\frac{2}{3}'$	$\frac{1}{2}'$	$\frac{1}{3}'$
C3	$2\frac{2}{3}'$	$2'$	$1\frac{3}{5}'$	$1'$	$\frac{2}{3}'$	$\frac{1}{2}'$
C4	$3\frac{1}{5}'$	$2\frac{2}{3}'$	$2'$	$1\frac{3}{5}'$	$1'$	$\frac{2}{3}'$
C5	$5\frac{1}{3}'$	$3\frac{1}{5}'$	$2\frac{2}{3}'$	$2'$	$1\frac{3}{5}'$	$1'$

Swell

Fourniture (V)

C1	$2\frac{2}{3}'$	$2'$	$1\frac{1}{3}'$	$1'$	$\frac{2}{3}'$
E2	$4'$	$2\frac{2}{3}'$	$2'$	$1\frac{1}{3}'$	$1'$
C4	$5\frac{1}{3}'$	$4'$	$2\frac{2}{3}'$	$2'$	$1\frac{1}{3}'$
E5	$8'$	$5\frac{1}{3}'$	$4'$	$2\frac{2}{3}'$	$2'$

Plein-Jeu (VII)

C1	$2'$	$1\frac{1}{3}'$	$1'$	$\frac{2}{3}'$	$\frac{1}{2}'$	$\frac{1}{3}'$	$\frac{1}{4}'$
C2	$2\frac{2}{3}'$	$2'$	$1\frac{1}{3}'$	$1'$	$\frac{2}{3}'$	$\frac{1}{2}'$	$\frac{1}{3}'$
C3	$4'$	$2\frac{2}{3}'$	$2'$	$1\frac{1}{3}'$	$1'$	$\frac{2}{3}'$	$\frac{1}{2}'$
C4	$5\frac{1}{3}'$	$4'$	$2\frac{2}{3}'$	$2'$	$1\frac{1}{3}'$	$1'$	$\frac{2}{3}'$
C5	$8'$	$5\frac{1}{3}'$	$4'$	$2\frac{2}{3}'$	$2'$	$1\frac{1}{3}'$	$1'$

Cymbal (VIII)

C1	$2\frac{2}{3}'$	$2'$	$1\frac{3}{5}'$	$1\frac{1}{3}'$	$1\frac{1}{7}'$	$1'$	$\frac{8}{9}'$	$\frac{2}{3}'$
C#5	$5\frac{1}{3}'$	$3\frac{1}{5}'$	$2\frac{2}{3}'$	$2'$	$1\frac{3}{5}'$	$1\frac{1}{3}'$	$1\frac{1}{7}'$	$1'$

Solo

Grand Chorus (IX)

C1	$8'$	$5\frac{1}{3}'$	$4'$	$2\frac{2}{3}'$	$2'$	$1\frac{1}{3}'$	$1'$	$\frac{2}{3}'$	$\frac{1}{2}'$
C4	$8'$	$5\frac{1}{3}'$	$4'$	$2\frac{2}{3}'$	$2'$	$1\frac{1}{3}'$	$1\frac{1}{3}'$	$1'$	$1'$

Carillon (IV)

C1	$1\frac{3}{5}'$	$1\frac{1}{3}'$	$1'$	$\frac{2}{3}'$
F2	$2'$	$1\frac{3}{5}'$	$1\frac{1}{3}'$	$1'$
C#4	$2\frac{2}{3}'$	$2'$	$1\frac{3}{5}'$	$1\frac{1}{3}'$
C5	$4'$	$2\frac{2}{3}'$	$2'$	$1\frac{3}{5}'$

Choir

Flute Mixture III

C1	$2'$	$1\frac{3}{5}'$	$1\frac{1}{3}'$

(non-breaking)

Echo

Mixture Aetheria (V)

C1	$2'$	$1\frac{3}{5}'$	$1\frac{1}{3}'$	$1'$	$\frac{2}{3}'$	$\frac{1}{2}'$
C2	$2\frac{2}{3}'$	$2'$	$1\frac{3}{5}'$	$1\frac{1}{3}'$	$1'$	$\frac{2}{3}'$
C3	$4'$	$2\frac{2}{3}'$	$2'$	$1\frac{3}{5}'$	$1\frac{1}{3}'$	$1'$
G4	$5\frac{1}{3}'$	$4'$	$2\frac{2}{3}'$	$2'$	$1\frac{3}{5}'$	$1\frac{1}{3}'$

Gallery Organ I

Mixture Mirabilis (VII)

C1	$8'$	$5\frac{1}{3}'$	$4'$	$2\frac{2}{3}'$	$2'$	$1\frac{1}{3}'$	$1'$

(non-breaking)

Gallery Organ II

Harmonic Cornet (III)

C1	$1\frac{3}{5}'$	$1\frac{1}{3}'$	$1'$

(made of harmonic flutes)

Fanfare Organ

Stentor Mixture (VII)

C1	$8'$	$5\frac{1}{3}'$	$4'$	$2\frac{2}{3}'$	$2'$	$1\frac{1}{3}'$	$1'$

Cymbal (V)

C1	$1\frac{1}{3}'$	$1'$	$\frac{2}{3}'$	$\frac{1}{2}'$	$\frac{1}{3}'$
C2	$2'$	$1\frac{1}{3}'$	$1'$	$\frac{2}{3}'$	$\frac{1}{2}'$
C3	$2\frac{2}{3}'$	$2'$	$1\frac{1}{3}'$	$1'$	$\frac{2}{3}'$
C4	$4'$	$2\frac{2}{3}'$	$2'$	$1\frac{1}{3}'$	$1'$
C#5	$5\frac{1}{3}'$	$4'$	$2\frac{2}{3}'$	$2'$	$1\frac{1}{3}'$

Harmonic Mixture (VI)

C1	$1\frac{3}{5}'$	$1\frac{1}{7}'$	$1'$	$\frac{8}{9}'$	$\frac{2}{3}'$	$\frac{1}{2}'$
C5	$3\frac{1}{5}'$	$2\frac{2}{7}'$	$2'$	$1\frac{7}{9}'$	$1\frac{1}{3}'$	$1'$

Fourniture (VI)

C1	$1\frac{3}{5}'$	$1'$	$\frac{2}{3}'$	$\frac{1}{2}'$	$\frac{1}{3}'$	$\frac{1}{4}'$
C2	$2'$	$1\frac{3}{5}'$	$1'$	$\frac{2}{3}'$	$\frac{1}{2}'$	$\frac{1}{3}'$
C3	$2\frac{2}{3}'$	$2'$	$1\frac{3}{5}'$	$1'$	$\frac{2}{3}'$	$\frac{1}{2}'$
C4	$3\frac{1}{5}'$	$2\frac{2}{3}'$	$2'$	$1\frac{3}{5}'$	$1'$	$\frac{2}{3}'$
C5	$5\frac{1}{3}'$	$3\frac{1}{5}'$	$2\frac{2}{3}'$	$2'$	$1\frac{3}{5}'$	$1'$

String Organ II

String Mixture (V)

C1	$3\frac{1}{5}'$	$2'$	$1\frac{3}{5}'$	$1\frac{1}{3}'$	$1'$

(non-breaking)

Brass Chorus

Tierce Mixture (III)

C1	$3\frac{1}{5}'$	$1\frac{3}{5}'$	$1'$

(non-breaking)

---

[1]   This cornet originally comprised eleven ranks, among them a stopped $10\frac{2}{3}$ rank which was disconnected.

[2]   This mixture is named the Schulze mixture, since it is modelled on the mixture in the famous Edmund Schulze organ in Armley.

Mixture compositions are provided by Jean-Louis Coignet, Organ Adviser to the City of Paris.

Measurements of the Great Organ Principals

Stop name	Diameter of C1		
Principal 32'	15" x 18"	380 x 460mm	double languid
Double Diapason I 16'	12" x 14"	305 x 355mm	double languid
Double Diapason II 16'	11 9/16"	294mm	
Double Diapason III 16'	9 3/4"	238mm	
Subquint 10 2/3'	9 5/16"	236mm	
Diapason I 8'	8 15/16"	227mm	double languid
Diapason II 8'	7 9/16"	192mm	double languid
Diapason III 8'	7 1/4"	184mm	double languid
Diapason IV 8'	7 9/16"	192mm	
Diapason V 8'	6 5/8"	168mm	
Diapason VI 8'	7 7/8"	200mm	
Diapason VII 8'	6 5/16"	165mm	
Diapason VIII 8'	5 13/16" – 6 15/16"	147/176mm	
Diapason IX 8'	7 1/4"	184mm	
Diapason X 8'	6 5/16"	165mm	
Quint 5 1/3'	5 19/32"	145mm	
Octave I 4'	4 15/16"	125mm	double languid
Octave II 4'	4 1/8" – 4 15/16"	105/125mm	double languid
Octave III 4'	4 1/2"	113mm	
Octave IV 4'	3 3/4"	95mm	
Octave V 4'	3 7/16"	87mm	
Gross Tierce 3 1/5'	3 9/16"	90mm	
Major Twelfth 2 2/3'	3 3/4"	95mm	
Fifteenth I 2'	2 7/8"	73mm	double languid
Fifteenth II 2'	2 11/16"	68mm	
Fifteenth III 2'	2 11/16"	68mm	

Great 16' 8' and 4' reeds forefront with 100 inches wind pressure Grand Ophicleide behind.
Note: springs to hold pipes in position.

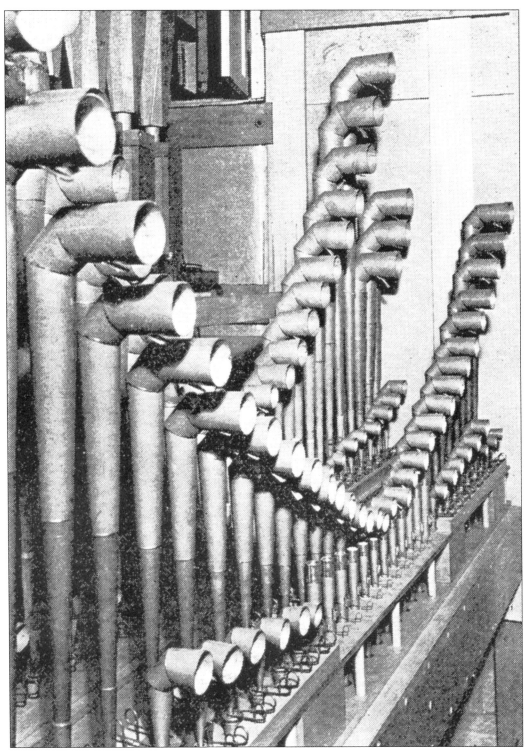

*Trebles of the Gallery I organ's reeds on 100 inches pressure. At the front is the Trumpet Mirabilis
with the Tuba Maxima behind.*

Twentieth Century European Organ Music – a Toast

by
Kevin Bowyer

for Tim and Annie

The scene: a tiny pub in a remote Cotswold village. Inside, a blazing log fire. The barman, a stout, moustachioed Yorkshireman, stands in command of the bar like a captain on the bridge of his ship. Two or three groups of people are already involved in early evening conversation – farmworkers, a local writer of some fame, an ex-poet. Suddenly the door is flung dramatically open, a blast of icy late February air tears its way into the warm interior and an organist of some notoriety, not to mention physical volume, strides gracefully inside. Three of his many adoring students appear in his wake.

Barman *(high-pitched shriek)*: Keveeee!!!!!

Notorious Organist: Ahoy there, Mr Landlord, sir! Drinks, snuff and a selection of your very finest crisps for my three acolytes, Jocasta, Hugo and Albert. *(introduces them with a flourish)*

Duly served, and that with accustomed courtesy, our heroes avail themselves of a small fireside table and chairs and launch forthwith, and eagerly, upon their topic of discussion…

Jocasta: Here we sit, at the gateway of the 21st century. In the next hour or two you've promised to give us a picture of European organ music, with an accent on that composed in these islands, over the last hundred years.

Hugo and Albert: Aye! That you have!

N.O.: And so I shall. You shan't be disappointed (I hope).
   At the turn of the last century things musical were already broiling. We tend to think of Modernism as something which occurred in music as the century progressed, but in the few years either side of 1900 things were already changing. Schoenberg and Varèse were already making names for themselves. The artistic air was humid with the storm to come…

Hugo: I studied English at Cambridge and I can tell you it's a good thing you're not writing this down!

N.O.: You can tidy things up from the notes you're taking. To continue: in France Vierne had just published his *First Organ Symphony* (1899), and Widor's *Symphonie Romane* appeared in 1900. What a visionary work that is! Like a lighthouse – built by musical tradition but turned askance from it – searching, shining, looking far out over the unknown, unmapped, ocean of the century to come. In some ways, certainly in artistic intent, I see this piece as the progenitor of much of the organ music that followed, not just from France, but from all over the world.

In Germany the leading light was Max Reger…

Albert: Who wrote *so* much! Where *does* one start?

N.O.: The famous D minor/major *Toccata and Fugue* from the Opus 59 set of *Twelve Pieces* is as good a place as any – and it's excellent music anyway. There are seven Chorale Fantasias. My favourite is the one on *"Hallelujah! Gott zu loben"* (op. 52, no. 3) – such exciting and moving music! The *Fantasia and Fugue on BACH* (op. 46) is another piece I've always loved – and the Opus 135b *Fantasia and Fugue in D minor* (1914/15), one of the most intense and powerful pieces of organ music ever written. At the difficult end of Reger's output is the *Symphonic Fantasia and Fugue* (op. 57) of 1901, nicknamed *"The Inferno"*; a maelstrom of notes which demands real intellectual rigour to disentangle.

Hugo: Yes. Sorabji must have studied that piece. Tell us about him.

N.O.: I'll come to KSS later. Have patience, boy. Let's start the ball rolling with events in England at the turn of the century as we have elsewhere. Much English organ music from this period is still not performed enough. German and French music from that period is more fashionable at the moment. How often does one hear either of the two splendid solo organ symphonies of Edwin Lemare (1865-1934) for instance? *Symphony No. 1 in G minor* (op. 35) was published by Novello in 1899. It's in four movements and is immensely satisfying when performed complete. Lemare had a real gift for melody as well as a tremendous control of form. As a recitalist he had a huge repertoire, and it's interesting to detect small traces of Liszt, Reubke and Guilmant in this work. The *Symphony in D minor* (No. 2, op. 50) appeared in 1906. I like it even more than the First. The *Scherzo* is a real treasure, light and genuinely gentlemanly – amusing in the best possible sense; and the final *Allegro Giusto* is a real barnstormer. The symphony finishes modestly and quietly – I rather like that too.

Hugo: You were going to bring some pieces along to show us. Do you have Lemare 2 with you?

N.O. *(reaching into his music case and withdrawing a number of items)*: Indeed I have. Here's the opening of the last movement of Lemare's Second. *(example 1)*

Jocasta: What about shorter pieces?

N.O.: There are lots of shorter works. The famous *Andantino in D flat* for example…

Albert *(singing)*: "Moooonliiight and Roses"…

Landlord: 'ere! Shut that b***** noise up!

Albert *(raising his hand in surrender, to the landlord)*: Sorry.

N.O.: There's a terrific *Toccata and Fugue in D minor* (op. 98, 1915) published by Schott that really ought to be played more. Moving away from Lemare, I have a soft spot for those modest little pieces that John Ireland wrote before the First World War, particularly the delightful *Villanella*, so charming, there's something of the flat cap about it that I find comfortable. The little *Menuetto-Impromptu* as well, and the softly spoken *Intrata*. These three pieces were brought together in 1944 and issued by Ascherberg, Hopwood and Crew as *Miniature Suite*. The not so modest *Capriccio* of 1911 is also a must (I hate that phrase…) *(descends into reverie)*

Jocasta: We're still listening. Tell us about some nice colourful ditties.

N.O.: J. Arthur Meale's *Fountain Melody* (1921) is a pretty little piece – not difficult – and he also composed other descriptive pieces: *Angelic Voices* (1901), *Abbey Chimes* (1901), *The Magic Harp* (1913), *At Sunrise* (1921) and *Serenade at Sunset* (1926). Dated, some would say (although I don't really know what that means – dated compared with what? Surely a thing is either of its age, or it isn't of its age. At what point does the word "dated" begin to apply? And when does it acquire a critical tone?)

Hugo: Stick to the point please.

N.O.: I *was* sticking to the point. That charming little *Evensong* (1910) of Easthope Martin (1882-1925) is another small delight. I'm very fond of it – be as critical as you want! Let him who is without sin cast the first stone!

Landlord: Keep yer b***** voice down or I'll chuck somethin' at yer from over 'ere!

Albert: Didn't you play that enormous piece by Ernest Austin a few years ago?

N.O.: Yes. Ernest Austin (1874-1947) wrote a huge narrative tone poem in twelve movements called *Pilgrim's Progress* (op. 41, 1912-20). The whole piece plays for about 2¾ hours and paints John Bunyan's book in music. It's rather like music composed to accompany a silent film. There are some wonderful moments: the death of Faithful at Vanity Fair, for instance. At performances of *Pilgrim's Progress* a leaflet was distributed to the audience describing what was happening in the music. At this point in the music we are told: "Thus came Faithful to his end – out of his death-agony .. a trumpet call breaks forth .. and Faithful is carried up in a chariot through the clouds". The organ swells, the Tuba rings out … glorious! At the end of the eleventh movement, *The Land of Beulah, and the River of Death*, the organ is joined by the sound of distant singing. The Twelfth Movement, *The Celestial City*, contains optional parts for SSATTB, bells and violin solo! Have a look at this! *(example 2)*

Jocasta: But those are mainly quite obscure pieces. What's really stuck in the repertoire from the England of that period?

N.O.: What about Herbert Brewer, organist of Gloucester Cathedral? His *Marche Heroïque* (1915) and *Cloister Garth* (1926). And Herbert Howells? The first set of *Psalm Preludes* and the three *Rhapsodies*, opus 17.

Hugo: I love Howells's music. I'm playing those two little pieces he wrote in 1959 for John Dalby to broadcast on the 1778 Samuel Green chamber organ in St Mary's Episcopal Church, Aberdeen. I particularly like the first one, *Dalby's Fancy* – it's so supple – that lovely, sinuous, winding oboe solo…

N.O.: Yes, I love that too. I remember, many, many years ago, long before you were born, when I was a student, something my organ teacher (who'd better remain nameless) said to me. I'd just played him

the Howells D flat major *Rhapsody*. He leaned over, enthused about the piece and then said, "Kevin, never buy the Howells *Sonata*," and told me what a poor piece it was.

Albert: This is the *Sonata* of 1932, not the early one?

N.O.: Yes, that's right. Well, being an obedient and respectful student, I instantly went out, bought it, learned it and found the most wonderful organ music that Howells ever wrote.

Jocasta: Piffle! You just like to be confrontational.

N.O.: Not so. Think of the climaxes to the first and last movements; hear for how long they're sustained! It's absolutely exhilarating! Those dramatic chords and pauses in the first subject of the last movement – the relaxed tread of the second subject. Throughout the *Sonata* the phrase lengths are so unpredictable, so sensuous, so lithe. And that marvellous fanfare in the middle movement, resolute but insecure, built on sand – it fades away without quite gaining a foothold in the music. And the wonderful gentleness with which that movement finishes – the sun sinks – warm twilight, and finally "soft stillness and the night".

Jocasta: "How sweet the moonlight sleeps upon this bank". Vaughan Williams is the man who makes my heart sing. Isn't the C minor *Prelude and Fugue* wonderful? Those discords built up in the *Prelude* like blocks of granite piled one on top of the other, those two long passages of semiquavers like birds flying around the whole thing – and the Fugue, blowing about like the wind around Stonehenge... It's like standing in a huge open space, the horizon flat all around and the vast windy sky above...

Albert: This is all getting rather colourful. Isn't it healthier to discuss music without recourse to such abstract Romantic notions?

N.O: Not necessarily. We're interpreters – lenses through which the composer communicates with the listener. It's the vividness of one's imagination that fashions the manner in which a piece is interpreted. It's not enough just to play the notes – even to play the notes in the full historical and/or biographical knowledge of the piece or composer in question. That's particularly true of pieces which have become part of the standard repertoire – pieces which have gathered around them the accumulated interpretational clutter of the years. Imagine a derelict country house (there's one just up the road from here) – the house has been empty for fifty years. Most of the windowpanes are gone. You stand in the road outside and try to penetrate the blackness inside with your eyes. You've stood in front of the house many times, perhaps over a period of years, wondering about the interior. It never changes, always looks the same, whatever the weather. Perhaps another pane of glass disappears or another tile falls from the roof from time to time. The house is a well-known standard repertoire piece – you only normally see it from the outside. And then one morning, in the early summer sunlight, you see a cat sitting on the windowsill, framed by darkness. You make eye contact with the cat. It gets up, stretches, turns – and drops down inside the house. That cat is your imagination. Then, walking down the long quiet path to the church, you startle two hares, which bound off through the undergrowth. While you practice there's a heavy fall of rain. Afterwards, again in the sunlight, you hear the water in the trees, cascading from leaf to leaf. Imagination is the key to music.

Albert: I hope you never startle a *lion* on one of your early morning practice sessions!

N.O.: But that's the kind of freshness of perspective that feeds a living performance – you have to have, or develop, the ability to hear even the most familiar things as if they were new, so that you can reinvigorate them for others to hear.

Jocasta: There are some composers, aren't there, who have become known for just one work but who may have written many more which we never hear?

N.O.: Frank Bridge is a good example. His *Adagio in E* of 1905 overshadows his other organ pieces. It's a wonderful piece, but the others all deserve to be played. The *Allegretto grazioso* from the set of three pieces published in 1919 is really lovely. His last three organ pieces are very interesting. They date from 1939 and are darker in tone than the early works. If Hindemith had been an Englishman he might have written music like this. The final *Processional* is particularly angular. I wish that Bridge had written an organ sonata along the lines of his piano sonata of 1924. That would have been very interesting indeed.

Albert: I predict the arrival of Benjamin Britten.

N.O.: Indeed. One five-minute piece only: *Prelude and Fugue on a Theme of Vittoria* (1946). Often under-rated. This is one of those pieces which really demands from the performer the kind of fresh thinking

I've just been talking about. That opening pedal solo is not just a line of notes – it's a stream of *intent* that moves from one state of being to another – it has sinews, muscles – its alive.

Jocasta: You haven't said anything about Percy Whitlock yet.

N.O.: There are a lot of really super pieces there. The *Plymouth Suite* for example – five movements. The opening *Allegro risoluto* has a wonderful second subject – you can just hear the full orchestral strings sweeping along with it alla Vaughan Williams. *Salix*, the fourth movement has a really beautiful melody, and the closing *Toccata* is full of fire and fanfare. I remember years ago doing the *Allegretto* from the *Five Short Pieces* for my Grade 8 (I wasn't put off it); and the other pieces in the set are charming, particularly the little *Scherzo* in G flat and the *Folk Tune* of course. For me, though, the best Whitlock of all is the C minor *Sonata* of 1935/6. I've played the *Scherzetto* many times, and that wonderful soaring melody in the last movement, flying ever higher on the rolling torrents of triplet semiquavers that carry it along, still moves me deeply. It never seems to quite arrive at its goal – I find that elusiveness very compelling.

Hugo: What about Sonatas by other English composers? You've mentioned Howells and Whitlock and the one Frank Bridge didn't write. Any more worth looking at?

N.O.: Hundreds! The 1937 *Sonata in E flat* by Edward Bairstow is well worth looking into. The splendid *Scherzo* can be played alone. Incidentally, his shorter pieces are good too. The *Toccata-Prelude on "Pange Lingua"* is very effective, very subtle (and requires careful thought…). Francis Jackson has written a tremendous amount of organ music including four sonatas. No. 1 (op. 35, 1971) was written for the opening of the new organ in Blackburn Cathedral and contains a brilliant and grotesque little *Scherzo*, which I can't recommend too highly. You'll all have to play that – in fact all my students must play it. The *Second Sonata* (op. 42, 1972) is subtitled *"per la renascità di una Cattedrale"* and celebrates the restoration of York Minster. – But I must choose this moment to rave about Francis's *Toccata, Chorale and Fugue* (op. 16, 1954). Everybody should play this piece! It's full of the most breathtaking warmth and spiritual honesty – as well as being quite ingenious – just look at the counterpoint in the *Fugue* – it really does boldly go where few fugues have gone before. And that delayed climax – you're made to wait – and wait – and then – Wow!!

Albert: But you need a BIG tuba…

N.O.: It helps. Sorry, my enthusiasm runs away with me. Let me get my breath back…

Hugo *(calling to the landlord and gesticulating in the direction of the Notorious Organist)*: This fellow needs liquid sustenance.

Landlord: So what's new?

Refreshments are provided for all and the discussion continues:

N.O.: John Somers-Cocks (1907-1995) wrote three organ sonatas, the first two in the thirties and the last, the shortest, in 1992. *Sonata No. 1* is particularly open-hearted – generous, sunny, music – with a touch of nostalgia. Robert Ashfield's 1956 *Sonata in E minor* is a good piece, concluding with a particularly effective and clever Rondo. Then there are the two organ sonatas of Alan Gibbs, but we'll talk about him later.

Albert: Meanwhile, in Europe…

N.O.: One of the mightiest organ works from mainland Europe of the early part of the century has to be the *Postludium* from Leos Janácek's *Glagolitic Mass* of 1926 – that bass line relentlessly rolling around. *Commotio* (op. 58, 1931) by Carl Nielsen is one of the greatest organ pieces ever composed. Such subtlety and endless invention, but not a note too many in its entire length.

Jocasta: People tend to think that it's a rather dry piece – is that fair?

N.O.: Not at all. Maybe the title puts people off. Perhaps it would be more popular if it were called "A Voyage to the Arctic Ocean, with sighting of Whales" or something. In any case you usually find that those who criticise it have either never heard it or have only heard it played badly. What's the quote? – "opinion is divided on this subject – those who *don't* know what they're talking about disagreeing with those who *do*."

Albert: You're an obnoxious old cynic.

N.O.: Possibly, but the fact remains that *Commotio is* one of the finest achievements in all organ literature. It takes more than twenty minutes for that opening pedal G to resolve into C major. The might of that final fugue is overwhelming, and the chromatic twists in the last few bars really do feel like turning a mountain over.

Jocasta: You began by talking about Widor and Vierne. Is there any other good French stuff from before the First War?

N.O.: Leaving aside Guilmant (I think he's really too early for our little chat – but you *must* do his *Fifth Sonata*) I have a soft spot for Roger-Ducasse's *Pastorale* of 1909. And Dupré's first set of *Trois Préludes et Fugues* (op. 7) date from 1911, although they weren't published until 1920. I particularly like the F minor *Prelude and Fugue* from that set. There's a later set of three preludes and fugues, opus 36, dating from 1938. I like it just as much as the earlier set, particularly the *Preludes* in E minor and C major and the Fugue in A flat. The *Symphonie-Passion* (op. 23) is a wonderful piece, particularly the third movement, *Crucifixion*, but my favourite Dupré of all is the understated and modest *Suite Bretonne* (op. 21, 1923). *Les Cloches de Perros-Guirec*, the final movement, is just heart-rending, and the spinning little *Fileuse*, of course, is wonderful.

   Moving on a little, the organ music of Maurice Duruflé is all magnificent – and very well known of course. Its tremendously subtle music – the *Sicilienne* from the *Suite* (op. 5) needs considerable thought if it's not to sound episodic (but an excellent performance can make it sound utterly wonderful); and how many times have you really heard all the accents and articulation marks in just the first two pages of the *Toccata*? Those details are usually ignored. Another justly popular piece is the *Prélude et Danse Fuguée* (1964) of Gaston Litaize (1909-91). You need nimble fingers and absolute rhythmic tightness to really make this work, but it can sound spine chilling. Eugène Reuchsel (1900-88) produced three books of *Promenades en Provence* (1938). He was a concert pianist, rather than an organist, and there's something very fresh about his way of writing. Just look at the offbeat bells in *Les Cloches de Notre-Dame des Doms en Avignon* from book 2 *(example 3)*. Moving away from France…

Albert: No, fire a shot over the bows of Langlais, Messiaen and Alain first.

N.O.: Okay. The best Langlais, for me, is the *Première Symphonie* (op. 37, 1941/2). Its not happy music – you can hear Paris under the Nazi jackboot. Even the rampaging *Final* in D major seems to sweat with unvoiced fear – it pretends to be a joyful and emphatic conclusion but there's something missing, something unresolved – you're still too aware of the skull beneath the skin. The whole *symphony* is a very human piece, full of human failings, human fears and worries. *Choral*, the third movement, is extraordinary, cavernous, like music in a dark space far beneath the surface of the earth.

Langlais's *Deuxième Symphonie: Alla Webern* (op. 195, 1976) is also strangely satisfying, even though it lasts for just five minutes. Apart from those pieces I like the well-known stuff: *Suite Brève* for example, especially the middle movements, *Cantilène*…

Hugo: Very sexy last two pages.

N.O. *(continuing)*: and *Plainte*.

Charles Tournemire is another major figure of course. The fifty-one suites of *L'Orgue Mystique* repay careful study, but my favourite Tournemire is *Deux Fresques Symphoniques Sacrées* (opp. 75/6, 1938/9). Fiery, unpredictable music.

The first thing to say about Jehan Alain is that his famous piece *Litanies* deserves better performances than it usually gets in England. It needs to be quick, breathless, pushing the limits of technique. It's usually heard in rather austere, misunderstood, fanfare-like, performances or, even worse, spiky neo-classical performances in which each stabbed left hand chord in the accompaniment sounds like a poke in the eye. This piece is more subtle than that. Alain is very icy – his music always makes me think of snowy mountains or remote mountain monasteries bathed in high altitude chilly sunlight. I particularly love his *Variations sur Lucis Creator*, and also the tiny *Choral Cistercien pour une élévation* – that really is eternity in a grain of sand.

Messiaen…

Albert: You're going to say that his best piece is *Livre d'Orgue*, I know it…

N.O.: I do find *Livre d'Orgue* very satisfying actually, but I enjoy playing *L'Ascension* and *Méditations sur le Mystère de la Sainte Trinité* just as much. There's something about *L'Ascension* that just doesn't age – I think it's something to do with serenity. There's something very fresh and yet very old, timeless, about the first and last movements in particular. The distillation of the Christian faith into sound – the translation into aural space of a state of mind in which time itself has no meaning. There's something approaching this in *Le Banquet Céleste*, but there the droplets of water portrayed in the pedal divide the space in a rather more human way. In a sense *Le Banquet Céleste* presents a picture of the Eternal from the point of view of he who contemplates it. In *L'Ascension* the music seems more to be a representation, a manifestation, of the Eternity which is contemplated. The human element is at one further remove. So, from that point of view, the music is impervious to age, ageing being a *human* frailty.

I suppose that's also why I feel so moved by *Livre d'Orgue*. Its very remoteness captivates me. On the other hand, *Méditations sur le Mystère de la Sainte Trinité* is a very human piece, full of the vibrancy of creation glorifying the Prime Mover of the Universe.

Jocasta: Any other French music we should know about?

N.O.: Of course – if only time permitted and licensing laws were already reformed… But André Jolivet (1905-74, a pupil of Varèse), for example. His music is full of turbulence and vibrancy. *Hymne à l'Univers* (1961) is the best known piece. Jean Berveiller (1904-76), too. His *Cadence, Étude de Concert* is great fun, really jazzy, and with a fiendish pedal part. The two middle movements of his *Suite* (1947) are marvellous; the *Adagio* in particular is breathtakingly beautiful. Jean-Jacques Grunenwald (1911-82) wrote some excellent organ music. His *Sonate* (1964) is very effective, particularly the *Final*. And then, of course, there's Jeanne Demessieux (1921-68).

Jocasta: *Six Études.*

N.O.: That's right – 1946. I remember wrestling with the last of those, *Octaves*, on the organ on which

I used to practise – not so long ago. It was very hard work and I thought my technique just wasn't really up to it. I felt that I was fighting the organ all the time. Then I took it off on tour to Australia and played it in Sydney Town Hall. It was easy – I was so pleased. It made me realise just what a difference it makes to have a good organ action – and also how much damage a bad one can do…

Jocasta: What about Naji Hakim?

N.O.: I particularly like *Rubaiyat* (1990), after Omar Kháyyám. Years ago, in 1984 I think, I heard Naji play a piece of his own called *Cosmogonie* in the Royal Festival Hall. I thought it was terrific. I wish he'd publish that.

  While we're on the subject of composers born in the Lebanon but resident in France, you ought to know about Raffi Ourgandjian (b. 1937). He studied with Grunenwald and Messiaen and produced a very effective, very original and challenging six-minute piece, *Interférences*, in 1984. It looks pretty unfriendly on the page but is so poetic and exciting. It's particularly suited to big acoustics.

  Moving along the road into Belgium, Joseph Jongen springs to mind. Many colourful and very rewarding pieces: *Scherzetto* (op. 108) for example, and the *Toccata* in D flat of 1935. *Sonata Eroica* is magnificent, of course, as you all know.

Albert: Okay. What about the rest of Europe?

N.O.: The three *Organ Sonatas* of Hindemith are essential pieces. No. 1 (1937) includes that magnificent fugue, which builds up so inexorably and then dissolves so charmingly – and the *Phantasie, frei* of course, with its wickedly biting harmonic ostinato at the end. *Sonata 3 "über alte Volkslieder"* (1940) is very beautiful. The middle movement, *"Awake, my treasure"*, is rarely played slowly enough – there should be a sense of almost total stillness – like waiting for the first hint of the sun on a distant horizon at dawn. And the last movement should zip along by the crotchet, not plod soggily quaver by quaver as it's usually heard.

  There's some lovely Flor Peeters. I particularly like the smaller pieces. The *Scherzo* from the *Suite Modale* (1938) is lovely, and the set of *Ten Chorale Preludes* (op. 68) contains much beautiful music.

  Sigfrid Karg-Elert (1877-1933) is a noteworthy figure of whose music I've only just skimmed the surface, although I did play his *Symphony in F sharp minor* (op. 143, 1930) a couple of times in Germany several years ago. There are some splendid things in *Seven Pastels from the Lake of Constance* (op. 96, 1919), *Cathedral Windows* (op. 106, 1923) and *Music for Organ* (op. 145, 1931). The smaller pieces are often very rewarding, even the little *Interludes* and sketches published by Hinrichsen. I recorded the first movement of his *Triptych* (op. 141, no. 1), a piece called *Legend*, in Blackburn Cathedral in 1986 to go on my first record, *A Feast of Organ Exuberance*, released on vinyl (CDs were only just starting to appear then). It wouldn't quite fit on either side so we left it off the record. I wonder where the mastertape is now? Perhaps it no longer exists. But I remember that it did sound terrific in that huge acoustic. I think I have a cassette copy somewhere…

Hugo: You've singled out Nielsen and Janacek for first prizes. Who else is in that league from the first half of the century?

N.O.: Arnold Schoenberg, of course. *Variations on a Recitative* (1940) rewards any amount of study and it's powerful, communicative music too. It's a pity that he left his *Organ Sonata* unfinished. And the *Passacaille* (1944) of Frank Martin – another understated and moving work – such subtlety.

Hugo: But it has been said that non-organists don't write good organ music. Is that accurate?

N.O.: I think I remember my old organ teacher (the anti Howells *Sonata* fellow) saying something like that. I wonder which pieces he was thinking of. If that idea ever had any truth it certainly hasn't now. It may be true to say that non-organist composers sometimes use the instrument in unorthodox or, in some cases, impractical, ways, but I find that those composers often bring a freshness of outlook to the organ which organists themselves lack. Can you imagine an organist writing Schoenberg's *Variations on a Recitative*? I played a recital in the Huddersfield Contemporary Music Festival in 1999, in which every piece on the programme was written by a non-organist: Iain Matheson, Donald Bousted, Brian Ferneyhough and Diana Burrell. The whole programme felt so fresh, and it suddenly occurred to me, towards the end of the concert, how out of place a piece written by an organist would sound. You would have suddenly become aware of the *organ*, rather than of the *music*.

Albert: Away with him! Away with him! You do us a disservice!

N.O.: I merely offer another point of view. A piece written by a non-organist can open up ways of using the organ that might never occur to an organist. The challenges set to the player by such pieces can encourage new and exciting ways of using the instrument. Organists tend to go for practicality, convenience and, often, stock figuration and keyboard patterns.

Albert: Controversial...

N.O.: I think a quick word about Kaikhosru Shapurji Sorabji might be expedient at this juncture, the more so as he was really a non-organist, in spite of having had a few early lessons.

Hugo: The biggest, mightiest pieces of all...

N.O.: Yes, it's true. Sorabji's three *Organ Symphonies* (1923/4, 1929-32 and 1949-53) are the most musically and technically demanding organ works ever produced...

Albert: I'm sure it's just as hard, if not harder, to give a really excellent performance of a piece by Mozart or a Sweelinck *Fantasia*, where you have to be really exacting about articulation...

N.O.: No, that's rubbish. Those things you're talking about – articulation, projection of form – I know all the arguments – apply equally well to Sorabji's music (or indeed any fine music), but here you have all the other difficulties as well: vast length, immense technical complexity of texture and rhythm, as well as the basic interpretational difficulty of rendering such density transparent for the listener. No – I don't mean to be confrontational when I say that KSS's music is the hardest of the lot – it just *is* the hardest of the lot – it's a simple statement of fact.

Jocasta: I read somewhere that *Symphony No. 1* was designed for an organist with six hands...

N.O.: It's all playable with two hands. Sorabji was a great composer – he knew the limits of physical possibility and wrote right up to them, not beyond. Of course the *First Symphony* was greeted with a mixture of confusion, silence and ridicule when it first appeared in print in 1925. Here's a page from the original publication *(example 4)*. Nothing like it had ever been seen before. Just remember – this was published three years prior to the appearance of Messiaen's first organ piece. The middle movement of the *Symphony* was played by E Emlyn Davies in 1928, but it had to wait until 1987 for its first complete performance. I've played it in public four more times since then. It isn't impossible – it's just very, very hard. But at a mere two hours it's far and away the shortest of the three. The *Second Symphony* plays for about six and a half hours – and the *Third Organ Symphony* is about the same length.

Albert: Six and a half hours? Unbroken?

N.O.: No, you take two intervals.

Albert: Have you played that?

N.O.: Soon. I've done the first movement – a mere snip at sixty-eight minutes. The middle movement (all these works are in three movements) plays for about three and a half hours.

Hugo: It doesn't look like anything I've ever seen before.

N.O.: It's like nothing else. If you imagine Bach, Reger, Szymanowski, Busoni and Schoenberg all mixed together you'll be ten per cent of the way to imagining the style. It's passionate, volcanic music – frightening in a way. When you play it it's as if you're involved in something universal, almost ideal, as if the music were close to the actual Platonic *idea* of music. The blueprint of music in the mind of God, from which all other music is a projection.

Albert: I just can't get over the length…

N.O.: There *are* longer pieces – one version of Tom Johnson's (b. 1939) *Mélodie de 6 notes* (1987) plays for 137 years…

Jocasta: Meanwhile, in the physical world…

Hugo: Okay, let's move forward to the sixties. But, just so that we keep everything in the right place, are there any other British pieces from the forties or fifties that you're enthusiastic about?

N.O.: Yes – some neglected items. Heathcote Statham's *Rhapsody on a Ground* (1944) is very fine, very atmospheric. Arthur Milner's *Toccata* (1962) really should be heard more – extremely effective and not very difficult to play (remember to keep those fingers curved, and play from the knuckles…). William Wordsworth (1908-88 and yes, he was related to *the* William Wordsworth) wrote a splendid *Fantasia in F minor* (op. 67, 1960) which is never heard. I have a soft spot for the organ works of Ernest Tomlinson (b. 1924). He was a chorister at Manchester Cathedral before becoming involved in light music as both composer and conductor. I wish he'd write some more – his music is so sunny and unworried. His *Paean* of 1958 and the *Berceuse* published in OUP's *Album of Preludes and Interludes* (1961) are both lovely pieces. In fact: let's drink to Ernest Tomlinson.

A toast is drunk.

N.O.: And don't neglect Herbert Murrill's *Carillon* (1949). It's easy to forget how original this little piece is; we know it so well. Remember my cat on the windowsill…
   Righto, Hugo! Moving forward as instructed. Two figures who rose to prominence in the organ world of the sixties were Kenneth Leighton and William Mathias. Although they both wrote organ music throughout the seventies and eighties, it's the music from the sixties that really attracts me. Mathias's *Partita* (1962) contains many of the motor rhythms for which he was to become known. After the initial fanfare the first movement washes along with considerable propulsion, and the middle movement features a spine-chillingly inhuman march. *Variations on a Hymn-Tune* (1962) is excellent – very cold and remote, a state of mind no doubt inspired by the wintry old hymn-tune ("Braint") on which it's based. *Invocations* (1966) was written for the opening of the new Walker organ in Liverpool Metropolitan Cathedral. It's quite exhilarating, full of vibrant rhythms and jazzy trumpet fanfares. The little pieces, too, all hit the spot: *Toccata Giocosa* (1967) written for the opening of the Hill, Norman and Beard organ in the old Royal College of Organists; *Jubilate* (1974) – very punchy indeed. And there are the pieces published in the various OUP albums, all concise and effective: *Postlude* (1962), *Processional* (1964) and *Chorale* (1966).

For me, Kenneth Leighton's Magnum Opus is *Et Ressurexit* (op. 49, 1966). The tension is brilliantly controlled throughout and there's a real sense of *emergence* on the last page – a terrific struggle, spectacularly won. This work was preceded by *Prelude, Scherzo and Passacaglia* (op. 41, 1962/3), also extremely fine. *Paean*, published in OUP's *Modern Organ Music, Book 2* in 1967 is, like the Mathias pieces, a model of conciseness.

We should also talk about Malcolm Williamson. *Fons Amoris* (1955/56) is wonderful and, like the rest of Williamson's organ music, is really crying out to be heard more often. The fabulous *Organ Symphony* of 1960 plays for more than half an hour and is very rewarding. *Vision of Christ-Phoenix* (1961, revised 1978) is based on the Coventry Carol and was composed in response to the sight of the new Cathedral of Coventry rising as if from the ashes of the old. It is devastatingly powerful music. The memorial pieces, *Elegy JFK* (1964) and *Two Epitaphs for Edith Sitwell* (1966) are intensely moving.

John McCabe was another major voice in sixties organ music. His *Dies Resurrectionis* (1963) used to be played a lot but I particularly like the *Sinfonia* (1961) with its boppy little *Capriccio*.

Alan Ridout produced some marvellous organ music in the sixties. *The Seven Last Words* (1965) is one of the most moving pieces of organ music written by an Englishman. Not difficult to play, it repays study a hundred times over.

Jocasta: All that music was rather different from what was going on in Europe wasn't it? György Ligeti wrote *Volumina* in 1961/2, a piece based entirely on clusters and written in graphic notation. Can't imagine that sort of thing being done in England.

N.O: That's right. In fact I have an example in my sack! *(example 5)*. It's really up to the performer to make this music work. It can sound breathtaking but you really *must* have a good imagination and a fully mechanical organ – registration as well as key action, so that stops can be partially drawn, or operated slowly. The *Two Études*; *Harmonies* (1967) and *Coulée* (1969) are highly effective, but *Coulée* is a nightmare to play. It's the fastest piece in the organ repertoire! – has to be over in not more than three and a half minutes. Ligeti's *Ricercare – "Omaggio a Frescobaldi"* (1951/3) is *not* difficult to play though, and is very satisfying – an early piece, but you can already hear the composer's fascination with clockwork mechanisms winding down.

In Czechoslovakia Petr Eben (b. 1929) had already produced *Musica Dominicalis* (*Sunday Music*, 1958) and the unique and brilliantly imaginative *Laudes* (1964). There are some wonderfully eerie effects in this, including the use of enclosed Nazard and Tierce at the bass end of the keyboard, producing a slightly microtonal effect. Much of this music really dances and is very exciting. There's a terrific jazz trumpet solo at the end of the third movement.

But, speaking of the way things weren't done in England; it's time to talk briefly about Alan Gibbs (b. 1932). Alan studied composition with Mátyás Seiber and organ with John Webster. He was Music Master at Archbishop Tenison's School in Kennington, next to the Oval cricket ground, for nearly thirty years. His first organ piece, an eight-minute *Sonata in One Movement* (since retitled *Sonata No. 1*) dates from 1955. It's a tremendous piece, quite unlike anything else written in English organ music at that time, possessing something of the strength and contrapuntal ingenuity of Carl Nielsen's *Commotio*. It was ahead of its time and no publisher would accept it. It was finally taken up by Bardic in the 1990s. This is great music that demands attention. Gibbs's second foray into organ music was in 1963 with the stunning seven-minute piece *Viewpoints*, broadcast by Richard Popplewell from St Paul's Cathedral. The climax is shattering with semiquaver sextuplets running riot in the right hand while the left hand, playing staccato quaver triads on the Tuba, jousts with the pedal *(example 6)*. Absolutely gold-plated stuff – and really not hard to play. It's taken decades for this music to gain a foothold – I just can't understand why. It should have been mainstream repertoire in the sixties along with Mathias and Leighton. Next came the three movement *Sonata No. 2* (1970), running at more than a quarter of an hour. I'm in danger of repeating myself in admiration, but the middle movement is crushingly beautiful. The last movement finishes with a terrific stream of fire for the Tuba. Next came *Hologram* (1984), finishing up with a marvellous fugue and, at well over twenty minutes, the composer's longest organ piece. After that there was a regular stream of organ pieces: *Jazzogram* (1986), a serial three movement sonata with more than a nodding acquaintance to jazz, blues and rag; the final *Rag-Toccata* is completely unique, like Scott Joplin made of titanium! You have to have your fingers screwed on well... *Oxford May*

Music (1987) is based on the Magdalen Tower Hymn and Oxford morris dances – wonderfully amusing and brilliantly well written music. Other pieces include *Magic Flutes* (1991), based on themes from Mozart's opera, and *Trio* (1991), a delightful, pastel piece for the white notes only. Alan has also written organ duets and several works for organ and other instruments. There are also several anthems and service settings. And there's an excellent little Christmas carol for boys' voices (although girls can sing it too of course), *Shepherds and Angels* (1976).

Hugo: You didn't mention the *Peacehaven Preludes* of 1970 – lovely, fascinating, little pieces for anyone with a modest technique (or anyone at all, for that matter…). Here's to Alan Gibbs!

A toast is drunk to Alan Gibbs, and glasses are replenished.

Albert: I won't let you get through the evening without mentioning Arthur Wills.

N.O.: I didn't intend to leave Arthur out! I've played his terrific *Introduction and Allegro* (1959) many times, and the very beautiful *Elegy* (1961). *Variations on "Amazing Grace"* (1974) is great fun – the final fugue builds up into a toccata that sounds like the music to *The Big Country*! And I have a soft spot for his *Hommage to John Stanley* (1974). There's a great deal of very original music in the later pieces too – *Missa Ad Hoc* for instance (1979).

Jocasta: A lot of organ music is quite fierce and grim though, isn't it? I mean – there's not much that actually laughs, not much that's really light-hearted.

N.O.: I don't know whether that's true or not. There *are* pieces that laugh. Ed Marsh's *Toccata "La Vallée Verte" sur le thème "Pat, le facteur"* (1996) is one such piece. I'll leave you to work out what it's based on… Christopher Steel (1939-91)? There's certainly plenty of humour in his *Six Pieces for Organ* (1975). And pieces that smile? What about the organ music of Adrian Jack (b. 1943)? There are four truly lovely warm-hearted little pieces: *Ringlet, Leaflet, Seraph* (all 1998/9) and *Hands and Feet* (2000). *Ringlet* is indescribable: sensuous, it twists and turns seductively in a kind of wispy chase. They're all so subtle, such perfectly formed and delightful miniatures. And Paul Fisher (b. 1943)? Again, so warm-hearted. His *Wild Spirits* (1997) contains a movement called *Vietnamese Pot-Bellied Pig*. I've always wanted to play it after a BBC Choral Evensong. Imagine switching on and hearing the announcer say, "*Vietnamese Pot-Bellied Pig* concludes Choral Evensong tonight, which came from …". The last movement, *The Whale*, is very moving. And I have a very soft spot for Ronald Watson's *Toccata* (1980, *example 7*). The music pursues the tonic chord of E flat throughout, but never quite reaches it until almost at the end, when it's cornered and grasped with both hands. The effect is so lovely – child-like and delicate in the best possible sense. It's a wonderful, heart-warming little piece. And what about Giles Swayne's *Riff-Raff* (1983), dedicated to "the one armed bandit who occasionally cheers me up"? There's real warmth there, as well as sophistication – and there's tremendous humour (as well as frightfulness) in his Organ Concerto, *Chinese Whispers* (1997). Incidentally, for a real sorting out of your right hand playing technique you should try Swayne's *The Coming of Saskia Hawkins* (1987)…

Jocasta: Alright. Point taken. Actually, now that I come to think about it, there's a lot of good humour in Gibbs isn't there? Those pieces by Nigel Ogden are good fun – *Penguins' Playtime*…

Hugo: Let's start to come bang up to date. Some loose ends to tie up, I think, dear master. You haven't mentioned *Essay* (1961) by Nicholas Maw, *Capriccio* (1966) by Hugh Wood, *Chaconne* (op. 34a) by Alexander Goehr, *Alba* (1973) by Richard Rodney Bennett, *Chorale-Sonata II* (1995) by Norman Kay, or anything at all by Sebastian Forbes, shame on you. Points away!

N.O.: You're right. I'm guilty as charged. Those are all vitally important pieces. The Forbes I'd choose is *Haec Dies* – visionary music. The opening sounds wonderful in a big acoustic – flying around on a quiet flute stop! And those other pieces have so much to say: the intellectual subtlety and rigour in the Maw and the Goehr, the spaciousness and physical excitement in the Wood and the Kay – and the sheer poetry of the Richard Rodney Bennett. I haven't even talked about Peter Racine Fricker's *Pastorale* (1959), one of the most sensual pieces of organ music there is! Just play the last three pages and try not to get hypnotised...

And Europe-wise, I really should have mentioned *Partita in honorem J S Bach* (op. 96, 1965) by Egon Wellesz. Wellesz taught in Oxford. One never hears his great organ piece.

Hugo: That's it! Time to come *right* up to date. Tell us about now, and events leading up to it.

Landlord *(approaching from the bar)*: Are you still 'ere?

N.O.: No, I'm a figment of your imagination.

Landlord: I knew there'd 'ave to be some explanation for it. Now it makes sense... *(returns to the bar)*

N.O.: Everyone should know the organ music of the Finnish composer Einojuhani Rautavaara (b. 1928). There are currently four pieces, including a straightforward *Wedding March* (*Häämarssi*, 1979) which plays for just two minutes. The more extended pieces are all very rewarding, especially the tremendous six and a half minute *Toccata* (op. 59, 1971). In its original form (it's been thinned out and simplified since) it contains some tricky keyboard writing and double-pedalling which demands an excellent sense of balance from the player. There are also some passages in which he seems to want a piano sustaining pedal in order to get a full wash of sound, so these need to be tackled using the same technique that Reubke demands in the *94th Psalm Sonata* – you know, where he directs that arpeggiated notes should be held as long as possible. Rautavaara's *Toccata* finishes with the most devastating Coda in C major, with the right hand palm sliding flat across the white keys, picking out notes of the melody at top and bottom *(example 8)*. It's well worth the effort. The early *Ta tou Theou* (*That which is from God*, op. 30, 1966) is very angular but equally rewarding – although it requires imagination from the player to make the, on the face of it, somewhat fragmentary style hold together. In *Laudatio Trinitatis* (1970, published 1999) you can hear the same kind of harmonic language that Rautavaara employed in his famous *Cantus Arcticus – Concerto for Arctic Birds and Orchestra*.

The Maltese composer Charles Camilleri (b. 1931) has produced much excellent organ music including two large scale (over half an hour each) suites based on the philosophy of Pierre Teilhard de Chardin (1881-1955). *Missa Mundi* (1970) is a work of tremendous spiritual strength and optimism, as is *Morphogenesis* (1981). In both works, diffuse matter (or thought, or pre-created spirit) goes through a turbulent period of organisation (or construction, or rebirth), reflected in the titles of the movements: *Fire over the Earth* and *Fire in the Earth* in *Missa Mundi*, and *L'Énergie Humaine, L'Atomisme de l'Ésprit* and *L'Activation de l'Énergie Humaine* in *Morphogenesis* – to arrive at a perfect state, a state of Grace: *Prayer* in *Missa Mundi*, *Le Monde de la Matière* in *Morphogenesis*. This vastness of spiritual thought is also found in the shorter works: *Invocation to the Creator* (1976) presents the same theme – pre-formed matter, or spirit, enduring catastrophic creative forces to reach a state of perfect equilibrium. There are some quite simple pieces: *Wine of Peace* (1976) and *L'Amour de Dieu* (1980). Don't let the complicated-looking left hand rhythm put you off – keep the slow crotchet pulse regular and you'll find, after a few days' practice, that the left hand isn't so difficult after all.

The Danish composer Per Nørgård (b. 1932) has produced a number of fascinating organ pieces including *Canon* (1970), which is written in proportional notation.

Henryk Mikolaj Górecki (b. 1933), of *Symphony No. 3* fame, has produced one organ work – the monolithic *Kantata* of 1968, a fearsome wall of sound.

Jocasta: This sounds healthy. These are all "mainstream" composers, rather than organist-composers. What about people like Henze, Xenakis, Berio? You mentioned Ferneyhough earlier I think?

N.O.: Yes, there's one piece by Brian Ferneyhough (b. 1943): *Sieben Sterne* (1970). It has the reputation in Europe of being the hardest organ piece of all. And it certainly is difficult – it's certainly the *blackest* organ score there is. The music is devastatingly powerful and demands a large instrument in a big space.

Hans Werner Henze wrote one piece, *Toccata senza Fuga* (1979), effective and fiery, concluding with a brief earth-shattering toccata over a ground bass, and a chord labelled *ffffff*!

The Berio piece, *Fa-Si* (1975) is not just fascinating music, but makes good theatre too. On the way through the piece the organist has to fix down notes on the upper keyboard (only two manuals are required); a total of eleven notes are fixed at one point – and the registrant has to execute trills on the stop knobs. I'm not sure this last technique is worth the trouble from a musical point of view – but it does *look* good!

The Xenakis piece *Gmeeoorh* (a free anagram of "Organon", 1974) is contrapuntally ingenious and extremely difficult – in fact it cannot be played by one person. At one point five hands are required. The notes to be played by the assistants have to be worked out according to what the main player decides he himself is capable of playing. I had eighteen months to learn this piece, so I was able to play everything that was physically possible, leaving the assistants to play only relatively straightforward passages at the extremities of the keyboards (the assistant on the bass end only had a few simple notes to play, but the treble end was rather more demanding, although not unreasonably so). Lots and lots of wind is required – at the end of the piece all stops, couplers (and tremulants!) are drawn and <u>all</u> keys (manual *and* pedal – with the help of specially prepared boards) are depressed.

The Dutch composer Jan Vriend (b. 1938 and now resident in England), a pupil of Xenakis, has written a wonderful three movement piece called *Jets d'Orgue* (1985/1991), which pictures the organ as a huge fountain of pipes. The whole piece plays for about fifty minutes and is a truly wonderful celebration of the organ itself *(example 9)*.

<u>Albert</u>: All those pieces are beyond the reach of mere mortals. What about something easier?

<u>N.O.</u>: There's Arvo Pärt of course, although his *Mein weg hat Gipfel und Wellentäler* (1989) is very tiring to play. *Pari Intervallo* (1976) is simple and creates an extraordinarily still atmosphere. A single, very quiet, grey, stop should be used, coupled down to a single sixteen-foot pedal stop. *Trivium* (1976) and *Annum per Annum* (1980) are also very effective and not difficult to play.

In a similar vein there's Christopher Bowers-Broadbent. He's produced two extended works in recent years: *Media Vita* (1996/7) and *Duets and Canons* (1996/7) both of which are straightforward (although there are a few corners here and there…) and highly effective *(example 10)*.

Wedding Introit and *White Note Paraphrase* (both 1994) by James Macmillan (b. 1959) are also easy, and very effective. And Howard Skempton's 1994 piece *Nature's Fire* is easy, with a good pedal tune in the middle.

If you want to look at something a bit Leighton-like and a little off the beaten track you should play the *Six Pieces for Organ* (1970-73) by Peter Inness (b. 1946), a pupil of Leighton and John McCabe. The whole set together makes a good concert work, but the pieces can be played separately. *Toccata alla Marcia* is a good, spiky, post-Leighton piece – and the *Intrada*, after a tremendous fanfare for the Great reeds, dissolves and recedes in a very satisfying way. There's a mighty *Sortie* too. No admirer of Kenneth Leighton should miss these pieces. Leighton is clearly the progenitor but Peter Inness has a distinct and unique voice of his own as well.

Patrick Gowers's organ pieces are essential items too. The *Toccata and Fugue* (1970/88) requires a pretty nifty keyboard technique but is well worth the effort. There's an excellent *Trio Sonata* (1995) as well, although that really *is* difficult…

<u>Jocasta</u> *(stretching and yawning)*: I'm getting tired. The evening's drawing to a close.

<u>N.O.</u>: Just time to tell you about some big pieces then!

<u>Albert</u> *(rising)*: Carry on. I'll get the drinks in.

<u>N.O.</u>: Wilfrid Mellers (b. 1914) wrote an excellent long piece in 1969 called *Opus Alchymicum*. He uses the concept of medieval alchemy as the philosophical and technical stimulus for the music. It's very colourful and tremendously satisfying to play – really quite moving too, the music growing from the opening sections – scattered fragments of sound – through various stages of transformation, until the final *Illuminatio* is achieved *(example 11)*.

In 1967 the Italian composer Niccolò Castiglioni (1932-96) published his *Sinfonie Guerriere et*

Amorose. This is an extraordinary work, playing for about forty minutes and in seven movements, each representing a day of the week, *Monday* to *Sunday*. The organist is asked to imagine a mythical garden in which the action of the piece takes place. *Monday* opens with a splendid march in C major. Less than a minute in, a small virus creeps into the music and gradually eats it, expanding, and infecting the whole texture in the most ghastly way, until there's nothing left! It is the most astonishing effect. There's a great deal of cynicism in the music throughout – and the end of the piece is left in the player's hands. The composer makes a number of suggestions: make a loud noise in the room next door, possibly on percussion instruments with a few friends; have a choir sing a Gregorian Alleluia off-stage and then appear before the audience "with violence"(!). He even suggests that the auditorium doors might be locked to keep the audience in!!

Then of course there's the organ music of Peter Maxwell Davies. I love the *Fantasia on "O Magnum Mysterium"* (1960), about twelve minutes of the most serene music imaginable; the last page alone plays for about four minutes (it's usually sped up in performance, but the player needs to have the courage of the composer's convictions). When I appear on *Desert Island Discs*…

Jocasta and Albert: arf! arf! arf!

N.O. *(continuing undeterred)*: … I may well choose this piece as my one record. The *Organ Sonata*, too, is truly wonderful – such subtlety, such space and control. I love the superhuman understatement of it all – it makes my heart sing!

Other pieces not to be forgotten: the *Trio in C minor* (1969) by James Iliff (b. 1923), a wonderful piece which carries on despite the fact that the assistant improvises registration all the way along, simulating the effect of a radio slipping in and out of reception. The organ works of Jonathan Harvey (b. 1939): *Laus Deo* (1969), heard by the composer played by an angel in a dream; and *Fantasia* (1991), a brilliantly telling piece notated against a metrical grid of passing seconds of time, and including a marvellous shimmering effect, a legato curtain of sound as in Ligeti's *Harmonies* but more quickly moving. Andrew Wilson-Dickson (b. 1946) has produced some excellent pieces. *Sonata 1* (1968) is particularly satisfying and is definitely not as hard as it looks – anyone with a good Grade 8 technique should be able to manage this quite easily. *Sonata 2* (1972/3) is based on "Praise him in the sound of the trumpet" (Psalm 150) and is for reeds only. *Passacaglia on a Song by Stevie Wonder* (1979) is most effective but quite hard. The subject "condenses" throughout the piece and just as the melody becomes obvious the music stops.

Diana Burrell's *Arched Forms with Bells* (1990) is an exhilarating sculpture in sound. The organist needs to imagine the visual image and make it clear for the audience, building as distinct a vision as possible, *rendering* the music into physical space.

Janet Graham's *Three Pieces for Organ* (1986) are marvellous, particularly the terrifying *Toccata* – probably the most soul-chilling three minutes in organ literature – devastating and utterly merciless.

Speaking of merciless music, *The Chair* (1994) by Gerald Barry (b. 1952) is a cracker. Very difficult – only a mechanical action will do it full justice – and the crispest possible playing technique. You need nerves of steel and considerable muscular control for this.

Hugo: So, who are the bright sparks now? And where do we go from here?

N.O.: We haven't touched on Francis Pott, of course – there's a whole new world in there. Iain Matheson (b. 1956) has written two ingenious organ pieces: *Wondrous Machine* (1998, very difficult) and *Through Thick and Thin* (1999). Donald Bousted has composed the intensely moving and passionate *A Woldgate Requiem* (1993, again very difficult). *The Archaeology of Air* (1998) by Peter McGarr is very marvellous. It's for organ and soprano (and there's a small tape part in the second movement, featuring sea-side noises and the distant sounds of Reginald Dixon playing the Blackpool Tower organ). In the fourth movement, *Ghost-Organs, Wind Chimes and the Ornamentation of c"*, the soprano enters the auditorium and makes her way amongst the audience quietly reading out the names of destroyed organs. It's all very eerie and very effective. The whole piece is deeply moving, full of remembrance and longing for things past *(example 12)*. Peter McGarr is currently working on a piece for solo organ. This is something to look forward to.

Robert Keeley (b. 1960) has produced an excellent set of four pieces entitled *Celebrations and Reflections* (1996). He studied with Oliver Knussen, Bernard Rose, Robert Saxton and Franco Donatoni (whose own organ piece, *Feria 2*, is a furious tour de force consisting largely of the organ part of his earlier work, *Feria* for organ, five trumpets and five flutes, played *backwards*!).

I played Janet Owen Thomas's organ piece *Rosaces* (1984) in the Proms in 1991. It's inspired by the medieval stained glass of Chartres Cathedral. The music is full of splendour and light, vibrant and shining, but sharp and dangerous, as if it were itself made of glass. That piece is already sixteen years old. I wonder what Janet might produce now?

Jeremy Thurlow (b. 1967) has written an excellent little piece called *Rising Dough* (1998) which demands discipline from the player if the texture is to remain clear. If the biting little rhythms are well controlled this can be very exciting.

Hugo: From whom would you like to see new organ pieces?

N.O.: Oh, the obvious ones certainly. Elliott Carter, Harrison Birtwistle, Michael Finnissy, Simon Holt, James Dillon... I'd like to see what Chris Dench might do with the organ. And I'd be very interested to see an organ piece from Rebecca Saunders. And I wish James Macmillan would write something substantial.

Albert: Where's organ music going now?

N.O.: Impossible to say. In a way it's become unfashionable to reject the past in the way that previous generations rejected their immediate predecessors, so reaction, revolution, is, in many ways, itself a thing of the past. Perhaps the next step will be to reject *everything*. Perhaps open-mindedness itself will be out of fashion (perish the thought), but for now organ music, in common with music in general, seems to be moving in many directions at the same time.

Silence from all

Hugo: You ought to write all this down.

N.O.: No. I couldn't possibly do that. It's okay to talk about with a few friends in my natural environment, but I couldn't possibly write an article about it.

Again, silence.

N.O.: Shall we go?

General murmur of assent. Our heroes rise and don outdoor gear. The Notorious Organist packs away his various musical examples and, in so doing, inadvertently drops a small leather-bound wallet on the floor. He fails to notice this. The party makes its way to the door, turns to bid adieu to the landlord and then, amidst a rush of cold night air, are gone. The landlord, surveying the recently vacated table, notices the small leather item lying on the floor. He sweeps over to it, picks it up, sniffs it, looks inside and then rushes to the door.

Landlord (*opening the door and calling out in a loud voice*): 'ere! Is this your stamp album?

Drawings by **Jeanne Bowyer**

Items of evidence drawn from the sack of the Notorious Organist

32

IV. Solo. (Reeds *fff*.)
III. Swell. (Full.)
II. Great. (Diap⁹ 16, 8, and Flute 4.) - III.
I. Choir. (8 & soft 4, with reeds 8 & Trem.)
Pedal. (Full.)

IV.

ALLEGRO GIUSTO.

Example 1: Lemare, *Organ Symphony No 2.*

Example 2: Ernest Austin, *Pilgrim's Progress, Movement 12.*

pour Marcel PAPONAUD
Organiste du Grand-Orgue de Saint Bonaventure à Lyon

19

4. Les Cloches de Notre-Dame des Doms en Avignon
THE BELLS OF NOTRE-DAME DES DOMS IN AVIGNON

Registration: Claviers fonds et Anches 16-8-4-2 - tous accoup^ts
Pédale   fonds et Anches 32-16-8-4 - tous accoup^ts
Indications: R (Récit) P (Positif) G (Grand-Orgue)

23.076²H.

Example 3: Eugène Reuschel, *Promenades en Provence.*

Example 4: Sorabji, *First Organ Symphony.*

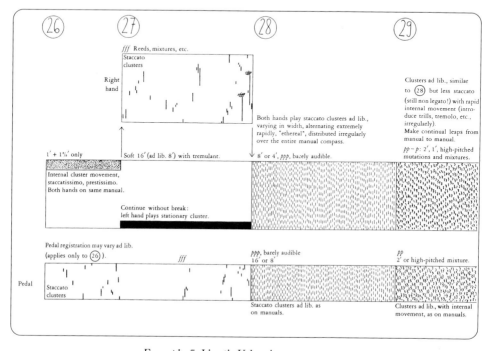

Example 5: Ligeti, *Volumina.*

Example 6: Alan Gibbs, *Viewpoints.*

Example 7: Ronald Watson, *Toccata*.

Example 8: Einojuhani Rautavaara, *Toccata.*

Jets d'Orgue

PART 1

Jan Vriend

Example 9: Jan Vriend, *Jets d'Orgue.*

Example 10: Christopher Bowers-Broadbent, *Duets and Canons.*

Example 11: Wilfrid Mellers, *Opus Alchymicum.*

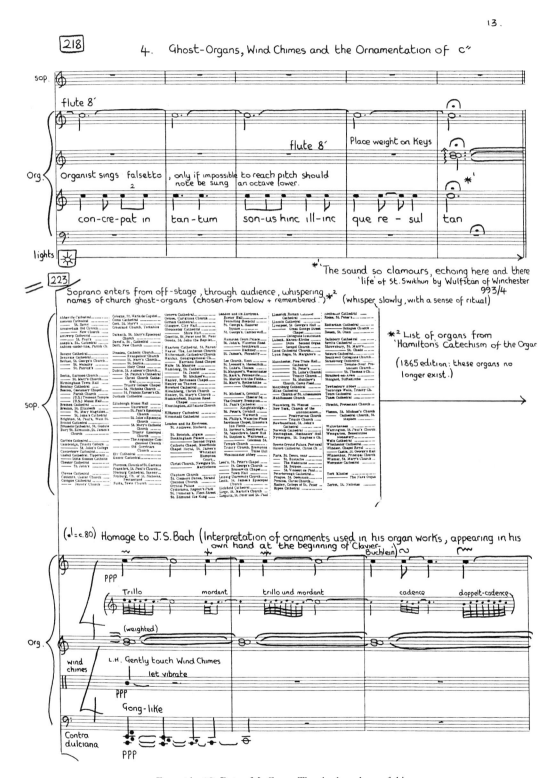

Example 12: Peter McGarr, *The Archaeology of Air.*

Improvisation: a Perspective

by
David Briggs

"Improvisation could perhaps be described as 'The Illusionist's Art'
– but then what would life be like if we were to lose our illusions?"

"When improvising you have neither pencil nor rubber –
so look on from afar, and don't go on for too long, otherwise
you could miss your way out…"

Two well-known quotes from the late Pierre Cochereau, one of the greatest organ improvisers of the twentieth century, who was titulaire at the cathedral of Notre-Dame de Paris from 1955 until his death in 1984 at the early age of fifty-nine.

Before examining, in some detail, the salient hallmarks of the history of organ improvisation in the nineteenth and twentieth centuries, I thought it might be interesting to look at the history of the art on a much broader basis.

The Broad Historical Viewpoint

Without doubt, the evolution of mankind has been marked by a consequent development of musical language. Only in the past few hundred years, however, has music been notated so that one performance could be repeated tens, hundreds, or even thousands of times. The idea of using neumes to write Gregorian plainchant represented the first major move towards specific notation in the history of Western music. In the sixteenth century, techniques moved on significantly with the development of staves. Prior to these developments all music making in the Occident was improvised. In other traditions, improvisation still plays a fundamental part – in Japanese and Indian music for instance where styles and techniques are often passed down through families. The development of music in the West was, of course, reliant on the sophisticated new notation but, interestingly, famous composers still seem to have been excellent improvisers until very recently, when a gulf between improvisation and composition appears to have arisen.

There are, for instance, many reports of J S Bach's improvisations. When visiting a new instrument, he would often improvise stunningly for two hours or more. The style was said to be exactly the same as that of his compositions, with music of great complexity, flair and contrapuntal finesse. It seems highly likely from looking at Bach's manuscripts that he composed very rapidly, almost like a slowed-down improvisation. The music of his North German predecessor Dietrich Buxtehude also strikes one as being particularly improvisatory, with flamboyant passagework and quite sectional form. One suspects that the difference between the written composition and the improvisatory style was negligible. The great George Frideric Handel is said by Charles Gurney to have improvised extensively in the organ concerti, even improvising complete movements in the sections marked *ad libitum* in the score. Mozart often embellished the slow movements of his piano concerti, in addition to improvising complete cadenzas. Moving closer to our own time, the Romantics Frederic Chopin and Franz Liszt were both known as superb piano improvisers, and the soirées with Serge Rachmaninoff in his New York apartment with the master improvising the night away must have been quite extraordinary. It is only comparatively recently that famous composers have not been known so much as famous improvisers – with a *few* exceptions!

The Psychology of Improvisation

Like composers, good improvisers have usually been so from an early age. Cochereau used to say, "Well, it is largely a matter of gift – but it a gift that has to be practised." When improvising your mind can never really be more than a second or two ahead of your fingers. Of course it is essential that the mind *is* leading the way – the other way round is rather like going to Hungary and expecting to get by without any Hungarian. My beloved teacher, the late Jean Langlais, in my first ever improvisation lesson, enquired firmly, "(*French accent*) 'Ave yoo studied harmonie, contrepoint, l'orchestration, forme...?" I was able honestly to say, "Oui, Maitre." His immediate response was. "'Ah... in zat case, you can improvise." This is an interesting standpoint, but I cannot say that it is necessarily true! The subconscious incorporation of compositional techniques into one's immediate musical memory bank takes many years to assimilate. A good improviser has usually developed the super-fast reflex action between the ears and the fingers (and the feet) from childhood days. Simply sitting at the piano and experimenting sharpens this reflex as the improviser discovers his or her reactions to particular sounds. Like the composer, the improviser is also influenced, whether he likes it or not, by the music he has around him at any given point. The great and liberating thing about improvisation is the balance of spontaneity with technique. All spontaneity and no technique produces very limited music making. All technique and no spontaneity is not true improvisation! When the balance is right then I believe that improvised music often has a remarkable ambience and excitement which is hard, if not impossible, to recreate with written music. The parallel with the public speaker is often drawn – many famous public speakers are able to communicate better without a formal text. However, they know precisely what they want to say, and have the grammar and the syntax to do so. Even more exciting is the element of the unpredicted – when the music can actually grow from itself and move on at an unexpected tangent. The successful improviser will nevertheless always be able to give his listener a strong sense of construction, even where this has actually evolved during the playing of the piece. *"Construite, mais non preparée"* was a favourite phrase of Cochereau.

The Liturgical Framework
Within the French Catholic Mass, it became customary from the sixteenth century onwards for the organist to improvise at specific points in the service. The tradition of the *Grand Orgue* at the west end commenting and embellishing on the liturgical mood of the day is centuries old. Nowadays the formula is more or less ubiquitous: the organist improvises at the *Entrée, Offertoire, Communion* and *Sortie*. The fact that the music is usually spontaneous allows the organist to expand and comment on the liturgical texts of the day, to incorporate themes (sometimes plainchant) which are being sung during the course of the Mass, and also, of course, to stop at virtually any time, thereby avoiding the unfortunate and arbitrary truncation of a piece of repertoire. At Vespers the organist alternates with the singing of Gregorian chant (e.g. the Magnificat) thus maintaining a tradition that goes back to Titelouze and even earlier. Great improvisers can create a satisfying musical and liturgical unity with their skill and sensitivity – the sense of theatre is intoxicating!

    In Holland and Germany a different tradition exists. Organists are trained to improvise introductions to the hymns and psalms. Sometimes styles will be classical (e.g. ornamented chorale preludes after Pachelbel) or frequently in a more romantic or contemporary vein. Thus the introduction can last for up to three minutes! It would be interesting to gauge the reaction of a middle-of-the-road English congregation...

César Franck: Founder of the French School
The organ class of César Franck at the Schola Cantorum was in fact primarily devoted to the teaching of improvisation. His students testified to the beauty and remarkable invention of the master's own improvisations. Registrations were far less conventional than those stipulated in his written compositions. His pupils also said that the Franck asked them to play his pieces as if they were improvisations. His most frequent criticism was that people played his music too rigidly and without due elasticity. So the gulf between interpretative eloquence and improvisatory freedom was very narrow. Langlais was a pupil of Adolphe Marty (who was himself a pupil of Franck). Langlais was fastidious in his teaching of Franck, particularly in terms of touch and rubato (lengthening the high notes of phrases, dwelling on sequential repetitions, proper treatment of *notes communes* etc.) and always dictated this improvisatory rubato with his index finger on your shoulder. Woe betide those who deviated!

Louis Vierne
Maurice Duruflé tells us that Louis Vierne, the great blind organist at Notre-Dame, improvised in a

style very close to the chromatic language of his symphonies. The influence of the great five-manual Cavaillé-Coll at Notre-Dame must inevitably have been very significant indeed, demonstrating a remarkable osmosis between instrument and performer. Vierne recorded three improvisations at Notre-Dame in 1930 which were later transcribed by Duruflé. They are intriguing from the point of view of performance practice as they have very little rubato – a real sense of "straight through". Perhaps this was to do with the limitations of recording techniques (78 rpm): Vierne could only play for about four minutes at a time! How fabulous it would have been to hear him without these mechanical constrictions, perhaps in the middle of a heartfelt *Adagio* or energetic *Final.*

Charles Tournemire

Tournemire was one of Franck's successors at Sainte-Clotilde and was a renowned and brilliant improviser with a uniquely impressionistic style. His impetuous and fragile nature is revealed in the music. His great cycle *L'Orgue Mystique* (music for each Sunday of the year based on the appropriate plainchant) was composed in 1930 and is extremely improvisatory. Great freedom of rhythm is combined with a voluptuous and individual post-Debussian harmonic language. The music is always changing in mood and texture – rather like an Impressionist painting in music. Essential listening for any serious student of improvisation are the famous examples recorded by Tournemire in 1930 at Sainte-Clotilde, which were later painstakingly transcribed by Duruflé.

Marcel Dupré

Dupré was appointed to Saint-Sulpice in Paris in 1934, in succession to Charles-Marie Widor. He already had a huge reputation as an improviser, having taken America by storm in 1923 with the original version of the *Symphonie-Passion* at the Wanamaker Store in Philadelphia. His treatise on improvisation remains a classic and his class at the Paris Conservatoire was justly famous – first prizes being held by such names as Jean Langlais, Marie-Claire Alain, Marie-Madeleine Duruflé, Pierre Cochereau, Jean Guillou and others. There were various elements to the course, varying from the very strict – say canon, or fugue with regular countersubject (a veritable crossword!) – to free form. How fascinating it would be to hear a recording of one of those classes!

A few Dupré improvisation recordings have been issued. They are curious in some ways, with the harmonic language being rather more akin to that of his teacher Guilmant than to his own compositional style, which frequently pushes tonality to considerable limits. One almost feels that he is trying to convince the listener that the form is in fact more important than the syntax. The sad point is that the recordings currently available were made in the 1960s when Dupré was nearing the end of his life. It would be most informative to experience Dupré the improviser in his thirties or forties.

Jean Langlais

My own teacher, Jean Langlais, was successor to Tournemire at Sainte-Clotilde from 1945. He had a worldwide reputation as an improviser/composer. He was a deeply spiritual organist – everything he played was an offering to God – and was rooted in the modality of Gregorian chant. As an improviser he revelled in large-scale symphonic frescos, which he called *"fantaisies"*, where the form was free but always on the move. The LP on the Motette label featuring improvisations on *Salve Regina* and *Veni Creator* is an excellent example.

As a teacher of improvisation Langlais was a genius, always encouraging and informative. One came away with the feeling that one had had a lesson in compositional skills, not "how to doodle"! The lessons took place either at his apartment (where there was a rather limited two-manual extension organ with a quarter-length 8' Dulzian on the top manual reminiscent of a duck in distress…) or on the inspirational Cavaillé-Coll at Sainte-Clotilde. At his apartment he used to talk mainly about the form (e.g. binary dance and so on), harmonization and fugue. At Sainte-Clotilde we were encouraged in a much free idiom, and, of course, the stunning Cavaillé-Coll provided an amazing aural stimulus. He frequently used to talk about modes (the theoretical side of which bewildered me), use of registration (he was very fond of Tournemire's ideas in this respect, favouring *mélanges* such as Récit Flûtes, Gambes, Célestes, Voix Humaine + Tremblant etc.), how to structure a fugue, and so on. The two phrases that used to crop up most often were *"pas trop long… pas trop long"* and *"beaucoup de choses"*, in other words the music was never allowed to become static.

He was very fond of canonic devices, usually at unison pitch and sometimes at other intervals. Langlais had the most astonishing memory and I recall my first meagre attempt at a Gregorian paraphrase, on *Veni Creator*, lasting perhaps two minutes. He slipped onto the bench immediately and played (so far as I could tell) *precisely* what I had played. I have never met anybody else who could do that! Of course he then proceeded to give some clear indications about how one could develop – perhaps by using more imitation, more counterpoint, more inventive harmony. As with Dupré, the brain always had to lead the fingers, never the other way round.

Pierre Cochereau

Marcel Dupré, the teacher of Cochereau at the Paris Conservatoire, described his protégé as "a phenomenon without equal in the history of twentieth-century French organ music". Born in 1924, he achieved great success at the Paris Conservatoire, where he was influenced strongly by Dupré and Duruflé (with whom he studied harmony). After a period as Organist at Saint-Roch, Cochereau was appointed to Notre-Dame in 1955 and remained in situ until his death on 5 March 1984. As an improviser he achieved a sort of cult status. Thousands would crowd into Notre-Dame and remain, spellbound, until the end of the *Sortie* of the High Mass. The clergy would even end the Mass, "Go in peace… *et maintenant, Pierre COCHEREAU aux Grandes Orgues"*.

Cochereau maintained that he never practised improvisation! There are accounts of him improvising at an early age (in the organ class of Marie-Louise Girod) and one suspects that it had always been his most natural way of expression. Cochereau had the keyboard technique of a concert pianist (he had been a piano pupil of Marguerite Long) as well as a stunningly rich harmonic vocabulary (showing the influence of Wagner, Debussy, Ravel, Vierne, Duruflé and, occasionally, his contemporary, Olivier Messiaen, for whom he had a huge regard). Marie-Claire Alain told me once how the whole Dupré class would wait with excitement for Cochereau to take the bench. He was known, even then, for *"le crescendo Cochereau"*, implying a harmonic as well as dynamic growth. A good number of Cochereau's improvisations have been released on the *Solstice* label by François Carbou, who recorded virtually all the Notre-Dame service improvisations since 1968. These recordings have become rightly very popular indeed and repay close daily study for the serious improviser. The osmosis between instrument and performer is total, producing music of staggering excitement as well as real emotional depth.

In the concert environment, Pierre Cochereau favoured symphonies, suites and variations. A typical plan for the last might have been:

Introduction:	(crescendo or diminuendo) hinting at the theme, but not presenting it in its entirety
Thème:	grand plein jeu/chamades
Fileuse:	the inimitable Cochereau "Spinning Wheel" all the 8' flutes coupled, Pedal 32', 16', $10\frac{2}{3}$', 8'
Fonds:	16', 8', 4' (*agité* or adagio – often using post-Wagnerian harmony)
Scherzando:	flutes and mutations
Dialogue on the	small chamade: (at Notre-Dame there is a Chamade 2/16' divided at treble C) accompanied by the Salicional/Unda Maris of the Positif
Trio:	right hand – flutes and mutations
	left hand – flutes and mutations
	left hand – 16' cornet (16', 8', $5\frac{1}{3}$', $3\frac{1}{5}$')
	Pedal – 4' and 2' reeds
Fugato:	(a) 8' fonds or
	(b) crescendo, or
	(c) plein jeu (chamades cantus firmus)
Ricercare:	cornets/cromornes/Pedal Divide
Final:	different plans and textures, but always leaving the listener stunned at the display of aural fireworks!

A typical plan for Sunday Mass might have been:

Entrée:	usually crescendo-diminuendo, starting and finishing with the Récit Tutti (box shut), with a crescendo via the fonds 16', 8', 4' (Grand Orgue and Positif)
Offertoire:	often a neo-classical texture with mutations, divided pedal etc.
Elevation:	*pp*
Communion:	fugato on the 8' stops or a luxurious Adagio, usually with a crescendo (up to Récit Tutti, box shut)
Sortie:	a veritable cascade of sound, sizzling with rhythm and excitement – music impregnated by an irresistible *joie de vivre*

Cochereau founded a new school of improvisation, probably without realising it. His influence amongst present day organ improvisers is enormous, even sixteen years after his death.

Competitions

Over the past forty years or so there has been an enormous growth in international competitions based around the art of organ improvisation. These competitions have increased awareness of improvisation and many of them, such as St Albans (UK), Paris, Chartres, Lyon, Strasbourg, Montbrison (France), Haarlem (Netherlands) and the AGO (USA) have a high profile. As well as testing performance of some repertoire, candidates are customarily encouraged to improvise in various forms and styles. The qualities of fluency and communication are essential, as is the ability to develop one's musical discourse within precise time limits without feeling truncated. Themes range from Gregorian chant to tone rows, from improvising on a scriptural passage to a piece of abstract modern art. For the members of the audience a high level improvisation competition can offer a stimulus which is uniquely exciting – music making at its most honest level, where the performers have no notated music to hide behind!

The Future

In the last twenty years or so there has been a great resurgence in awareness of the art of improvisation. The fact that many recordings of great improvisers have become easily available may well have something to do with this. I also believe that the ability to improvise or to enjoy improvised music, where spontaneity and technique merge into one, is an incredibly freeing psychological phenomenon. It can inform and enhance the element of controlled freedom with which players perform repertoire. The idea of "lifting the music off the page" by using one's own innermost musical personality and imagination is surely very close to improvisation.

It is certainly to be hoped that this renewed enthusiasm for improvisation will give rise to many more performers in the future who are prepared to improvise in public – and not just on the organ – thereby promoting truly spontaneous music making.

Theatre Organ Playing

Some suggestions for achieving a good technique with particular reference to the art of registration

by
Roy Bingham

In the early days of cinema entertainment the piano provided the musical support to the showing of silent films, then with the addition of a violin and cello the piano became a trio, eventually developing into small orchestras. However it was the introduction of the pipe organ that made the greatest impact, as with its full body of sound it could not only give support to the orchestra but was an acceptable alternative to it.

These early organs which started to appear in cinemas shortly before the first world war were church type instruments and although more orchestrally voiced instruments later came on the scene, it was the introduction of the unit type Wurlitzer organ which arrived in Britain in 1925 that heralded the era of the true cinema organ. This one man orchestra proved ideal for accompanying silent films, and later with the advent of talkies, became a solo instrument in its own right.

But what about the players of these instruments? After all, the church organist lived in a hidden world of diapasons, mixtures, choral works and Bach. Not so the cinema organist who had to contend with the likes of tibia clausa, krumet, glockenspiel and drums, might even be spotlighted in mid air, not to mention having to be conversant with the diverse fields of marches, overtures, musical comedy, novelties, popular tunes of the day, opera, orchestral transcriptions, and even the odd straight organ composition – and a signature tune!

The cinema organ or theatre organ as it has perhaps been better known during the past fifty years or so, certainly became one of the most popular forms of musical entertainment particularly during the 1930s, and with the ever-increasing use of radio a great number of organists became household names. This certainly proved that the best of them successfully mastered these instruments, and the art of registration as applied to the field of light music, which resulted in the production of sounds that not only appealed to the listener, but which could also be musically tasteful. After all playing all the correct notes is only part of the story.

Many of the organists who officiated in these early days were extremely competent and week after week would exhibit a playing quality that reached "the very heights of artistry and musicianship". Listen to the recordings of Quentin Maclean and judge for yourself the man who was once invited by the Royal College of Organists to give a recital of the test pieces at a distribution of diplomas. After all many of these organists held the FRCO, for example George Tootell, Rowland Tims, Reginald Foort, Charles Saxby, Edgar Peto, G T Pattman and Frank Newman. But there were many others not necessarily FRCOs but with ARCOs and/or good musical training and playing standards that did much to ensure that the theatre organ was taken seriously.

In this country approaching 500 of these unit type organs were originally installed in cinemas. Today fewer than twenty remain in playing condition in their original locations. But all is not lost; there are still 150 or so that have been saved, fully restored and rehoused, and played regularly either privately, or for the benefit of the public. The public ones can be seen and heard in halls, churches, schools, museums, ballrooms, theatres and leisure centres, whilst there are about thirty organs which have been dismantled and will no doubt be fully restored and rehoused in the fullness of time. There is also keen interest overseas including Australia, New Zealand, South Africa and Holland. The United States is particularly active and the American Theatre Organ Society has been in operation since 1958. In fact collectively the United States and Canada have in the region of 300 theatre organs in use in public places alone and there is a regular exchange of players between Great Britain and overseas.

In this country The Theatre Organ Club (founded 1938) and The Cinema Organ Society (founded 1952) continue in operation, and with people like the respected Nigel Ogden to spread the gospel via the BBC's *The Organist Entertains* together with his countrywide recital work, interest is maintained. Ensuring that this situation continues in the future is dependant on a number of factors, one of which is that the sounds coming from the organ must be musically acceptable.

In order to achieve this, good registration not only plays a major part, it is a must.

A   Preliminary Considerations

The art of good registration is where the correct selection of stop combinations results in satisfactory musical sounds. In order to achieve this it is essential that before considering such aspects as stop combinations and piston settings we need to be fully conversant with what is available on a theatre organ.

Generally speaking except with very small or large organs, everything that makes up the instrument is usually located in two separate chambers, one containing pipework and effects used for accompaniment purposes (Main on a Wurlitzer) and the other for solo work (Solo on a Wurlitzer).

So now let us establish what pipework etc is used for which purpose, what different types of pipes there are and what are their characteristics.

B   Details of Pipes used in Theatre Organs

Pipework
In order of volume, start from pp<ff

a.	*Type of Flue Pipes*	
1.	Dulciana	
2.	Unda Maris	
3.	Flute	
4.	Concert Flute	
5.	Harmonic Flute	
6.	String	Generally used for
7.	Violin	accompaniment purposes
8.	Violin Celeste	
9.	Viol d'Orchestre	
10.	Viol Celeste	
11.	Salicional	
12.	Quintadena	
13.	Tibia Clausa – Mainly used for solo purposes but also for accompaniment	
14.	Gamba	
15.	Gamba Celeste	
16.	Open Diapason	Generally used for accompaniment purposes
17.	Horn Diapason	
18.	Diaphonic Diapason	
b.	*Type of Reed Pipes*	
19.	Vox Humana	Used for both accompaniment and solo purposes
20.	Orchestral Oboe	Generally used for solo purposes
21.	Clarinet	Used for both solo and accompaniment purposes
22.	Saxophone	
23.	Kinura	Generally used for solo purposes
24.	Krumet	
25.	Oboe Horn	Generally used for accompaniment purposes

26.   Trumpet
27.   Tuba Horn
28.   Tuba
29.   French Trumpet   Generally used for solo purposes
30.   English Horn
31.   Tuba Mirabilis

c.   *Flue Pipe Characteristics*

1.   Dulciana – a small scaled Diapason
3.   Flute
4.   Concert Flute
5.   Harmonic Flute

The Flute and Concert Flute are both wooden pipes fully extended from 16' to 1' although the 16' extension may stop short at Tenor C. The Harmonic Flute is a metal pipe with a brighter tone than that of a wooden flute.

2.   Unda Maris
6.   String
7.   Violin
8.   Violin Celeste
9.   Viol d'Orchestre
10.   Viol Celeste
11.   Salicional
14.   Gamba
15.   Gamba Celeste

2, 6, 7, 8, 9, 10, 11, 14, 15 – All these are metal pipes producing varying shades of string tone. The celeste units are tuned slightly sharper so that when used with their 'parent' unit a fairly fast beat is produced which gives the impression of a collection of strings. The Unda Maris is tuned flat and is used in conjunction with the Dulciana which has a slight string quality.
    String units are rarely extended fully to 16' but are almost invariably playable to Tenor C in that pitch.

12.   Quintadena – A stopped metal flute pipe voiced to sound a fifth overtone. Often used to bind together flue pipe combinations.

13.   Tibia Clausa – On Wurlitzer Organs the Tibia is always a wooden stopped pipe of large scale with a very big mouth and a leathered upper lip. The tone (without tremulant) is likened to a dull flute. It is invariably extended fully from 16' to 2' +. this is the foundation stop of the theatre organ and when used with the tremulant is immediately recognised as the characteristic tone of a theatre organ. It blends well with the Vox Humana. British organs tended to use metal Tibias but it is the wooden Tibias of, for example, a Robert Morton (USA) organ and particularly a Wurlitzer that produce that rich full round unique tone.

16.   Open Diapason
17.   Horn Diapason
18.   Diaphonic Diapason

The Diapason is the foundation tone of the classical or church organ. In a theatre organ it is a metal pipe giving a full sound but with a somewhat lesser clarity than the Classical Diapason. It is usually extended to 16' and 4' with the lower octave being diaphones.

The Horn Diapason has the essential tone of an Open Diapason but as the name implies is voiced to give a more reedy quality to its tone; its pipes are slotted.

d. *Reed Pipe Characteristics*

19.   Vox Humana – A metal pipe giving a moderately reedy, bleating, rather plaintive effect. This stop always has its own tremulant and is rarely used without it. Used in this way and played in chorus it creates a choir-like impression. It is extremely useful in combination with Strings and the Tibia Clausa. It is usually extended to 4' with a Tenor C 16'.

20.   Orchestral Oboe – A narrow-scaled metal pipe with a slightly penetrating raspy tone. It is useful to give build up to some chord ensembles and also to add to other carefully chosen pipework for individual solo work.

21.   Clarinet – This approximates very closely to its orchestral counterpart. It is usually available in 8' pitch but may be at 16' down to Tenor C. Without the tremulant the tenor and lower middle octave is quite realistic.

22.   Saxophone – A brass pipe which can be likened to a stronger form of Vox Humana but with rather temperamental characteristics. It bears only a slight resemblance to the tone of the orchestral instrument but nevertheless if correctly regulated gives a rich crooning tone which is quite colourful. It is sometimes extended to a 4' with a 16' terminating at Tenor C.

23.   Kinura – A pipe with very small resonators producing a distinct nasal sound. It is hardly ever used by itself being designed for use with other pipework. Used with the Tibia Clausa in the middle octaves it can produce quite a novel buzzy sound without tremulant.

24.   Krumet – This also gives an edgy nasal tone midway between a Clarinet and Kinura. It blends well with string units and gives the impression of an additional String ensemble. Used without tremulant in conjunction with a limited number of carefully chosen stop footages it can be very effective.

25.   Oboe Horn – This has a quality rather like a soft English Horn. Almost always used as an excellent accompanimental stop for fine note definition. It is very good when used with Flute, Quintadena, Horn Diapason, Clarinet etc for clean sounding harmony in the accompaniment and a change from Strings.

26.   Trumpet – A Wurlitzer style D Trumpet gives with the tremulant a mellow round sound with not too much edge but with enough bite to be effective without the tremulant. A brass Trumpet, usually made from spun brass, has more edge and can be used for solo and chorus work or a loud snappy accompaniment without tremulant. Even so it can still sound melodic with tremulant plus, for instance, Tibia 8' or 4' and played in single notes.

27.   Tuba Horn
28.   Tuba
31.   Tuba Mirabilis

The Tuba and Tuba Horn give a fairly powerful smooth trumpet or trombone sound. The rounded tone of the Tuba Horn makes it a very useful solo combination stop giving build up to the majority of ensemble formulations. Both types are usually extended to 4', the 16' terminating at Tenor C. The Tuba Mirabilis is a larger and more powerful form of Tuba. It produces a very powerful fat round sound being a sonorous fanfare stop and a magnificent solo voice. It is rarely extended beyond 8' pitch.

29.   French Trumpet – A coarse rasping type of trumpet. If regulated correctly it is quite useful with tremulant particularly in the tenor range (à la Joseph Seal).

30.   English Horn – A very penetrating stop although it bears no relation to the orchestral Cor Anglais, nor the Cor Anglais or English Horn as found in church organs. It can cut through a barn door but can also impart a scintillating brilliance to a full organ. Whether strikingly melodious or sharply biting it is invaluable in combination with other pipework and is especially effective without the tremulant, but it must be used with discretion. Without the tremulant it is very good at 16' in full combinations. If there is no 16' available use the 8' with sub octave coupler. Also very useful for 'riffs'.

General Comment
Although it is basically true to say that Solo & Main/Accompaniment organ chamber pipe ranks are used for solo and accompaniment purposes there are exceptions. With particularly large organs similar to those found in the USA the Main Tibia Clausa, Main Vox Humana, and Main Tuba Horn are all used primarily for solo purposes, as is the Diaphonic Diapason. Also the larger instruments quite often have other Celestes additional to those already referred to above e.g. Quintadena, Horn Diapason and Flute, the latter being particularly effective.

C   Percussions and Special Effects
All theatre organs irrespective of size have in addition to pipework Tonal Percussions, Non Tonal Percussions (traps) and Special Effects. Here is a list of those most commonly found: of course only a large organ will contain them all.

Tonal Percussions	*Non Tonal Percussions (traps)*	*Effects*
Xylophone	Snare Drum	Steamboat Whistle
Glockenspiel	Tom-Tom	Train Whistle
Sleigh Bells	Wood Block	Police Whistle
Cathedral Chimes	Tambourine	Thunder
Tubular Bells	Castanets	Surf, Rain
Muted Chimes	Jingles	Wind Howl
Harp	Sand Block	Aeroplane
Marimba	Triangle	Phone Bell
Chrysoglott	Crash Cymbal	Fire Gong
Carillon	Choke Cymbal	Pistol Shot
Vibraphone	Cymbal Tap	Birds
Piano	Cymbal Roll	Bird Scale
	Bass Drum	Horses' Hooves
	Bass Drum Roll	Siren
	Tympani	Ratchet
	Chinese Gong	Crockery Smash
		Cow Bell
		Anvil
		Cock Crow
		Motor Horn

The normal procedure with organs in cinemas has been to have all these units, like the pipework, contained in a shuttered chamber, with the exception of the piano on the stage. In recent years some organ installations, for instance in pizza parlours, have had their Percussions and Effects located outside the chamber and visible to the audience. Such arrangements can provide added interest but as the volume of sound produced is at a constant level, a correct balance between them and pipe sound is essential.

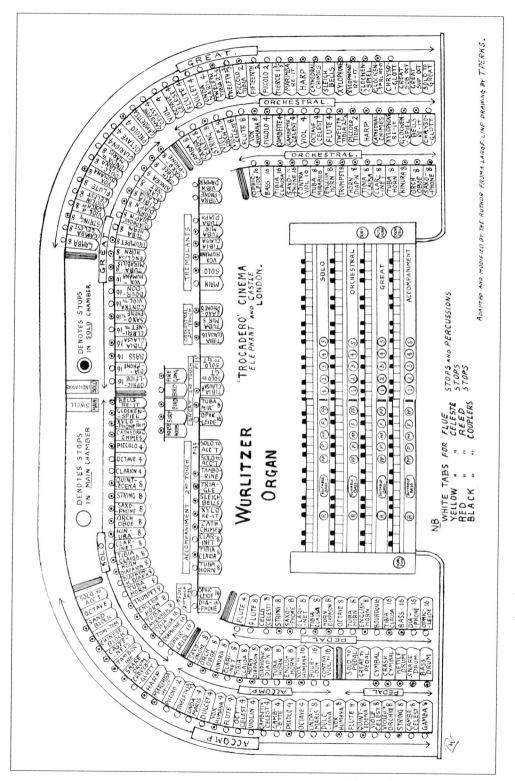

A typical large Wurlitzer console layout – here the "Trocadero", Elephant & Castle, London

(drawing by Reginald Whitworth)

D   Registration

We now turn to the most important aspect of this assessment of theatre organ playing – registration. We are conversant with the wide range of properties and characteristics of what is contained in the organ chambers and the next step is to see how we can harness all this information together, in order to produce the right theatre sounds.

Here are some practical suggestions on what stops and combination of stops to use for solo work (or provide the melody) and the supporting accompaniment and pedal stops required to give the correct musical balance and complete the whole ensemble.

The essence of good playing as George Wright said is to "use the minimum number of stops to achieve the desired effect". Some registrations are for single note melody, some for chords, and some are for certain parts of the keyboard, whilst some can be used as general sounds to which stops can be added or subtracted at will.

a. *Solo*

The basic difference between the classical organ and the theatre organ is that whereas in the former the foundation stop is the Open Diapason, in the latter it is the Tibia Clausa. So not only is the Tibia Clausa the main featured stop it is available at many pitches viz 16' 8' 4' $2\frac{2}{3}$' 2' $1\frac{3}{5}$' 1' and also as a quint at $5\frac{1}{3}$'.

It is not surprising therefore that without a Tibia Clausa there would be no true theatre organ sound, particularly in so far as Wurlitzers are concerned. No wonder that it is featured in so many different combinations in solo playing.

i.   *Some useful Tibia Clausa combinations; chords or single notes. (with tremulants)*

8'+4', 8'+2', 8'+4'+$2\frac{2}{3}$' + sub octave coupler
(for open harmony – 8' + 2')
16'+4', 16'+2', 8'+$2\frac{2}{3}$'.
The Tibia Clausa with other additions:-

A
{
Vox Humana 16' + Tibia Clausa 8'
Vox Humana 8' + Tibia Clausa 4' (play an octave lower than usual)
Tibia Clausa 8' + Flute 8' + Vox Humana 8' + Flute 4' (an effective combination)*
Add to * Tibia Clausa 4' and then Vox Humana 16' or 4'
Vox Humana 8' + Strings 8' + Tibia Clausa 4' (very useful for chords in the middle range)
}

ii.   *Lush Strings (with tremulants)*

Both hands on Strings + Vox Humana at all available pitches.

All Strings and Vox Humanas at 8' and 4' Tibia Piccolo 2' + sub octave (This combination is for chords but it works well in the tenor range on second touch with Tuba or Diapason)

String and String Celestes at 16' and 8' + Violin and Viol d'Orchestre with Celestes + Vox Humana all at 16' and 8' and 4' + Tibia Piccolo 4' (The Tibia gives just the right amount of body for this combination).

iii.   *Block Chords (with tremulants)*

In addition to A referred to above use any combination of Flute and Tibia Clausa at 8' and 4' and add the Vox Humana 8' or Orchestral Oboe at 8'. To build on this add higher pitches of Flutes and lower pitches of Strings and Reeds.

Remember that the Tibia Clausa at too many adjacent pitches will create a muddy sound except in the largest combinations.

iv.   *Amplification of Tibia Clausa sound. Some examples with tremulants*

Tibia Clausa/Vox Humana ensemble + Saxophone 8' + Orchestral Oboe 8' or Krumet 8'.
Tibia Clausa 8' + 4' + $2\frac{2}{3}$' (+maybe 2') + sub octave coupler.

Then add Saxophone 8', Orchestral Oboe 8', Vox Humana 8' and maybe octave coupler, but avoid a screeching effect when the Tibia Clausa 2' is used, particularly when playing at the upper end of the keyboard.

Tibia Clausa, Saxophone, Oboe, Vox Humana (all at 16') + Saxophone, Oboe, Vox Humana, Kinura (all at 8') + Tibia 4' $2\frac{2}{3}$' and 12th (use for single notes in the mid range).

For a 'sleazy' effect try Tibia Clausa, Vox Humana, Colour Reeds, Flute & Strings (as necessary) (all at 8') + Tibia Clausa, Flute and Strings (as necessary) (all at 4') + Tibia Clausa 12th 2' $1\frac{3}{5}$' + Flute 12th + Fife 1' (if possible). Play single notes in the tenor range.

v.   *Use of Reeds*
All the following combinations are (except for the English Horn) used with tremulants. However some excellent sounds can be achieved with careful tremulant selection and even with no tremulants being used at all.

Individual solo Reeds at 8' are satisfactory. For a fuller sound add the Open Diapason or Tibia Clausa at 8'. For more colour add a Flute or Tibia Clausa at 4'. (The Open Diapason must tremulate satisfactorily for these combinations)

A good solo combination – Tuba Horn 8' + Tibia Clausa 4' (or 8'+4')

Reed solo (improved) – Add a $2\frac{2}{3}$' (Flute or Tibia Clausa) to improve the Reed harmonies.

If there is no Tuba available, Trumpet 8' + Open Diapason 8' is a useful alternative. For a pleasing sound with tremulants, played in single notes, try Trumpet 8' + Tibia Clausa 4'.

English Horn – used in the main without tremulant (see later).

vi   *Useful combinations (with all tremulants off apart from c)*
To be played in chords:-

a.   Krumet 8' + Tibia Clausa 8' + 4'
b.   Krumet 8' + Open Diapason 8' + Tibia Clausa 4'
c.   Krumet 8' (or Kinura 8') without tremulant + Tibia Clausa 4' with tremulant (common in the USA)
d.   English Horn 8' + Tuba Horn 8' (or Tuba 8' or Trumpet 8') – a brassy sound
      (This combination is good in block chords against Strings and Flues with tremulants).
e.   8' English Horn + full combination
f.   Strings and octave and sub octave couplers (may be with Chrysoglott)

vii   *Church or Classical Organ Sound (tremulants off)*
a.   Use Diapasons, Flutes, Strings (no Celestes) and Reeds (carefully chosen) and maybe octave coupler.
b.   Strings and Celestes in combination
c.   Flutes and Celestes in combination
d.   Avoid colour reeds e.g. Orchestral Oboe, Saxophone and Vox Humana. Also the Tibia Clausa.
e.   The Krumet and Kinura would normally be also avoided. However a straight organist could find the Kinura useful as a solo stop in certain situations. When he needs a Schalmei perhaps?
f.   To get a full organ plus mixture, Trumpet 16' with the Solo swell box partly open could be considered.

A typical Compton console, complete with illuminated surround.

The theatre organ does not set out to be a straight organ but there are occasions when such a sound is required. The specification of many theatre organs particularly the larger ones is such that they can give a good account of themselves in this direction, but only if the correct pipework is used. Even with a 2/5 Wurlitzer acceptable sounds can be obtained using carefully chosen footages of Flute, Flute/Salicional and Salicional with sub and/or octave couplers, without tremulants of course.

On a theatre organ it is not just a question of switching off all the tremulants on whatever stop combination is being used. Too many organists do this and a combination of Vox Humana, Saxophone and Tibia Clausa in full flight is not the answer; it sounds like a harmonium and does not command respect.

Even if a straight combination is used for only a short space of time in a recital programme, its formulation should be given as much care and consideration as for music of a lighter nature.

viii   *Fast Playing*
The use of a Reed or Percussion to carry the melody is recommended, as in some combinations a confused sound results from using the Tibia Clausa with tremulant.

A light combination using the Tibia Clausa which is effective is Tibia Clausa 2' (or to a lesser extent 4') + Chrysoglott + Glockenspiel + Tremulant.

ix   *Couplers*
Use couplers with extreme care and only when you cannot obtain the sound you require from the stops available. An Octave Coupler can in the right situation give added brilliance and a 16' Coupler gives a fuller bodied sound when playing in the top octaves. In the main do not play below middle C with the 16' Coupler on and only play in the top 1½ octaves if both 16' stops and 16' Couplers are in use. One combination using the Sub Octave which could sometimes go down to Tenor G is the buzzy sound

associated with Joseph Seal and Reginald Dixon. In this case the registration is Tibia Clausa up to 12th + colour Reeds + Sub Octave + tremulant.

Remember that couplers affect every stop at every pitch and can on the one hand give added body and brilliance but on the other hand can transform a pleasing combination into a musical disaster.

The 'screech' effect caused by misuse of the Octave Coupler should be avoided at all costs.

x   *Full Organ*

For a brassy full sound do not include the Vox Humana. Leave the Krumet and English Horn off until you have set up a good orchestral ensemble. If you must use them to add some 'sass' do not use the 4' Coupler and do not register any Reeds at 4'.

Also take advantage of 16's or Sub Octave for a rich full sound.

b.   *Accompaniment*

i
- Flute 8'
- Flute 8' + 4'
- Flute 8' + String 8'
- Flute 8' + 4' + String 8' + 4'
- Flute 8' + 4' String and Celeste 8' + 4'

(For a warmer sound use *more* Flutes and *fewer* Strings)

Add the Open Diapason 8' to any of these combinations and also to Strings at 8' and 4'. The Open Diapason gives solidarity but if it is too pronounced the general sound can be heavy.

For a shimmering String sound use the Vox Humana 8' with various String combinations.

To increase the loudness of the Accompaniment after putting down the loudest combination indicated at (i) add the Open Diapason 8', then the Tuba Horn 8' and other Reeds as required.

The Octave Coupler could also be used in any of these combinations but should not be overdone. Bear in mind that with a loud Accompaniment combination, particularly if this includes an 8' Reed such as the Tuba Horn, playing legato chords could ruin any solo combination being played.

If a legato Accompaniment is required use the 4' Tibia Clausa instead. The Tibia Clausa should not be used with the left hand when playing a rhythmical Accompaniment. Where the Tibia Clausa is used on the Accompaniment is in the technique developed by Reginald Dixon. Here the Tibia Clausa is played legato with the left hand in conjunction with untremmed English Horn either singly or with other Reeds, played staccato with the right hand.

General Comment

In the case of small or medium sized organs there is a limit to the number of different accompaniment combinations that can be used, hence the predominance of Flute & String voices.

However with larger organs there are other stops which can be invaluable for accompaniment purposes. In particular I would refer to Oboe Horn, Horn Diapason, a Quintadena all at 8'. These coupled with the Flute 8'+4' form an extremely useful neutral body of sound suitable for general use including ballads and rhythmic offerings. So for a change use Flute 8' 4' and 12th + Chrysogott. Then try adding Oboe Horn 8', Quintadena 8' and Horn Diapason 8'.

Where a Harp or Sub Harp is available this is very effective with non string quiet registrations.

c.   *Pedal*

Generally speaking the Pedal stops are designed to match the Accompaniment stops and the colour Reeds such as Saxophone, Krumet and Orchestral Oboe; the heavy Reeds such as Tuba Horn and English Horn would only be used in special circumstances.

The softest stop is the Bourdon 16' (useful for ballads). To increase the volume add the Tibia Clausa 8' or Cello 8' and then both together. Next add the Diapason 8'. Finally add the Diaphone 16', and for completion the Accompaniment to Pedal (very useful) and Solo to Pedal. Obviously the latter coupler would only be used occasionally.

The Tuba 8' should be rarely used and the English Horn 16' retained for a sustained pedal note for effect, or for a final flourish.

The addition of the Tibia Clausa 8' and/or Open Diapason 8' and the Tibia Clausa 16' enhances the base line and makes it easier to follow, especially in conjunction with fast pieces. Also with fast pieces where more body is required, instead of the Tibia Clausa 16' use the Diapason 16', which will result in a faster speech response.

Another point to bear in mind is that using the Accompaniment to Pedal coupler automatically builds up the Pedal, though remember of course still to use the 16' Pedal stops as required.

d. *Percussions and Effects*

Tonal Percussions should always be used with discretion. Quite often there is a tendency to overuse them, especially the Glockenspiel and Piano. However good and entertaining effects can be obtained with them, for example:

i *Solo*

Tibia Clausa 4' + Glockenspiel or Xylophone
Tibia Clausa 8' + 4' + Glockenspiel or Xylophone
English Horn 8' + Glockenspiel or Xylophone
(no Reed tremulant)

At the end of playing –   an arpeggio on the Glockenspiel,
Chrysoglott or both together or
alternatively a single note Chime.

In the main use single notes only, avoiding large chords and Couplers.

A few other suggestions:

Strings 8' + 4' + Tibia Clausa 2' + Glockenspiel/Chrysoglott, + Tremulant (common in the USA)

All Strings + Octave Coupler/Sub Octave Coupler + Glockenspiel, no Tremulants and played on chords.

Tuba 8' + Diapason 8' + Glockenspiel, no tremulant. (For jazzy playing à la Dan Bellamy)

English Horn 8' + Xylophone and/or Harp/Sub Harp + Sub Octave Coupler or maybe Octave Coupler played in single notes. (For jazzy playing à la John Seng)

ii *Accompaniment*

A soft registration + Chrysoglott or Vibraphone

Care must be taken when using Non Tonal Percussions (Traps) especially the reiterating type. The rhythm must be maintained otherwise inadvertently holding down a note can result in any good effect being immediately wiped out. Nevertheless Traps can be used to enhance playing, particularly in dance numbers.

Effects were originally part of theatre organs because of their use in the accompaniment of silent films. They are still retained today on the organs and in novelty numbers for example can be useful and amusing.

E   Combination pistons – operation and registration settings

The great advantage of combination pistons is that so many different registrations can be made available to the player without the necessity of changing the stop keys directly by hand. In this way the exact registrations required are immediately available at the touch of a finger or thumb resulting in a far better musical presentation by the organist. In fact in so far as serious quality concert organ playing is concerned the use of combination pistons is a MUST.

One appreciates that organs vary in size and make; pistons can be manually and foot operated and even feature double touch. Also the number of pistons available may vary. Fully unified organs for example will have pistons on each manual, whilst a three manual coupler instrument may have no pistons on the coupler manual. Small two manual instruments may have as few as half a dozen pistons for the whole console, whereas a fully unified four manual instrument could have forty or more.

Add to this the fact that no two organists' thoughts on piston setting registrations are the same, and it is not surprising that many recitalists on a strange instrument make use of what is on offer and leave well alone. However there are occasions when the organist may be able to set up pistons before a recital. Also the increasing availability of modern electronic piston setter systems means that players' own special settings can be programmed in seconds, thus leaving more time available for a practice session.

All this leads me to suggest that some knowledge of the basic principles of piston setting together with some examples would not be out of place. Here are a few ideas.

a   *Two Manual Instruments – Small*

On a small instrument with possibly three pistons only on each manual, the tonal build up on the Solo Manual would be from a soft combination on piston 1 to loud on piston 3. Similarly the three pistons on the Accompaniment manual would use the same procedure in providing suitable support for the melody line on the Solo manual. Any registration adjustments such as Vox Humana/Tibia Clausa combination or a non-tremmed brass effect on the Solo manual could be achieved by hand registration.

With six pistons on each manual the same principle could apply for the first three pistons on the Solo manual, the other three being used for special combinations.

Similarly on the Accompaniment manual all six pistons could range from soft on No 1 to loud on No 6 or alternatively pistons 4 5 and 6 could be used for special combinations e.g. a String/Vox Humana setting and on No 6 piston full organ without tremulants.

b   *Two Manual Instruments – Large*

In these cases one could expect to have available ten pistons on each of the Solo and Accompaniment manuals giving far more flexibility and variety of tone colour.

Here is one basic suggestion for the Solo manual (Tremulants on all except 3 and Clarinet on 2):-

1.   Tibia Clausa 8' + 4' + Vox Humana 8' (or Tibia Clausa 16' + 4' + Vox Humana 8')
2.   Tibia Clausa 8' (with tremulant) + Clarinet 8' (without tremulant) – a popular combination in the USA.
3.   Reed combination e.g. English Horn 8' + Tuba 8'
4.   Half full organ excluding Trumpet/English Horn types
5.   Full Organ
6.   Tibia Clausa 8' + 4' + Tuba 8' (good solo combination)
7.   Tibia Clausa 8' + 4' + $2\frac{2}{3}$' + sub octave (also with Krumet 8')
8.   As for No 4 but with 2's added
9.   Tibia Clausa 16' + 8' + 2'
10. Tibia Clausa 8' + 4' + Glockenspiel (or Xylophone)

c   *Comments on the above settings*

i   No 3 piston is set for an easy registration change. Had this setting been for example on No 10 piston a quick manipulation would have been more difficult.

ii   A No 3 piston alternative would be to make this piston a Krumet 8' + Tibia Clausa 8' + 4', (or Tibia Clausa 4' + Diapason 8') combination without tremulant. This would then give two contrasting untremmed reed combinations, easy to operate, in the midst of tremmed settings.

iii   A good straight organ combination is sometimes useful and if so this could be on No 10 piston in view of it being used to a lesser extent than the other settings.

iv   Another alternative to the ten suggested piston settings detailed under (b) above could be to have the first five pistons set to give a gradual volume build up, with the remaining five pistons being used for specific settings.

v   All the above piston settings would require suitable support on the Accompaniment manual and the same principle would apply here as for smaller organs, but obviously the greater number of pistons available results in greater flexibility.

d *Larger Organs*

These would range from three manual coupler types up to five manual fully unified giants. The larger the organ the greater the number of pistons and the wider choice of registration settings at ones disposal. The choice really is unlimited but it does allow the position of perhaps a few choice settings not already mentioned. Examples would be a rich sub octave combination, a full string/Vox Humana setting at all pitches and a quint coupler mixture. There would also be room for a few simple registrations based on specific solo stops e.g. Tuba or Trumpet 8' + Tibia 4' or the Tibia Clausa alone at e.g. 16' + 4' or 16' + 2' or at 8' + 4' + $2\frac{2}{3}$' + sub octave coupler.

General Comments

In addition to the suggested piston setting combinations put forward in this section consideration should also be given to the examples detailed under 'D *Registration*'. Collectively this should help to guide the players into an appreciation of registration colour and an awareness of what stop combinations produce a good theatre organ sound. Any that are then particularly suitable could, if the situation arises, be used to make up a series of organ console piston settings which are acceptable and musically satisfying to the player.

F *Second Touch*

Like combination pistons second touch (or double touch) is also a most valuable facility and its use can contribute greatly to good theatre organ playing. Basically it allows an organist to play both a melody and its accompaniment simultaneously with one hand on the same manual, whilst the other hand is available to play musical variations on another manual. It is useful for playing counter melodies, or to provide a sforzando effect when a particular sound emphasis is required, and it is usually available on other than the Accompaniment manual and also the Pedals.

When playing on the Accompaniment manual if we consider the normal playing pressure on the keys as 'first touch' then by pressing below this a different stop or group of stops can come into operation which sound above the Accompaniment registration resulting in two distinct different tone colours. Let us assume that the Flute 8' + 4' stop keys on the Accompaniment manual are 'on' and also that the Tuba Horn 8' second touch stop key on the same manual is also 'on'. The first touch on the manual will give the Flute 8' + 4' combination but by depressing the key down to second touch the sound produced will be Flute 8' + 4' plus Tuba Horn 8'. This would enable a melody to be played on the second touch combination with the first touch sound providing the accompaniment, all on one manual.

Stops which can be useful on second touch include Reeds, Open Diapason, Tibia Clausa (usually all at 8') Cathedral Chimes and Triangle.

Worthy exponents of Second Touch include Jesse Crawford, Reginald Dixon, Joseph Seal and Reginald Porter Brown.

G *A few relevant comments*

i We must not be carried away by certain sounds that appeal to us and then use the same combination at every available opportunity. The constant use of Piano or Glockenspiel irrespective of the type of music being played is an example of this. We should not overdo anything whether a single stop, or a combination of stops. It is monotonous and tiring to the listener.

ii We should ensure that we like every combination of stops that are used. An unsatisfactory sound to the player will result in an unsatisfactory approach. However if by design or accident we obtain a particularly pleasing sound from a combination of stops, we should make a note of what was used as it could be useful again.

iii We need to remember that we are playing a theatre pipe organ and not an electronic instrument. Thus we should not try to produce sounds that make it sound like an electronic organ by being tempted to use the Flute and Tibia Clausa at all pitches.

iv A theatre organ can make a lot of noise. We do not have to use full organ for long periods or play full combinations when delicate phrasing using a few stops is required. Do not be afraid to use simple registration e.g. Tuba 8' + Tibia Clausa or Open Diapason or Flute. This idea could work just as well for the Orchestral Oboe or Trumpet.

v   Many of us have had to rely on information given on sheet music to detail what the registration should be for a particular composition. Unfortunately this information usually relates to either a particular make of electronic organ or electronic organs in general. Often the information is vague and even when referring to a church organ is still not particularly helpful. In no sensible way should this information be used as a basis for playing a particular composition on the theatre organ and thus do full justice to the music itself. Where available piano conductor copies of music are considerably fuller than piano solo copies and give admirable hints on what instruments were used by the composer; with strings, brass, flutes and reeds such as the clarinet even on small organs one can give a good impression of the various orchestral effects. However whilst this may be possible with orchestral music, in the main the majority of us have to be satisfied with piano copies of music only. This is where our knowledge of what is available on an organ can be so helpful.

vi   To help fully appreciate what sounds good on the organ we need to listen to recordings of top rank performers, past and present. American organists of note include George Wright, Lynn Larsen, Ashley Miller, Ron Rhode, Jim Riggs, Jesse Crawford, John Seng, Tom Hazelton and Walt Strony. British organists would include Simon Gledhill, Douglas Reeve – a good orchestral player employing clean sounding ensembles, Dudley Savage (usually on a Compton) – a good solid player, and Joseph Seal (usually on a Wurlitzer) – well worth listening to and an expert on good registration. Listen to his contrast changes from tremmed Tibia Clausa/Vox Humana registration to untremmed Reeds. For general light music, including dance music, recordings by Phil Kelsall and Robert Wolfe can be helpful. Also we must not forget others whose records are still available and show that they were truly masters of their art. I refer to Reginald Dixon, Horace Finch, Reginald Foort, Hubert Selby, Sidney Torch and Quentin Maclean.

We can learn a great deal from all these organists' performances, by observing how they interpreted different melodies. It also helps to listen to orchestras and bands to identify the instruments used and know where and when they are featured in a particular composition.

vii   This article details some of the main aspects of playing a theatre organ. It cannot cover everything so some omissions (e.g. pizzicato couplers and sustainers) may no doubt come to mind, but hopefully what information has been given is sufficient to encourage those of us who play the theatre organ to continue to improve our performance.

To achieve a satisfactory standard takes time and practice but being able to play every note correctly is not the full story. Theatre organ music basically consists of a tune, an accompaniment and a bass and it is how we combine these all together and what sounds we make come out of the organ chambers that matters.

We must never be entirely satisfied with our playing but always endeavour to improve our standards. There is still today a place for an organist who is technically competent, has had adequate musical training, plays correctly and musically, uses good registration and can present a well balanced programme.

Today the Blackpool sound developed by Reginald Dixon is very popular but not all performers in this style match up to the quality of its originator. The sound is very enjoyable but the theatre organ is capable of giving more.

Unfortunately some recitalists tend to string together a collection of popular tunes with little variation in registration and call it an organ recital. There is so much more to it: a good performer should be capable of playing to a satisfactory standard overtures, musical comedy, marches, opera, waltzes, ballet and good novelty numbers etc. in addition to pops and light classical organ pieces.

The sound of a theatre organ can give pleasure to performer and listener alike, always remembering that the player's contribution should be of the highest standard.

In connection with this article on theatre organ playing I would like to express my appreciation to theatre organist David Lowe, Hon. Musical Adviser to the Cinema Organ Society 1986/87, for his constructive comments and helpful suggestions.

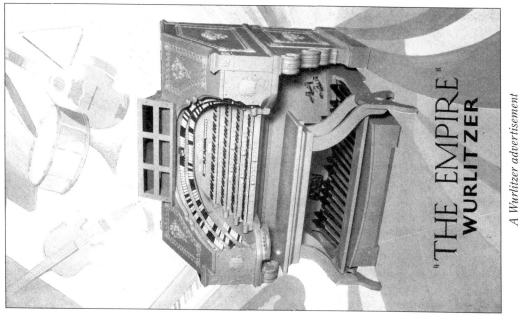

A Wurlitzer advertisement

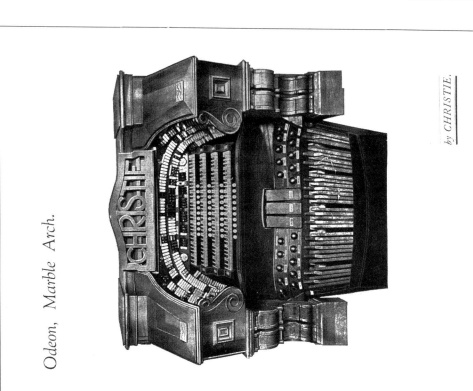

A large Christie console,
from Hill, Norman & Beard publicity

Church Music in the Twentieth Century – a Rise and Fall?

by
Dr Lionel Dakers

THE GENERAL OVERVIEW

It would be no exaggeration to say that there has been more change in the Church during the past fifty years than in the whole of the preceding five hundred. This, moreover, applies to virtually every denomination, not just to the Church of England or the Roman Catholic Church. Not surprisingly, this reflects the world at large with its ever increasing thirst for change at all costs. In the past half century we have experienced enormous advances to our great benefit in areas such as medicine, electronics, communications, computers, fax and E-mail, in the speed and ease of worldwide travel and the wholesale emergence of supermarkets and take-aways, while the influx of immigrants has brought new cultures encompassing new religious needs.

In the Church, while major thinking and changes have seen the escalation of new and often divisive issues such as the ordination of women to the priesthood and the gay/lesbian debate and their being for ever highlighted in the media, far greater issues in the matter of liturgical change and how we opt to worship today are, as we shall see, far more contentious and the more damaging.

Such then is the all-encompassing momentum and urge for change, not least within the political arena. One cannot help but wonder how long this can be realistically sustained at its present level for it has become something of an in-thing phobia which we cannot easily escape.

In order to fully understand where we are today, and why, we first need to consider some of the many departures from the norm that have taken place in church music during the 20th century and which account in greater part for the prevailing *status quo* which confronts us. Much of what I shall survey will necessarily hinge on the Anglican tradition and the distinctive dual role of the cathedrals and the parish churches. The cathedrals with their long rooted firmly established traditions may in some ways be too comfortably secure, though overall they have probably experienced far less drastic change than have the parishes. In both instances change is not a word always to the forefront in the ecclesiastical dictionary. For the traditionally orientated it is the resistance stemming from 'we know what we like and we like what we know', while for others it can be a matter of pursuing change willy nilly, and often for its own sake.

At the beginning of the 20th century the Church soldiered on for the most part in a mainly tranquil and uneventful way in terms of its music, with two of the most significant parallels to the worship songs and charismatic music of today being the music of The Salvation Army and the hymns of Sankey and Moody. While the reforming zeal of S S Wesley and Maria Hackett was significant, liturgical change was not even remotely on the horizon, though churchmanship was sharply divided into three areas – centre of the road, evangelical and Anglo-Catholic, with the distinctive ritual (or lack of it) and the music of each a significant factor.

A mere glance at cathedral music lists of the early 1900s (see over) reveals a mostly monochrome diet, much of it, particularly in settings of morning and evening canticles of the Kempton, Aldrich and Travers mould being dull in their pedestrian and uneventful chordal structure, devoid of rhythmic interest and with only minimal key contrasts. To our ears it is distinctly insipid, as is much of the heavily larded sentimentalism of the anthems of the period, as probably in the way they were performed. Anyhow, the chances of hearing any of this today are virtually non-existent, though we are currently rediscovering the best of the period, of which there is a considerable amount. Some of this is published by the Church Music Society, while in hymnody *Common Praise*, the new edition of *Hymns Ancient and Modern* due to be published this summer, will include a number of examples from this period and from the 19th century.

With the emergence of composers of the stature of Stanford, Parry, Elgar, Charles Wood, and then their pupils who included Vaughan Williams, Britten, Howells, Harris and Walton, a new and influential

A LATE NINETEENTH-CENTURY CATHEDRAL MUSIC LIST
May 31st – June 6th, 1896

	Services	Anthems	
TRINITY SUNDAY	*M.* Sullivan in D Kyrie: Sullivan in D Creed: Goss in D *E.* Stainer in B flat	Holy, Holy Lord God of Hosts I saw the Lord	*Spohr* *Stainer*
MONDAY	*M.* Tours in F *E.* Tours in F	Teach me thy way O come, let us worship	*W H Gladstone* *Mendelssohn*
TUESDAY (Men's voices in the morning)	*M.* Plainsong *E.* Russell in A	Let all creation Wherewithal shall a young man?	*Mendelssohn* *Elvey*
WEDNESDAY	*M.* Nares in F *E.* Nares in F	– O Thee each living soul	*Haydn*
THURSDAY	*M.* Barnby in E *E.* Barnby in E	See what love hath the Father Stand up and bless the Lord	*Mendelssohn* *Goss*
FRIDAY	*M.* Tallis (Dorian) *E.* Tallis (Dorian)	– Lighten our darkness	*W H Gladstone*
SATURDAY	*M.* Wesley in F (chant) *E.* Walmisley in D minor	O Father, blest O how amiable	*Barnby* *S S Wesley*

From E H Fellowes: English Cathedral Music

perspective came into being with its resulting influence soon firmly established. This was the more remarkable in that the church music of Stanford was only a small part of his output which included symphonies, concertos, chamber music and opera.

This turnaround was implemented by pioneer scholarly work, particularly in music of the Tudor period. Initiated by E H Fellowes and others, this made available, mainly in the early days through Oxford University Press, a whole wealth of material previously unedited and unpublished. This whole new ethos regarding music of the 16th and 17th centuries readily found its place in the repertoire. Much of the promotion and performance of this music was to a great extent made possible through an emerging breed of cathedral organists whose musicianship and artistry were exemplary. Some, such as Bairstow at York and Bullock at Exeter and Westminster Abbey, were in themselves composers of considerable expertise and gave a further ongoing new look to the scene.

Even so, a Sunday Eucharist as we know it was a rare occurrence in the early years of the 20th century, as it was in the 19th, for the emphasis on the centrality of the Eucharist had yet to emerge. The singing of psalms to Anglican chants was the sole method employed, though the earliest psalters such as *The Cathedral Psalter* and *The New Cathedral Psalter* put the cart before the horse by making the words subservient to the claims of the music. Speech rhythm pointing was aeons away in the future. Hymn singing only began to be a regular part of Anglican worship following its introduction at St Paul's Cathedral on Sunday evenings during the latter part of the 19th century, much of this due to the impetus created by the advent of *Hymns Ancient and Modern* in 1861.

Since then hymn singing has never looked back and now every few minutes punctuates many forms of public worship. Hymns are also much more prominent in cathedrals where they fulfil a distinctive role for congregations. They not only corporately involve all concerned, musicians, congregations and clergy alike, but are freely shared across the board by all denominations as opposed to the strict separatist approach which prevailed a century ago, or even less. For example, Anglicans sing the hymns of the Roman Catholic Cardinal Newman and *vice versa*. Because of this, hymns should ideally be a major means of promoting ecumenism, though this is not always by any means realised or taken advantage of.

LITURGICAL DEVELOPMENTS

While the Book of Common Prayer reigned supreme a century ago, for there were then no rivals or opposition, things changed with the adoption of the 1928 Prayer Book which, though never approved by Parliament was therefore illegal, but was in use mainly in Anglo-Catholic parishes. The first revision of the main services in recent times, known now as Series 1 and Series 2, was a fairly guarded and mild updating, after which liturgical revision swiftly developed, with *The Alternative Service Book 1980* being a major restructuring using contemporary language. This has now been revised and, as *Common Worship,* will be with us this millennial year. The multiplicity of what is now on offer is confusing for many laity, even for some of the clergy. It is certainly controversial, as is the current fashion of devising DIY services to be found in the more liberal areas of the Church which reject formal acts of worship and ritual in favour of the informality now so prevalent in many aspects of our secular national life. Even so, the ongoing work of the C of E's Liturgical Commission is as nothing compared with the Roman Catholic Church which at Vatican 2 generally abandoned Latin for the vernacular and threw out not only the bath water but the baby as well.

Nevertheless, these factors overall have led on to growing contact between the denominations and have shown how much we in fact share in common. Today the various parts of the Anglican Communion are much more bound and linked together than ever before as is the exchange of liturgical scholarship, this in itself a new and major 20th century departure. This means that although texts may vary in detail, the shape of the Eucharist is basically the same worldwide. This, moreover, extends to other denominations where texts are now much more freely, and willingly, shared with the Free Churches who themselves are much more liturgically orientated, and consequently more formal, in their worship patterns.

During my time as Director of The Royal School of Church Music I experienced this more and more both at home and as I travelled to many countries. I felt quite at home attending a Roman Catholic Mass, though I was initially somewhat surprised to hear the Prayer of Humble Access and other Anglican extracts in a Baptist Communion service. Today there is happily much less liturgical exclusiveness, even if some of the C of E changes have proved contentious, particularly the introduction of the Peace which is less acceptable to many stiff-lipped Anglo-Saxons than it is to Frenchmen who readily embrace each other at the slightest provocation. Although many of the newly structured Anglican services are now widely used, *ASB* Mattins and Evensong have not generally caught on.

THE 20TH CENTURY IN MORE DETAIL

In order to fully assess where we are today – and the reasons for this – we need to examine as far as possible each and every aspect, of which there are many. The influences, and by no means least the pioneer work of the past century have exerted a tremendous impact within the Church as a whole and, as we shall see, not always for the best.

By far the greatest changes have been in parish worship where Sunday Mattins, and to an extent Evensong, have been more or less sidelined to such a degree that the Parish Communion has become *the* Sunday service. In this the Anglican church has mirrored what was always, and still is, fundamentally the Mass of the Roman Catholic Church as its all but exclusive form of worship. While this is understandable, it has assumed such a prominence in the C of E that almost every specially constructed service, whatever the occasion, is very much moulded on the Eucharist, exceptions being events such as the Battle of Britain Commemoration, national organisations holding an annual service, and the plethora of school carol services which often take place in cathedrals.

In the light of these 20th century developments it is interesting to recall that until the middle of the century the Eucharist was in many instances a virtually private priestly matter, a survival of the chantry chapel and of the monastic clergy who would daily celebrate the Mass in their personal chapel with no congregation present. I can remember in the 1950s Anglo Catholic clergy who would say the Prayer of Consecration and the Prayer of Humble Access so softly that the congregation could hear virtually nothing, for it was considered at that time to be something conducted solely between the celebrant and his Maker. By sharp contrast the Eucharist has now become a very public act of worship with all concerned corporately saying the prayers in the plural. More of this and the reasons for it when we discuss how we use our churches today.

In the C of E the Parish Communion movement is a fairly recent innovation, some of it originating in the problems arising when celebrating Holy Communion in the trenches in the First World War when Eric Milner White (later to become Dean of York) sought new ways expedient to this. Its subsequent growth demanded music which could be sung by the congregation as well as the choir. Martin Shaw saw the need for this in the 1930s when he wrote his Anglican Folk Mass and his going round England teaching it to congregations, particularly in country areas. He sought to provide something readily singable by rank and file ordinary people who were probably musically uneducated. In doing so he mirrored Merbecke whose system of one musical note for every word or syllable was a way, which proved to be very successful and lasting, of providing simple music for the then new Book of Common Prayer, and as a contrast to the florid contrapuntal music of the Latin Mass. Palestrina, Vittoria and Byrd were but three composers who wrote elaborate and lengthy settings for choirs, whereas Merbecke sought to provide simple music for congregational use, music which continues to be as locked into Anglican worship as *Greensleeves* is to the secular world.

Other composers have increasingly provided simple settings with congregational needs very much in mind, especially John Rutter, Peter Aston and Richard Shephard. Their music is eminently suitable at the present time particularly when the demise of so many SATB choirs is for one reason or another in the ascendent. Martin How, in his *Music for Parish Communion* (published by the RSCM) built much of the music on a simple ascending five note motif as the basis of each movement. In the Gloria this is sung every so often by the congregation while the choir, or soloist, provide the non-repetitive narrative. This approach is the sort of thing which Gelineau and Dom Gregory Murray did in order to make psalm singing more readily congregational in much the same way as the *animateur* in Roman Catholic churches on the continent.

By no means all of the Rite A Holy Communion settings have in the long run proved successful. This is especially true of some of the earlier examples which, in their aiming to be simple to sing and play, proved to be somewhat mundane and trite. In their chord by chord progression they frequently failed to incorporate any rhythmic interest or melodic memorability. As with many pioneers they did at least point the direction which was more successfully realised by later composers. A further innovation has been in those churches where the organist has put pen to paper and contrived to provide for the needs of that church.

A significant change brought about by the need for the involvement and togetherness so much at the heart of 20th century liturgical thinking has been the awareness that if this is to be fully achieved we need to be able to use our churches in a more flexible way. The Oxford Movement in the late 19th century saw the focus of worship moving both spatially and visually towards the chancel and sanctuary, together with the clergy, choir and other assistants. With this the organ superseded the orchestra in the west gallery so vividly portrayed by Thomas Hardy in his Wessex novels. The resulting crowded situation was made the worse by filling every conceivable space in the body of the church with pews, much of it of bulky pitchpine and maybe functional in an age when people went to church in greater numbers than now. Much of it was neither beautiful nor worthy, unlike the box pews which they replaced. Most of this furniture was firmly screwed to the floor, for the Victorians were convinced of what they believed to be the permanency of this new approach to worship.

What also materialised was the growing realisation later on that worship for people seated in the nave was often something of a distant spectator sport visually and in terms of participation. This was particularly so if a screen divided the congregation from the chancel and sanctuary, producing a 'we and they' situation. The altar, as the focus of eucharistic worship, was in most instances so remote from the people, the more so when the priest celebrated with his back to the people. In the 1950s the first change to come about was to place the celebrant behind the altar facing the congregation, though this was not possible in many instances when the altar, often a stone one, was firmly fixed against the east end of the church. The next move was to place a portable altar in a more central area which, when on a raised platform or dais, was the more visible to the people wherever they are seated. The next problem was what to do with the choir isolated in the chancel and probably singing collegiate fashion across to each other instead of to the congregation. Where to accommodate the choir in parish churches has frequently proved problematic, the more so when failing to try out different places on an experimental basis so as to find the best position for all concerned. The same problem has been experienced in cathedrals when the entire building is being used, though no problem for weekday services when the congregation are seated around the singers.

The geographical demands of contemporary worship in parishes where re-ordering has taken place has proved a challenge, and sometimes a nightmare, which has never before affected and influenced matters musical. One advantage we now have is that most of the furniture is mobile and can be re-sited as and when needed, not least in clearing the central area for concerts.

For various reasons of which we are all too aware, choirs, as mentioned earlier, have greatly diminished during the latter part of the 20th century. While commitment and loyalty was once virtually part and parcel of choir life there are now so many rival activities and attractions on offer, for we live for the most part in a five day working week with Sundays now much more dedicated to socialising and sporting activities. Non-churchgoing parents even discourage their children from joining a church choir, seeing this as an obstacle to their secular weekend activities. Nor are matters helped by clergy either intent on disbanding a traditional style choir or who see no place for what they consider to be élitist and contrary to the mania for informality. Gone for the most part are the days when we donned our best Sunday clothes for churchgoing. The attitude of mind this engenders sees men in open-neck shirts, jeans and sneakers striding up to make their communion as if they were doing the Almighty a good turn instead of as a humble penitent.

The frequently encountered lack of partnership between clergy and organist, the two key figures in a worship situation, is a further detrimental factor. While there are many difficult organists and choir members in circulation, many clergy are becoming increasingly autocratic and dictatorial. Maybe some feel threatened, even jealous, when they perceive what the music is achieving where perhaps their own ministry has failed, and who react accordingly. It is small wonder that job satisfaction is for many church musicians at an all-time low, the more so when security of tenure is increasingly on the line and summary dismissal can be a very real prospect. When clergy and organist see eye to eye and work as colleagues on the same wavelength, the one aiding the work and ministry of the other, such parishes (and cathedrals) flourish in equal proportion to the unhappiness, even misery, which results when the musicians are given what can only be called sub-Christian treatment. On balance, the situation has much worsened in recent years. Regarding this there is a little prayer which says 'Lord, though we may disagree, help us not to be disagreeable'.

Dissatisfaction with what are perceived as the constraints and ritual of liturgical worship patterns, together with the quest for informality, have contributed towards paving the way for charismatic renewal worship. While the Church has from time to time in its long history seen bouts of fringe revivalist movements, it is doubtful whether any have caught on with such fervour, and so rapidly, as the current charismatic vogue which spread from The United States and the Far East to virtually every part of the Christian world and not least in our own country where this is the fastest growing part of the C of E. The attraction of informal ever-changing DIY worship, the use of heavily amplified instruments other than the organ are attractive to the many weaned on Radio One. Even so, choruses and worship songs are in many instances little more than trite phrases repeated *ad nauseam*, often with accompanying body movements, yet it is often given much more preparation and rehearsal than can be said of some more traditional parishes where hymn singing can be unexcitingly pedestrian. Having said this, informality and excellence are by no means incompatible bedfellows, but only if the musical excellence is a priority.

One of the less acceptable aspects is the self-assurance of many who have been renewed which can engender an arrogance condemning those who have not been so renewed as virtually second class Christians. Whether in the long term there will be a degree of staying power is another matter, though for the foreseeable future the charismatic church is with us.

All in all, while we may have gained much in the pursuit of music as an integral part of worship in our rapidly changing world, we have equally lost much *en route*, and much that we can ill afford to lose. Summing it up we could say that we have considerably abrogated our sense of responsibility and being increasingly encouraged towards liberalism and egalitarianism as much in the Church as in life in general. In our personal attitudes we have veered towards being self-indulgent. We need to be constantly reminded that the pursuit of excellence is crucial to the wellbeing of worship, and is not élitism (whatever that much vaunted word means). The only problem lies in the way each of us interprets excellence, be it in the quality of the music or in its performance.

ORGANS

Although organs as such are not my brief here, mention must be made of their role in parish churches during the past century. Following the influence of the Oxford Movement virtually every Anglican church installed a chancel organ, invariably boxed in on three sides and not speaking down into the body of the church. These were one or two manual instruments with a predictable stop list which was bound to include only one pedal stop, a woolly and characterless Bourdon. This stereotype more or less prevailed into the 1950s and is still to be found in many a country church. With the emerging vogue for the Baroque, some new instruments, although admirable for certain types of music, proved unsuitable for the romantic treatment demanded for most liturgical needs.

An attendant problem has been the mistaken one of installing organs too large and too loud for the church particularly if free-standing. This situation is not helped by organists who regard the status symbol of having an instrument of almost cathedral proportions. The colourful Sidney Smith, Canon of St Paul's Cathedral, remarked that organists are like "jaded cab drivers, always looking for another stop".

The organ is probably the largest single piece of furniture in any church and expensive in upkeep, the more so when the time comes for a major overhaul or rebuild. Because of these constraints some parishes are attracted by what they see as the advantages of an electronic or digital instrument, which is generally less expensive and considered cheaper to maintain. This delights the organist as master of a console, pistons, gadgets and all, probably larger than the cathedral organ, though the merits or otherwise of the electronic instrument, which tonally has developed out of all recognition since the days of the Hammond organ in the 1930s are not my concern here. Even so, there are churches, especially modern ones, where there is little or no space for a pipe organ.

INSTRUMENTS OTHER THAN THE ORGAN
While I touched on this when discussing charismatic worship, there is also a happily growing tendency to use orchestral instruments, especially in cathedrals on occasions such as the great festivals when this can greatly enrich the liturgy in the Masses of Haydn and Mozart. A brass ensemble can provide thrilling highlights in hymns, though it needs to be used sparingly.

This use of orchestral instruments has proved to be one of the biggest revolutions of the past fifty years as witness the thousands who attend the Sunday Eucharist in St Paul's Cathedral each summer. In some ways this is the 20th century turning full circle back to the 19th century village orchestra in the west gallery. There are also situations where instrumental groups are used because no organist is available. This can be an admirable way of employing young players by giving them the platform which school carol services have offered. Would that this happened more frequently at other times though the crunch can come when guitars, rhythm sections and other highly amplified instruments are introduced and when the resulting noise level is anything but an aid to contemplation and worship for many.

This conveniently leads on to

HYMNODY
Here we have experienced arguably the greatest change of all during the past hundred years. Just compare the first edition of *Hymns Ancient and Modern* (1861) and its contents with the multiplicity of material now on offer, and in every denomination. Today hopefully caters for all tastes, needs and persuasions, not least in language where, in the pursuit of political correctness and gender, some editors have recast splendid poetry of previous ages in order to avoid the exclusive use of 'man', while anything militaristic is taboo even, in some instances, 'Onward, Christian soldiers' and 'God rest you merry, gentlemen' becoming 'people all'.

The editors of *Common Praise*, the millennium edition of A and M, were at pains to maintain the traditionally orientated ethos of previous editions, for there are many churches looking for such a book. Apart from removing some obscure words not now currently used, this new book basically retains pre-1880 language as it is, for it was deemed as wrong to tamper with the magic of Isaac Watts and George Herbert as it would be to modernise the language of Shakespeare.

The sheer volume of hymnody now on offer and the number of books appearing with increasing profusion is, to say the least, confusing. The Hymn Explosion of the early 1950s, as Erik Routley so aptly termed it, heralded the work of the 20th century Church Light Music Group which centred on Beaumont and Appleford. This well intentioned effort to popularise hymnody caught on in schools weaned on *Songs of Praise* and *The Public School Hymnbook*. Redolent of the songs of Fred Astaire and Ginger Rogers and the music of Ivor Novello and Noel Coward, much of it was a sort of update of the 19th century Sankey and Moody. As with many innovators, much of what they set in motion was to be fulfilled with better integrity and success by their successors.

From the first edition (1861) of Hymns Ancient and Modern
The treatment of the plainsong tune is a far cry from today's scholarship.

While many choruses and worship songs revolve round a particular statement and brief musical phrase, presumably to make matters simple, what invariably results is a trite phrase repeated *ad nauseam* and far removed from the sequence of events undergirding most traditional hymns. Whether these innovations are here to stay is questionable. Maybe they will prove to be as transitory as the music of previous evangelistic missionary revivals. Time will tell, though at present they are virtually unassailable in many areas of Christendom. It is sad that in many churches, so great is the lure of this type of material, traditional hymns are seldom, if ever, heard.

However, the 20th century saw a steady and commendable expansion of traditional hymnody, both in words and music. Prior to the Hymn Explosion there were but a handful of good new tunes, including *Abbots Leigh*, *Down Ampney*, *Sine Nomine*, *Thornbury* and *Love Unknown*. More recently *Coe Fen*, *Guiting Power* and *Corvedale* are but three finely moulded examples which have done much to enrich the texts to which they are set. The use of folk tunes, begun by *The English Hymnal*, now include *Waly Waly* and the *Londonderry Air*. A significant number of fine authors have contributed much, not least Timothy Dudley-Smith, Albert Bayley, Brian Wren, Cyril Alington and Brian Foley. It is also interesting to see the prolific Free Church author Fred Pratt Green twice speak of adoration in 'God is here', an indication of how hymnody straddles the denominations as an interesting aspect of ecumenism. In many 20th century hymns good theology and teaching are to the fore, unlike some Victorian examples.

Finally, in terms of performance it is deplorable that so many church musicians, singers and organists alike, approach hymnody in a perfunctory, unimaginative, even seemingly reluctant way, the more so as hymns are pertinent to most worship situations and involve all concerned. Such people have much to answer for.

PSALMS

Following the pioneer work on Anglican chanting mentioned earlier, and the later emergence of speech rhythm, a number of new psalters appeared around the 1930s, including the *Oxford, English* and *Worcester*. These were used mainly in cathedrals while Sydney Nicholson's *The Parish Psalter* admirably provided for the needs of the parishes and continues to be widely used. Because fewer choirs are now operating, new methods have evolved, pioneered by Gelineau and later by Dom Gregory Murray, with the choir given responsibility for the ongoing text, interspersed with a congregational refrain repeated every few verses.

A notable exception is of course the cathedrals where the singing of the psalms happily continues to be a crucial mandatory part of daily Evensong, though the style of performance and the interpretation of speech rhythm varies so much between one cathedral and another, and not always helped by exotic flamboyant chants which sometimes detract from the words.

One regrettable outcome of liturgical change is that the psalms have to all intents and purposes become an endandered species in the parishes.

CANTICLES

As with psalm singing in parishes, so have canticles become a rarified commodity, with fewer opportunities now to use them. Despite the virtual demise of Mattins and Evensong there are some parishes with the musical resources to make their use possible, mainly at Evensong. Compared with the beginning of the 20th century the number of simple and rewarding settings has greatly increased, with those by Stanford, Ireland, Charles Wood, Sumsion, Moeran, Watson and others being valuable contributions. For the cathedrals, what was admirably set in motion by Stanford and his contemporaries has been added to by Herbert Howells with settings tailor-made for the characteristics of various cathedrals, of which *Collegium Regale* is the best known. There has been a marked growth of specially commissioned works such as Vaughan Williams' splendid Te Deum for the enthronement in 1928 of Cosmo Gordon Lang as Archbishop of Canterbury and Britten's Jubilate for St George's Chapel, Windsor Castle. The last century also saw greater use of the Benedicite in place of the Te Deum during Lent and Advent. This brought splendidly ebullient settings by Francis Jackson, Sumsion, Ashfield and Harris. Humphrey Clucas broke new ground with his delightful setting of the Venite, little of it rising above *mf*. There is also a new departure in singing canticles as anthems, not least the Te Deum as a thanksgiving at Evensong on great festivals such as Easter. There is every reason for encouraging the use of canticles as anthems.

MUSIC FOR HOLY COMMUNION

With the emphasis on the Eucharist as *the* main Sunday service, a wide cross-section of settings are in use. Stanford, Darke and others spear-headed the 20th century repertoire with the added use now in cathedrals of the Masses of Mozart and Haydn, also the many unaccompanied settings by 16th and 17th century Italian and Spanish composers. It is not all that long ago that singing in Latin was banned in many establishments, deemed as being popish. This is now as widely accepted as is applause at concerts in church. There is nothing sacrilegious in saying thank you in this time-honoured way. Mercifully, whistling and catcalls have not yet been taken on board, even by the most reactionary clergy. The 20th century has also seen a rich harvest of contemporary settings for cathedral use, though Rite A and ASB texts generally have not greatly attracted composers who cite 'Glory to God in the highest' as not having the rhythmic impetus of 'Glory be to God on high', though it is debatable how valid an excuse this is. Kenneth Leighton and Richard Shephard are two composers to have successfully met the challenge. As with anthems, commissions are more prevalent today, often for special occasions such as the Three Choirs and Southern Cathedrals Festivals.

Turning to the parishes, greater congregational participation with simple music is needed, and by right. Extended settings are not always appropriate when resources and expertise may not be of a high order. Merbecke understandably continues to hold a special place, as in the past, for his one note for

every word or syllable principle was specifically to provide simplicity in contrast to the flamboyancy of the great polyphonic settings, even though most of us sing his music as if it were plainsong.

The parishes have on the whole been better catered for in Rite A though some results have been short on artistic qualities, not always fully taking into account the three essential ingredients of melody, harmony and rhythm, the latter considered in Victorian times, and until quite recently, to be too secular, even frivolous, for worship situations. Local efforts written specifically for a parish, often by the organist, have not always produced the happiest of results, sometimes because they are not instinctive composers, a shortcoming which as we saw was that of not a few composers of previous generations. John Rutter's pioneer setting proved popular and paved the way for Martin How, Peter Aston and others whose attractive simple music has admirably met parish needs.

ANTHEMS

Taking an overall survey of the 20th century, the worst examples of Victoriana have by and large disappeared from the repertoire, though some of the works of Mendelssohn and Stainer are now seen in a new light and prove acceptable when shorn of the sentimentalism once given them. The influence of Parry and Stanford and

Charles Villiers Stanford, by Spy (1905)

their contemporaries cannot be too highly rated nor the influence they exerted on their pupils, Vaughan Williams, Walton, Howells and Britten being four of those who have provided for the contemporary scene in a richly rewarding way. They were, and continue to be, influential, in writing music for needs right across the board. What could be simpler, or more effective, than Vaughan Williams' *O taste and see*? Although fewer cathedral organists have put pen to paper as compared with the 19th century, they are on the whole much abler composers and craftsmen, and this despite the poor quality hymn-anthems some of them wrote around the 1930s.

The parishes were further catered for by Novello and in recent years by Oxford University Press with their extensive series of easy anthems. Their *Church Anthem Book* and its recent successor *The New Church Anthem Book*, have proved best sellers, while their collections for seasons of the church's year have provided useful material. Scholarship and editing have always been high OUP priorities such as their Tudor Church Music Series, as was done by Stainer and Bell in *Musica Britannica*. Oxford's greatest scoop is John Rutter, one of the most prolific and significant of 20th century composers of church music whose originality is amply seen in everything he has written, not least in the three *Carols for Choirs* which he edited in conjunction with Sir David Willcocks. The writing of carols has been revolutionised as a consequence.

THE CATHEDRALS IN GENERAL

In terms of drawing power the cathedrals have never been more popular, with many attracting a large and regular Sunday congregation in addition to visitors. As a counterblast to the noise level in many parish churches as much in the services themselves as before and after, many who wish to worship silently through the interlock of visual and musical beauty find their spiritual needs met through the cathedrals. Whereas many parishes have moved away from traditional music, the cathedrals have provided the very opposite with most divesting themselves of any lingering Barchester traits.

The musical life blood for trebles is the cathedral school or associated local schools. While a few of the smaller schools such as Eton and All Saints, Margaret Street disappeared some years ago most have expanded in order to be financially viable, some having as many as 200 pupils, often with a pre-prep department. In the parish church cathedrals the choristers are usually drawn from local schools.

Despite ever increasing school fees the cost of the musical establishment is invariably the single greatest burden facing most cathedrals. All praise to those Deans and Chapters who realise the value of the daily *Opus Dei* and how impoverished this would become without the musical ingredient. Even greater praise to those who raise large sums of money to safeguard the musical foundation, though there are some who view such a choir as an expensive and outdated luxury.

As many parents find it hard to provide the fees, grant giving bodies such as The Friends of Cathedral Music, The Ouseley Trust and The Sons of the Clergy direct sizeable sums towards subsidising fees for individual cases. Another contemporary factor is the pressure which can be encountered over the rival claims of the music and the demands of the school curriculum. Give and take between the Director of Music and the Head Master is crucial if both aspects are not to suffer. Happily, this generally works though special services, broadcasts, television and recordings make inroads on the school timetable. A further problem is that holidays are generally much longer nowadays and can have adverse effects on the continuity both of the musical and scholastic needs. When I was organist of Exeter Cathedral in the 1950s, the choir remained after Christmas until the Epiphany and at Easter until Low Sunday. There is also the hazard today of parents not wishing to send their children to a boarding school at an early age, with promising singers being lost to the Church. Parents are now less willing to make family sacrifices than a generation ago and thus penalise the musical prospects of their children.

Whereas until quite recently cathedral organists invariably conducted the local choral and orchestral societies and maybe taught part-time at a school or college, while many examined here and overseas for The Associated Board, the increased demands of the job such as the use of a cathedral for many musical events and special services, necessitates the organist being much more in his cathedral.

Moreover, with the widened role and responsibilities, and following the Cathedral Organists Association now having working links with the Deans and Precentors Conferences, some organists have now become virtual members of the Cathedral Chapter, a great advance from some years ago when organists were kept very much at arms length. As a result, much better working relationships generally pertain though, as with parish organists, both sides need to adopt a give and take attitude if this is to succeed. When one reads of the conditions which applied a century ago, let alone when S S Wesley was campaigning for better working conditions and salaries, one realises that matters have progressed a long way over the years. Even the cathedral assistant organists now have their own independent body, while the parent organisation is actively involved with Deans and Chapters ensuring better salaries, housing conditions, pensions, and contacts with the BBC and The Incorporated Society of Musicians over fees.

Local festivals of music involving the use of a cathedral are now much more widely in evidence than a century ago when the Three Choirs Festival was virtually the only such event. Another major innovation unthinkable until recently – and by no means fully accepted by everyone today – has been the introduction of girl choristers, not as a substitute for boys but in their own right, and giving them identical opportunities. The ramification of the pros and cons are an explosive issue for many and will probably continue to rumble on for the foreseeable future in much the same way as the ordination of women to the priesthood. This makes additional responsibilities for the organist and his assistant by virtually doubling the workload of rehearsing. It is interesting to compare this growth with the rapid falling off in recent years of boys and girls in parish choirs. What conclusions can be drawn from this?

In some cathedrals, as at King's College, Cambridge, lady minor canons now take their share in singing the weekday offices. Not only is this perhaps looked on as equal opportunities but has been brought about in part by the decline in young clergy wishing to become minor canons for a few years as part of their priestly progress. It is sad that there are so few takers for this important and interesting role. It is perhaps reflective of the reluctance of some clergy to become residentiary canons, deans and even bishops, this another sign of the times.

REPERTOIRE AND PERFORMANCE

As with many other aspects this has greatly changed and been much enhanced especially during the past fifty years. Studying and comparing cathedral music lists is revealing in the growth of their wide-ranging contents. Today much of the music is as technically demanding as it is artistically, with the resulting standard of performance adding much to the completeness of worship for all concerned. A comparatively recent departure has been as much the addition of non-English music as the inclusion of works by composers not primarily connected with the church music tradition. This brings new breadth of interest and variety. Into this category come Kenneth Leighton, William Walton, John Tavener, William Mathias, Jonathan Harvey and Francis Grier to name but six. By the reverse token relatively little church music is being written by today's cathedral organists or those recently retired, Francis Jackson, Philip Moore, Arthur Wills, Stanley Vann, Richard Lloyd, Barry Ferguson and John Sanders being notable exceptions.

The standards of performance overall are exceptionally high bearing in mind the demands of much of the repertoire and made possible by the expertise and quickness at reading of today's choristers. In doing so they mirror the professionalism of the major orchestras. Do we always realise the extent of what has been achieved in this respect during the past hundred years? If we had recordings of those earlier years it could well be quite revealing. There is however a danger in the tendency to relax discipline, having repercussions in outward signs such as choirs rehearsing minus cassocks and in their general bearing, something not countenanced previous to the current informality of life generally.

CATHEDRAL ORGANISTS

A significant change which took place during the 20th century was the demise of the old style articled pupil whereby those wishing to become cathedral organists were given full-time training working with an established cathedral organist. In its place we have seen the emergence of the organ scholar, initially at Oxbridge but now including the red brick universities and some parish churches. At the major Oxbridge colleges there can be two or three such people at any one time while many cathedrals now have not only an assistant organist but an organ scholar on a short-term contract probably during a gap year. The potential field is thereby greatly increased, with high standards of expertise achieved at an early age, though a snag is that the work is mainly confined to organ playing while the director of music rehearses the choir, conducting at most services and consequently doing less playing.

Sir William Harris KCVO, Organist of St George's Chapel, Windsor Castle 1933-61.

In the early 1950s when I was assistant at St George's Chapel, Windsor, this extended even further to my sitting beside the organist, Sir William Harris, at every rehearsal and at the console for services, turning pages, helping with the registration and giving the chord for an unaccompanied anthem. It was only on Mondays when he taught at the Royal College of Music or when examining for The Associated Board that I was in sole charge – and how I relished taking the rehearsals – even if he seldom chose any demanding music for me, though for certain broadcasts and recordings I would play the organ. In comparison with today this seems a strange way of life but I and others certainly learned a lot through this observing process and from general conversation. At that time the order of progress was to move after a few years to a small cathedral and then if you were lucky to a major post. After Windsor I went to Ripon where there was no choir school and a run-down choir, so I learned much the hard way and made my inevitable fledgling mistakes in a small market town environment which taught me much of value when I arrived at Exeter three years later. One notable exception to this type of progression was Henry Ley who was appointed to Christ Church Cathedral, Oxford, while still an undergraduate.

The long-established title of 'Organist and Master of the Choristers' tends now to be replaced by 'Director of Music' which is more accurately all-embracing, with the assistant now called 'The Organist', again more realistic as he usually plays for most of the services.

Where there is a university cathedrals are increasingly employing undergraduates as choral scholars, as for many years have the Oxbridge colleges. The old style lay clerk has in some instances all but vanished in favour of young voices of high quality rotating every three years or so and replacing singers whose main occupation was elsewhere and some of whom stayed in post well past their sell-by date. A further bonus with choral scholars is that they are available for more rehearsals than was ever possible under the old system when it was frequently difficult to get away from places of work.

Salaries of cathedral musicians have in many instances not only kept up with inflation but have been considerably increased, sometimes with accommodation or an allowance provided for singers. Until only a few years ago remuneration was deplorably low, the prestige of the job sometimes being made the excuse. When there is a cathedral organist vacancy there is nowadays no shortage of applicants. As yet, although there are some lady assistants, there are no ladies in the top job in England. Being an FRCO was once an obligatory qualification for being on a short list but this is of seemingly less account today, Deans and Chapters relying much more on experience, personality, and the general impression created at interview which is generally far less formal and more relaxed for all concerned including wives who are now sometimes included in a couple of days of conversation with members of the Chapter in their homes, all of which is deemed to be a better way of getting to know and assess candidates.

The status and kudos of being a cathedral organist still retains its element of mystique in musical circles, though gone are the days when the Director of The Royal College of Music and the Principal of The Royal Academy are likely to be chosen from among the cathedral organist fraternity, nor is there the likelihood of a cathedral organist being knighted as not a few were in the 1930s. An interesting recent departure has been the appointment of Anglican organists to Catholic cathedrals and *vice versa*. Further evidence of ecumenism?

THE PARISHES

Here we have an entirely different ball game as, apart from a few major parish churches, choirs and organists are amateurs. It is sad that many of the older generation have not in many instances taken advantage of refresher courses such as those provided by the RSCM and have consequently become dyed in the wool, though some stay too long in one post simply because there is no one to take over. Choral festivals, many of them long established annual events often held in a cathedral, and where being part of a choir of some hundreds and working, possibly with their cathedral organist, in different surroundings, can be a stimulus, inspiration and renewal when they return to routine week by week work. While the zenith of these occasions was in the 1930s and again after World War 2, numbers are now falling, mainly because parish choirs are in decline, to which must be added the cost of the music and transport.

The remuneration for parish organists has not generally kept up with the times, some being so minimal that any attempt to better the reward has achieved little in an inflationary age, particularly if the organist does not live in the parish and the cost of petrol eats into his meagre honorarium. Some parishes even contest the view that the labourer is worthy of hire and so get their organist on the cheap, though expected to be on duty week by week without fail. There are however some signs of improvement as advertisements in the *Church Times* show. Even so, while there is no shortage of applicants for the cathedrals, parishes are harder to fill. People are less willing to take on these assignments when it is far from easy to maintain a choir and when job satisfaction, even security of tenure, is too often at a premium with clergy/organist relationships often at a low ebb and with little sign of improvement. As with most disagreements there are often faults on both sides for it takes two to make an agreement as it takes two to make discord such as when these two key figures are not on speaking terms and communicate through notes – a not unknown sorry state of affairs.

An encouraging factor in recent years has been the growth of parish choirs and other groups doing duty in cathedrals during the resident choir's holiday. This new departure has become a much sought after attraction both here and for choirs from overseas, although the choice of music can become too demanding an assignment bearing in mind unfamiliar surroundings and the organ being perhaps some distance from the singers. If choirs could sing simple music well rather than ape the cathedral repertoire they would have less prospect of meeting an embarrassing Waterloo – and would be more likely to be invited back.

RELIGION IN SCHOOLS

In the independent sector and particularly in boarding schools, chapel services (although not generally mandatory any more) are productive of some admirable standards, made possible in many instances through the number of very good Directors of Music. Between the wars a clutch of stirring hymn tunes such as *Thornbury, Ladywell*, and *Wolvercote* proved most effective for teenage singers *en masse*. In order to further school music the RSCM promotes annual festivals which include preparatory and girls schools. The state sector provides a rather different picture with morning assemblies now largely abandoned despite the 1944 Education Act. Many schools being ethnically mixed, Christian music is deemed to be unacceptably exclusive. Whereas from the 1930s to the 1960s the primary and church schools would probably include hymns from *Songs of Praise*, today for the most part worship songs and choruses have taken their place, often involving instruments. As such they are superficially more attractive, certainly rhythmically, than many traditional hymns.

OTHER DENOMINATIONS
A mixed and varied situation prevails. Since Vatican 2 the Roman Catholic Church has greatly changed, not least in its music and the abandonment in many instances of plainsong which was its musical bedrock. The cathedrals, particularly Westminster and Liverpool, maintain a very high standard of traditional music as does Brompton Oratory. The Methodist and United Reformed Churches have made great strides in recent years through the work and influence of their church music bodies. They take the subject seriously, though in some aspects are not averse to the less traditional types of music.

One thing is certain, namely that liturgical worship in recent years has increasingly shown what the denominations now share in common, rather than in where they differ. This is particularly true of eucharistic worship which is basically identical worldwide. Music, especially hymnody, is very much part of this.

MUSICAL HELP FOR THE CLERGY
This is not a good news area. With far fewer theological colleges than fifty years ago, little or no provision is made for music and its role in worship. At one time the RSCM regularly visited the colleges and even had a full time Clerical Commissioner. Nowadays the colleges by and large claim there is no space in the timetable for music, and few value it as an important subject. The same applies to NSM courses. While this situation persists there is scant hope for the future particularly when so many clergy wash their hands of music and fail to emphasise its power to enrich worship, as to impoverish it when the music is slovenly. It is the responsibility of the clergy to safeguard music as an integral part of their ministry.

THE ARCHBISHOPS' COMMISSION ON CHURCH MUSIC
This high powered body, set up by Lord Runcie when he was Archbishop of Canterbury, met for two years, surveyed every aspect and came up with *In Tune With Heaven*, a 300 page report which was adopted by The General Synod. It was greeted with great expectancy though in the event the interest was shortlived except that it resulted in the RSCM being given the status of the C of E's official church music body. The report also helped in some measure towards security of tenure and salaries, though many of the proposals found little, if any, implementation as happened with the previous Commissions in 1922 and 1951.

OTHER CHURCH MUSIC ORGANISATIONS
The 20th century saw the rise of a number of bodies each dedicated to the furtherance of church music. The Royal School of Church, founded in 1927 as The School of English Church Music, brought about by the vision of Sir Sydney Nicholson, uniquely sought to help amateur musicians whose needs had previously been seldom catered for. Its work in the field has over the years greatly extended and is now worldwide and ecumenical. The small residential College of St Nicolas catered for the profession and was very much part of its earlier work. In the 1970s the College was closed and Addington Palace became an ecumenical education centre promoting more than seventy courses each year including a six weeks summer course for overseas students. Resident training courses are held in various parts of the world. The publishing of simple music of quality has always been to the forefront as has been the promoting of great festivals beginning at the Crystal Palace in the 1930s which drew some thousands of singers. More recently these have taken place in the Royal Albert Hall and throughout the country.

At one time the RSCM was viewed by some as a somewhat inward looking precious body but that is no more. Today part of its work is directed towards less traditional types of music and in helping the growing number of churches using it.

Other bodies such as The Church Music Society, The Friends of Cathedral Music and The Guild of Church Musicians have proved influential in their various ways. The IAO has in recent years homed in much more on church music while not neglecting its fundamental role. The Royal Academy of Music has a wide-ranging church music course, as much an innovation as the expansion of the RCO's role in church music and choir training. A few dioceses have set up schemes for helping church music though financing these is proving difficult.

MUSIC GROUPS

These are relatively new departures gaining much prominence in the past thirty years or so. Although not specifically church orientated, the work of John Eliot Gardiner, The Sixteen, The Tallis Scholars, The King's Singers and others have through their concerts, broadcasts and particularly their CDs, heightened our awareness of the breadth of repertoire now to be experienced. High standards of authentic performance have been much to the fore. The innovation of these groups has done much in recent years to promote church music in high profile concert performances.

THE BBC

In the earlier part of the last century the Religious Broadcasting Department was a high powered missionary part of the Corporation. One of its best sellers was, and continues to be, the weekly *Choral Evensong* broadcast. Begun in 1926 it is the single longest running outside broadcast, though it has had its ups and downs and was saved some years ago only through vigorous public intervention. While *Sunday Half Hour* goes on in much the same way as always, television's *Songs of Praise* has developed into a very mixed bag with some of its programmes featuring popular contemporary music at the unjustified expense of the traditional. Well known hymns can be subjected to bizarre harmonic and instrumental embellishment resulting in sounds – and sights – far removed from the norm, which is probably the object of the exercise. No doubt its policy is to try to please all, and from time to time it produces some notably more traditional programmes.

At the present time the BBC is coming in for justified criticism for its continual retracting and dumbing down on religion which, by and large, gets far less than its fair slice of the cake other than on special one-off national occasions and the King's College Festival of Nine Lessons and Carols on Christmas Eve, which can now also be seen in a specially televised form.

RECORDINGS

Those featuring church music, having started in a very small way, have now mushroomed out of all imagination both in quantity and quality. Church music has been widely and increasingly recorded in recent decades. Beginning with Columbia's sizeable output on 78s of a comprehensive cross section sung by leading cathedral choirs, today virtually every church and cathedral choir has added to the sum total, often again and again. Much of this is of an extremely high quality, such are the advances in recording techniques.

GENERAL CONCLUSIONS

The past century has seen enormous changes and advances in liturgy, choral expertise, composition, and in a heightening of standards with, by no means least, the opportunities these have afforded. Recent ecclesiastical policies have resulted in the demise of many traditional parish choirs which have been replaced by the popularity deriving from choruses, worship songs and the instruments associated with them, particularly in churches promoting charismatic renewal worship. By marked contrast, this has only marginally influenced the cathedrals. All these changes are a far cry from the prevailing *status quo* pertaining at the beginning of the century despite Rupert Brooke being prompted at that time to comment on 'the modernness and the desire to shock'.

One of the most regrettable and harmful of contemporary cancers is the seemingly stubborn inability of some clergy and musicians to appreciate the point of view of each other, with the resulting failure in far too many instances to work in partnership. Could this be jealousy and envy of the one for the other? In any event, this is causing untold harm to the Church as in many quarters is the headlong helter-skelter phobia to be at all costs popular or 'with it' by playing to the gallery. An Australian organist summed this up when he said to me "So much of the Church here is heading towards the lowest common denominator as fast as its little legs will carry it" and which is equally true of many situations in England. This is fodder for the media all too ready to highlight any bad news, real or perceived, concerning the Church. The fact that much of this reflects our restless, violent and discordant world is very much a reality which affects church music. The global pursuit of informality and resorting to near gimmicks has made questionable inroads, for it inevitably offloads standards. Where, on the other hand, these are high, worship flourishes, for worship demands the very best in every aspect – and from everyone concerned. Excellence is not élitism, though the impact of the 'Honest to God' syndrome of the 1960s continues to rumble on and has a lot to answer for.

Much of what is happening is disturbing to many, even if it is a matter of merely reinventing the wheel which often dictates saying the same things but in a different way. Nor is the outlook helped when the overall number of churchgoers is falling. This is inevitably reflected in choir membership.

THE FUTURE?

I recently read that 'The past is history – the future mystery'. That just about sums it up. Without speculating rashly or resorting to crystal ball gazing, one thing is for certain, and constant, in the welter of change that confronts us and not least the secularisation of the Church, and this is that everything today is questioned and contested. Nothing is taken for granted. Perhaps this is good for us and keeps us on our toes. Those of us of the older generation will doubtless continue to reminisce and, as is inevitable in thinking back to the past, to remember the good things, for time has a knack of eradicating the less wholesome. What we must never do is to look back in anger, for there will always be 'things new and things old' (and note the order in which St Matthew placed them). Inevitably, there will always be tension between the old and the new. We must seek to overcome clergy and musicians working in virtual isolation instead of as colleagues. We must also lay greater store on the education of both, the more so with the many liturgical changes and often confusing contemporary worship patterns which confront musicians, clergy and congregations alike, and will probably continue for the foreseeable future.

Composing for the Church today

by

Richard Shephard

Was it Mr Prendergast in Evelyn Waugh's *Decline and Fall* who had doubts? If I have remembered the correct character, Prendy was a parson whose doubts were pretty fundamental: he could not understand why God had ever bothered to create the world and so, he was unable to believe. In a similar way, there are many who would ask what is the point in writing music for the church at a time when, if we are to believe the statistics, church attendance is at an all time low; when it is far from clear what it is that many clergy believe in and when the churches which are fuller seem to be peddling choral music which is pretty bereft of theological content and almost entirely free from any musical creativity.

For a composer to write about these matters is risky. Anything which I write about music can be used as a critical stick to set about me. But we are all far too mealy-mouthed. We none of us dare utter a word of criticism lest we should be thought to be either politically incorrect or elitist or any other of the presently unacceptable positions. If, for example, one were to take a popular hymn such as *Make me a channel of your peace* and apply rigorous critical methods to it, one would come out with comments about the poor word-setting, the gauche harmony and the general paucity of invention. But to criticise such an evidently poor piece of work is akin to asking for a gin and tonic in the Pump Room at Bath. One becomes a Batemanesque character: "The man who dared to criticise *"Make me a channel"*. And so, more and more becomes acceptable at both extremes of writing: the avant garde cannot be criticised because it represents an attempt to bring so-called serious composers and the church together, and the guitar, tambourine and chorus fraternity have played the trump card: as one Charismatic Musician once said to me, "You cannot appreciate this music unless you have been re-born in the Spirit". A remark, I have to admit, which sent me rushing for the sick bag.

What a state we are in, partly because of the attitude of composers. The high-art brigade tend to regard the composer as nature's aristocrat, attempting to educate the poor, ignorant huddled masses. The chorus composers play the Holy Spirit as a trump card and make any criticism appear blasphemous. The truth is that composers are, or should be, craftsmen whose skills are put at the service of the church. What we, as composers are doing, in our imperfect way, is to provide *gebrauchsmusik:* music which can be useful. If, by chance and good fortune we write something which has a life far beyond the occasion for which it was written, well, so much the better, but we can none of us produce a masterpiece simply by trying: we have to do our best and leave posterity to judge our efforts.

So the composer has, in some respects, a humbler path to tread, not unlike that trod by the anonymous mediaeval masons who built our great churches and cathedrals. They sought to serve, not to push back the frontiers of artistic appreciation, not to demonstrate some agenda of their own, but in a simple way to endeavour to assist the people of God in their devotions by providing a glorious canopy for worship. This seems a high and noble calling. Composers for the church have an enormous privilege and responsibility because before they put pen to paper they have to ask themselves why they are writing at all. They are not writing to express their inmost *angst;* they are not writing to push back the boundaries of musical taste; they are not writing on their own agenda at all. They are writing for the glory of God and to assist the people of God in their devotions.

Now that may well sound rather pretentious, but it has to be the truth. Music in church is merely the medium by which the message is conveyed, it is not the message itself. There are countless examples of pieces which have served their turn in their generation and have now been consigned to the eternal waste-paper basket. I remember Cyril Taylor telling me that when he was a chorister at Magdalen, in the days of Varley Roberts, there used to be a queue of people round the quad waiting for evensong on the day when Roberts's *Seek ye the Lord* was being performed. Roberts had, evidently, a high opinion of his own place in the scheme of things. He used to say of the inheritance of English composers, "Twixt Purcell and Roberts, there's nowt". Perhaps his purgatory is to listen to a ceaseless tape of Boyce, Greene, Croft, Battishill, Walmisley, Wesley (both S & SS) and other composers who, coming twixt Purcell and Roberts have not reached the genius of the former, but have undoubtedly surpassed the latter. Which underlines the fact that composers are servants who, when they cease to be of service, are dismissed.

Service is not a popular concept at the present, and in musical terms, the idea that a composer should subjugate his creative genius in order to provide a work which is both useful and helpful, receives little support. Why then, like Mr Prendergast's god, bother at all? Each writer must work out his own answer to that question. I think it was E M Forster who said that he wrote in order to win the respect of people he admired. Others have written because they feel compelled to do so; still more, in order to win a small acreage of immortality; more still to earn an honest penny. None of these motives is ignoble and most composers would probably own up to more than one of them. More dangerous are those who believe that the Holy Spirit is directing them to write in a certain way.

A few years ago I was lucky enough to help direct the splendid choral course in Sewanee, Tennessee. If you have not been there, it is certainly worth a visit. Part of my brief was to go through compositions with the students and to offer critical comments which were supposed to be helpful. A number of students produced very good offerings and I hope I was able to give small pieces of advice on technical matters. One student, however, was impossible to help. She had written a chorus which, both melodically and harmonically was impoverished, or even inept. A few alterations would have made it at least competent, but she would have none of it. This was what the Holy Spirit had told her to write and changes were not allowed. My knowledge of the Holy Spirit is, alas, sketchy, but I find it difficult to believe that part of the Holy Trinity can direct people to write badly. Composers with a mission are dangerous and any attempt to cite the Holy Spirit as a witness for the defence should be viewed with considerable scepticism. At the same time it is vital that critical judgement of musical works should not be suspended merely because the music is to be sung in church. What message does that send about the importance of worship or of the music within the context of worship.

So what is to be done? Clearly composers have to tread a very narrow path. On one side lies the morass of eclecticism and on the other the desert of the avant-garde. Is there a *via media* which enables composers to write what they believe in while at the same time avoiding the alienation of congregations which much modern music would appear to aiming at? The first thing to be said is this: in writing music, competence is infinitely more important than sincerity. This is not a cynical *bon mot* designed to amuse or even infuriate. Incompetent music can never be worthy of a place in public worship, so any arguments which underline the sincerity of the composer are almost always suspect. Orthodoxy of belief does not equip a composer to write competently but musical competence does. A brief look at composers of the past will show that Bach and Haydn are exceptional in the fact that they were sincere believers: many other composers who wrote for the church were much less sure of their beliefs. By contrast, there appear to be at the present time many composers who are undoubtedly sincere in their beliefs but who are less than competent in their craft.

In an article such as this it would be wrong to name names and, as far as composing is concerned, I can speak only for myself. Perhaps I should, before explaining how I approach the whole matter, issue a disclaimer. I am one of those journeyman craftsmen who write for the present. Look at the paper covers of old Novello editions and read the names of those who have gone before: T Tallis Trimnell and Athelstan G Iggulden are two of my favourites. These men, and countless others like them, wrote for their day and are become as though they had never been. It is the lot of most composers to disappear into oblivion and this is as it should be. In music, only the best survives. Would that the same could be said about architecture......

So I face the task of composing with the realisation that my music may have a short life. Of course I hope for my little piece of immortality, but I realise that no effort of mine can ensure this. When writing for the church I feel that I have four responsibilities: to God, to the congregation, to the performers and to myself. In one's duty towards the Deity one is bound always to fall short of the ideal. I know when I start a piece that I want it to be the best of me but constraints of time and energy make certain that for me, and I suspect most composers, the piece which one wants to write is virtually always the one that got away. I look back on some of my anthems and services with shame. Did I really write that? How did I let that through? And this is a healthy attitude. Composers should be their own fiercest critics.

Next to the composer as critic comes the congregation. The taste of congregations is conservative, so one must expect some new music to take a time to be clasped to the congregational bosom. I remember singing as a chorister at Gloucester the *Gloucester Service* by Howells and Jackson in G, both of which seemed very modern and discordant to the ears of the congregation in the late 1950s. Both pieces have deservedly become part of the stock repertoire so there is at least a grain of truth in the old adage that all music was modern once. What we have to remember is that congregations are not specialist musicians, neither are they going to a concert to hear the latest novelty, so there has to be a degree of modernity beyond which it is not wise to tread. In the concert going world, many works written at the beginning of the last century have failed to become loved by the general audience. True, Webern gets a number of performances, but his works lack any endearing qualities and so do not tend to be taken to the desert island. In the same way, many of the church pieces which have sought to reconcile modern techniques with worship demands have failed to find a place in the repertoire of the cathedrals and churches of the land. This is not to imply that all composers have to do is to produce *ersatz* Stainer or J B Dykes in order to produce something to which congregations will relate. The task is much more difficult. Composers have to be true to themselves while taking the pragmatic view of the requirements of public worship. If this is an impossible position for some to take, then they had better leave church music alone. The most basic requirement of all is that music should not impede or interrupt the devotions of the people. This is evidently a negative requirement and there are plenty of positive things which could be said: music must be appropriate to the building, to the style of worship, to the liturgical requirements; it must enhance the worship.

Responsibilities to performers are clear. The music must be appropriate to the skills of singers and players and it must be competent. This may appear obvious, but during a long period as a singer in cathedral choirs and at the Three Choirs and Southern Cathedrals Festivals, I had to sing in a number of first performances which were appallingly written for voices. Happily, these pieces (which I shall not name) have not made it into the general repertoire, but my experience serves to underline the fact that performers need to be properly treated and given material which is appropriate to their vocal range and ability. In the same way, accompanists need to be provided with material which is realistic. Years ago I wrote a congregational setting of what was then Series 3. I kept the vocal parts simple but went to town on the accompaniment, thinking that I might as well dress up a fairly plain vocal line with a glitzy backing. The afore-mentioned Cyril Taylor gave me advice which I have never forgotten. He told me to consider where the piece might be performed and cited several parishes in the backwoods of Dorset where virtuoso organists were in pretty short supply. The lesson was learnt and I have tried over the years, with varying degrees of success to write for my performers and audience in an appropriate way.

The fourth responsibility, to oneself, is at one level pretty simple. The very fact of writing puts composers in the firing line. Works which are very personal things are heard in public and dissected, criticised and analysed. And this is all fair enough; but it does mean that the composer has to attempt to produce works which will not make him a target for ridicule. With the plethora of writing styles available, this is not easy. Is anything except the latest electro-acoustic music derivative and eclectic? Is post-modernism the way forward? Is there an English choral tradition which traces a line through Stanford, Parry, Vaughan-Williams, Howells, and others? It is all rather bemusing and worrying, and there is no one answer, which is why it is easy to succumb to the temptation of believing that there is no point in the exercise at all. Yet there is a point. Each generation has an obligation to add to the tradition of the centuries. Frequently, as in the nineteenth century, compositions become a sort of musical compost, rotting down to provide the base in which the next generation's pieces take root. And occasionally, in a musical Sahara, there appears an oasis: here I think of Jonathan Battishill's two masterpieces, *O Lord Look down from Heaven* and *Call to Remembrance*. They are both superb works; but I wish we could hear more performances of the latter.

In the end, there is little composers can do except their best. We all have to sow our handful of seeds and hope that they bear fruit. The long-term results, if indeed there are any, of our musical husbandry will not be seen in our lifetime and some of us, like Salieri in Peter Shaffer's *Amadeus* may live to see ourselves become extinct. Happily, for the church, there seems to be a sufficient number of composers coming forward to add to the heritage of the past. Long may this continue.

The Rise and Rise of the Recording Industry

by
Terry Hoyle

The earliest recordings date from the latter quarter of the nineteenth century. These were acoustically produced, i.e. did not use microphone or amplifier; they were cylindrical in shape. Earliest sounds recorded included on 'Edison's Improved Phonograph' in 1888, excerpts from Handel's *Israel in Egypt* from Crystal Palace and, from Westminster Abbey, Frederick Bridge on a two minute cylinder though it is not clear whether as soloist or accompanist. These were recorded by Colonel Gouraud, Edison's London agent. Edison's cylinder eventually succumbed to the flat discs – or 'plates' as they were known – of Emil Berliner and from Rome in 1904, nine 78s of Gregorian chant were made on HMV, which also included music by Palestrina. These were easier to copy, and still made acoustically, by means of a diaphragm which oscillated at the narrow end of a conical horn; the signal was transferred to a stylus cutting a wax-covered disc. Although called 78s, the speed was originally anything between 72 and 80 rpm.

By 1907 the same company had also recorded Westminster Cathedral choir *Easter Hymn* and Gounod's *Ave Maria* and music from the Leeds Festival choir. The first British discs of the organ were of Easthope Martin, from the City Road studios of HMV, recorded on January 13th 1913. Pieces include the Widor Toccata, Martin's own *Evensong*, a Lefébure-Wély *Sortie*, arrangements of *The Lost Chord*, the Bridal and Wedding Marches, the *Hallelujah Chorus*, *Cuckoo & Nightingale* concerto movement [Handel] and music by Batiste, Lemmens and Guilmant. EMI Archives have no mention of an organ in the studios; the labels of Martin's 78s simply state 'English Pipe Organ'. Adolfo Bossi (brother of Enrico) recorded Bach for Italian HMV [BWV 559 & 560] in 1917, and acoustic discs were made for Polydor by Walter Fischer (organist of Berliner Dom) – Mendelssohn, Guilmant & Reger, and Kurt Grosse – Bach and Liszt.

During the period of acoustic recording, another form of reproducing keyboard music was the player-piano invented in 1849 by Michael Welte in Freiburg. His grandson Edwin, with Karl Bokisch, developed the player-organ which created paper rolls; these could then be played back by anyone utilising the automated player mechanism. Rolls were cut by Max Reger, Karl Straube, Dupré, Lemare, Reginald Goss-Custard, Lynwood Farnam and Gigout among others, whilst other similar systems were constructed by Austin and Aeolian organs.

The first known electrical recording is from 1920, using a system adapted by George Guest and Horace Merriman from a microphone to detect underwater objects by sound. The crude result is heard in the hymns *Abide with Me* and *God of our Fathers* from Westminster Abbey – the service of interment of the Unknown Warrior, where the massed choirs and bands are barely discernible. The Gramophone Company had improved its technique by 1925 when the first electrically recorded discs were made by the Western Electric system, Victor and Columbia (USA) and HMV (England).

The first English organ record

Photo courtesy of EMI Recorded Music

With the epoch of electrical recording, the next problem to be solved was the portability of equipment, allowing for more than studio venues. Originally this was overcome by use of GPO landlines, linking musician to the engineers cutting the disc. Thus strength of signal, occasional interference, etc, could affect the outcome. The HMV mobile studio was the answer to this, and by 1927 choral music was recorded; for instance at Hereford Cathedral during that year's Three Choirs Festival – not Worcester as Fred Gaisberg mentions in his autobiography *Music on Record*. Elgar conducted *The Dream of Gerontius* with Margaret Balfour, Tudor Davies & Horace Stevens, the LSO and Herbert Brewer at the organ. Other recordings using the van include the Royal Choral Society at the Albert Hall and concerts from the Crystal Palace, though extraneous noise – coughing etc – resulted in many never being issued. Indeed, the selection from *Gerontius* issued by HMV was that recorded by the Royal Choral Society and Royal Albert Hall orchestra on February 26th 1927, again under Elgar, from the Albert Hall.

By 1930, cathedral organists recorded by HMV and Columbia outside London include Edward Bairstow at York, W G Alcock (Salisbury), William Prendergast (Winchester), C C Palmer (Canterbury), H Goss-Custard (Liverpool), A W Wilson (Manchester) and Herbert Walton (Glasgow). In London several churches, cathedrals and public halls were put on disc. Of these, Queen's Hall is notable as the venue for the first players from Europe on HMV – Marcel Dupré & Albert Schweitzer, plus the organist of St Michael Hamburg, Alfred Sittard. From this period, of course, comes the most well-known of all 78s recorded in a church – Ernest Lough singing *Hear my Prayer* with the Temple Church choir under George Thalben-Ball. This was produced on April 5th 1927 –

Photo courtesy of EMI Recorded Music

later sessions included organ solos, from Festing to Reubke by Thalben-Ball, who also recorded for HMV on Alexandra Palace's Willis. Best known is Wagner's *Ride of the Valkyries* [arranged by Lemare]. Other players were Dupré, R Goss-Custard, Cunningham, Alcock and Herbert Ellingford. Music ranged from Bach and Widor, to arrangements such as the Wagner already mentioned, Saint-Saëns' *Swan* and *Finlandia* to Karg-Elert *Chorale Improvisations* by Ellingford.

Music recorded on the organ in the first few years of electrical discs was diverse, from arrangements of orchestral or choral works to 'real' organ music. The very first piece recorded electrically by Cecil Whitaker-Wilson on Kingsway Hall's 1913 Binns, was Handel's *Largo* – matrix CR8. This was issued as one side of HMV C1327. (Kingsway Hall was much used – seven organists recorded there before 1930.)

In the USA the first 78s were similarly broad in musical content, from hymns (one series released 'for use in Funeral Parlors' by Charles Cronham on the Major label) to the earliest release of American organ music per se, also played by Cronham, at Trinity Church, Camden, New Jersey [Victor] of *The Bells of Ste Anne de Beaupre* by George Alexander Russell.

During the late 1920s and 30s recording became a major industry, with many players and organs throughout Europe, America and beyond – though not all were available in Britain. Today it is of interest to hear instruments and players no longer with us, especially when old recordings are put on compact disc and treated by modern noise-reduction technology. In Britain Thalben-Ball, G D Cunningham, Reginald Goss-Custard, Arthur Meale and Herbert Dawson were most conspicuous in catalogues of the time – and organs, including those now destroyed, rebuilt or moved (besides those already mentioned) are:

Whitefield's Tabernacle; St Mark's North Audley Street; Westminster – Abbey, Cathedral, Central Hall, St Margarets's and Christ Church; All Hallows Barking; St Thomas Wandsworth; St Paul's Cathedral; St Michael Cornhill; Eleventh Church of Christ Scientist; Brompton Oratory; the Liberal Synagogue; St Mary-le-Bow, BBC Concert Hall, and Aeolian Hall – and that is only London!

French organists on record, after Dupré, include André Marchal, Georges Jacob, Noelie Pierront, Edouard Commette, Gustave Bret and the famous Paris discs of Louis Vierne, Charles Tournemire and C-M Widor from Notre Dame, St Clotilde and St Sulpice respectively and Schweitzer at Ste Aurelie Strasbourg. From Germany came Alfred Sittard at St Michael Hamburg [Walcker organ], Kurt Grosse [Berlin Garrison church], Walter Fischer [Berliner Dom's Sauer], Günther Ramin [St Thomas Leipzig], Paul Hebestreit [Paderborn Cathedral] Otto Dunkelberg [Passau Cathedral], Hans Bachem [Cologne Cathedral]; Fritz Heitmann, [Kaiser Wilhelm Gedachtniskirche, Charlottenburg and the Dom, all in Berlin.]

Organists sometimes appeared only as pianists, as in the case of Pierné and Saint-Saëns, or may have made records as solo pianist or accompanist years before solo recitals were issued – Maurice Duruflé, Olivier Messiaen etc. Others were already putting some of their own compositions onto disc, an invaluable learning aid to anyone wondering what music should sound like – although some players became renowned for disregarding their own dynamic markings, tempi and so on.

Alcock played his *Toccatina* at Salisbury Cathedral, R Goss-Custard's *Chelsea Fayre* which the composer plays at Kingsway Hall & *Nocturne in D* at Queen's Hall; Dupré's many works – on 78s Prelude & Fugue in G minor and *Cradle Song* also from Queen's Hall – all on the HMV label, as are many of Arthur Meale's played by the composer. On Parlophone, Edward d'Evry plays his *Meditation* and *Album Leaf* [Brompton Oratory]; Vocalion has William Wolstenholme at Aeolian Hall playing his *Prelude in F, Carillon in B♭, Rondino in D♭* and *Sketch in G*. Many pieces were arrangements [transcriptions of either vocal or orchestral works], and the Bach played in those days sounds very dated now, with colourful changes of registration, rubato, reeds added at the climax of fugues, etc – the 'politically incorrect' of the music world!

Among French composers presenting their own work on 78s, following Dupré, are Commette at Lyons Cathedral; Widor; Tournemire; Vierne, and later Joseph Bonnet [*In Memoriam Titanic, Romance sans Paroles* and *Matin Provencal*, played on the organ of Hammond Museum, Gloucester, Mass in 1941] and Jeanne Demessieux at St Mark North Audley Street, London, with her *Etudes* Nos. 2 & 5 [1948 Decca]. American 78s include Edwin Lemare playing his famous *Andantino in D♭, Chant de Bonheur* and *Aloha Oe* as early as 1927 for the Victor Company at Trinity Church, Camden, New Jersey. Leo Sowerby plays his own works on the Austin organ of 1920 in St James's church, Chicago – *Carillon & Prelude on The King's Majesty* [Diapason Records].

In the early 30s the Organ Reform movement began in Germany but it was in the U.S. that this most affected listeners via recordings. In 1936 Carl Weinrich visited the Continent in the company of G Donald Harrison (of Aeolian-Skinner) and as a result of this the organs of the Germanic Museum, Harvard University and Westminster Choir College, Princeton were

Magazine advertisement, 1930

designed and built. The sound of the 'neo-Baroque' was heard in 1938, with Weinrich playing Bach at Westminster College and E Power Biggs (also Bach) at the Germanic Museum – although Biggs' very first 78 on this organ contains the Allegro from Handel's *Cuckoo & Nightingale* concerto and D'Aquin's *Variations on a Noel*. These first pieces (and his first five 78 Bach set) are on the Technichord label; Weinrich's on Musicraft. After the Technichord, Biggs went over to the Victor label until 1947, then to Columbia for his LPs.

Also during the '30s, the first large historical reviews of music appeared; in Britain and America the *Columbia History of Music* started in 1930 and continued until 1939; this is not to be confused with the issue of an *Anthology of English Church Music* also on Columbia. This latter totalled two volumes each of twelve 78s by seven choirs – St Paul's, conductor John Dykes-Bower; Westminster Abbey [William McKie]; Canterbury [Gerald Knight]; St George's, Windsor [William Harris]; York [Francis Jackson]; King's College, Cambridge [Boris Ord] and New College, Oxford [H K Andrews]. Music ranged from mid sixteenth to twentieth centuries – Fayrfax to Howells.

By the mid 1930s Church music in the HMV catalogue alone included Anglican Morning Service and Evening Canticles from St George's choir Windsor, Stanford's Magnificat and Nunc Dimittis in Bb [Westminster Abbey choir], Benediction [Westminster Cathedral], Plainsong from Ampleforth Abbey, a Scottish service from St Columba, Pont Street, London, Gregorian music from the Sistine choir and Solesmes, the Russian Creed from the Metropolitan Cathedral Paris and Christian Science hymns from Boston, Mass.

In France, Anthologie Sonore began a series in 1934. The Columbia set included no organ music whereas the French collection has Dupré playing G Gabrieli & Frescobaldi, Pachelbel & Scheidt on his house organ in Meudon. Bonnet plays Cabezon, Santa Maria & Cabanilles, Couperin & de Grigny in the Paris music-room of Mme Gouin, and Marchal recorded Sweelinck & Bach at St Eustache, Paris. Pathé issued a set of twelve 78s from Mme Gouin's residence [organ by Gonzalez], the first of which is a stop demonstration by Marchal complete with spoken commentary. Another French label, Lumen, produced *Seven centuries of Church Music*, actually a selection of tenor arias, etc, sung by Yves Tinayre. Use of speech on recordings is as old as the groove itself – Edison's very first cylinder of 1877 is of the inventor reciting *Mary had a little lamb*. Occasionally speech is in evidence on organ records – Marchal particularly, in the above mentioned instance plus later LPs containing conversations with Norbert Dufourcq – again stop demonstrations – at St Eustache, the Palais de Chaillot [both Erato] and St Merri, Paris [EMI], then his house organ [on the Zodiac label].

As 78 rpm discs provided more and more music, the problem for listeners was mainly that of having to change records every five or six minutes, and to the musician the impossibility of editing. Issues of Handel's *Messiah* or Bach's *St Matthew Passion* for instance lasted for about 36 sides. One innovation of note was the change from recording onto discs at the master stage to the use of tape – in England HMV had, by September 1949, moved to spool recordings for all masters. In 1948 the long-player was produced in USA. The first organ disc was of Richard Key Biggs at the Church of the Blessed Sacrament, Los Angeles [1928 Casavant] with a mixture of music from Bach [*Toccata & Fugue in D Minor* BWV 565 & *Fugue in E Minor*], Dandrieu, Boex, *Finlandia* & Schubert's *Ave Maria*. Also in the USA, Virgil Fox made LPs from Riverside Church, New York; he and Charles Courboin were leaders in the recording of large instruments there. Fox's earlier 78s include his arrangement of *Komm süsser Tod* by Bach on the Girard College 1933 Skinner organ; Courboin recorded Widor's transcription of Bach's final chorus from the *St Matthew Passion* on the even larger Wanamaker organ. Both were eventually out-sized when on LP *Bach on the Biggest* was issued on the Atlantic City, New Jersey organ played by Robert Elmore [1956].

Robert Elmore at Atlantic City

However in 1947 Deutsche Grammophon began their Archiv series, including Helmut Walcha's Bach – from the Jakobikirche, Lübeck [Stellwagen organ]. These were 78 rpm but in microgroove format, allowing fifty per cent extra time per side called variable micrograde. They were also issued as LPs, combined on some with Bach from the Schnitger at Cappel. Recording *Bach's Complete Organ Works* has been the dream of many firms and organists, from Walcha who later recorded at St Lauren Alkmaar [twice] and St Pierre-le-Jeune Strasbourg, to the many on LP & CD which still continue today – Hurford, Rogg [three times!], Rubsam, M-C Alain, Stockmeier, Chapuis, Fagius, Bowyer, Koopman, etc. Fernando Germani played, at All Souls, Langham Place London, the six *Trio Sonatas*; according to an HMV advertisement in *Gramophone* magazine "Germani has undertaken the recording of the whole of Bach's organ music" which, however, was taken no further as a complete series. Germani began recording for Victor in 1928 – Wanamaker Store, New York – not the larger Philadelphia instrument – and later on 78s at S Ignazio Rome [SEMS – the 'Vatican label'], Turin Academy [Cetra], Westminster Cathedral and All Souls [HMV]. He also made LPs from Westminster Cathedral [HMV, Cathedral and Philips Fourfront], Alkmaar, Selby Abbey, Royal Festival Hall, Colston Hall Bristol [all HMV], Naples Conservatoire [a six LP set of Reger for Fonit Cetra] and Sta Maria del Riposo Venice for Deutsche Grammophon Archiv.

The years leading up to the LP era showed just how the number of players and instruments on record was growing and soon after the long-player became the standard method of reproduction the barriers were pushed even further back. In the late '40s and early '50s EMI recorded Geraint Jones at Steinkirchen, Germany, on the Schnitger; in England Pall Isolfsson from Iceland [All Souls Langham Place]; Guy Weitz [St Thomas Wandsworth and Westminster Cathedral]; and Hans Vollenweider from Switzerland [All Souls]. Decca used St Mark, North Audley Street, London to record Jeanne Demessieux and Marcel Dupré [where Thalben-Ball also made discs for EMI] – the organ [1930 Rushworth & Dreaper, since removed to Holy Trinity Brompton] was first recorded by its then organist, Maurice Vinden, in 1931 for Parlophone.

One of the most adventurous projects of its time was that of Columbia with E P Biggs on his European tours. After his U.S. 78s and some LPs from St Paul's Chapel, Columbia University, New York and Symphony Hall, Boston, LPs released between 1955 and 1971 feature organs in England, Germany, Holland, Denmark, Italy, Spain, Sweden, Norway, Austria, Portugal and Switzerland – but France is represented by only two Silbermann organs. Indeed, when Biggs made LPs of music by Franck, Widor, Vierne & Dupré he did not use a Cavaillé-Coll, but an Aeolian-Skinner and a Möller in New York. In Paris, Dupré recorded LPs at St Sulpice issued by Mercury and Westminster – from Couperin and Bach to his own compositions and Messiaen, while Messiaen played his own works for Ducretet-Thomson at La Trinité.

Smaller companies have been vital to those collecting LPs of religious music, both choral and organ. Abbey, managed by Harry Mudd [and its sister label Alpha] produced many such including hymns, anthems, music for service and organ recitals. They recorded in several English churches and cathedrals, as did Guild, Cathedral Recordings under David Woodford, Wealden, Ryemuse and Michael Smythe's Vista label. Mudd's pioneering work, for which he was awarded the MBE, combines ground-breaking recordings with a continuation of the long choral tradition. Cathedral and church choirs had of course long been on disc, but Abbey increased the number significantly with such as St Matthew Northampton and St Mary Warwick, many volumes being issued in the series *In Quires and Places*. Other records

'In Quires and Places . . .'

The Choir of the Parish Church of St Peter, Leeds,
directed by Donald Hunt   Anthems, England, Solo Organ

were made by college choirs [New and Magdalen, Oxford, etc] choral scholars and school choirs for nearly thirty years – LPs and CDs. Organ records include excerpts from a concert *Organ in Sanity and Madness*, Peter Hurford and Francis Jackson demonstrating the organ in Cecil Clutton's house, and from the 1969 St Albans Festival an LP of selections ranging from the party cabaret to music by McCabe and Ridout. Ryemuse included the only commercial recordings by artists such as Geoffrey Tristram [Christchurch Priory – old pipe organ] Huskisson Stubington [Tewkesbury Abbey] and Derrick Cantrell [Manchester Cathedral]. Many interesting discs came from Vista including two from Thalben-Ball; Tristram played the electronic organ in Christchurch Priory, Raymond Sunderland recorded at Bridlington Priory and other venues include St Martin-in-the-Fields, London, Wakefield and Sheffield cathedrals and the Royal Northern College of Music.

Wealden, under four series titles – *London, College, Parish,* and *Cathedral* – issued some interesting combinations of player and instrument: Jack Hindmarsh at Haileybury College; Bryan Hesford – Melton Mowbray parish church; Susi Jeans – St David's Cathedral; Richard Coulson – Arundel Cathedral; Holy Trinity Sloane Square [two LPs by Jonathan Rennert & Robert Gower], St Stephen Bournemouth etc. Cathedral produced among others discs of Nicolas Kynaston at Westminster Cathedral, Gordon Phillips at All Hallows Barking – the Harrison organ which replaced that upon which Schweitzer recorded, Brian Runnett at Norwich Cathedral and Jiri Ropek at Sussex University & Queen's College Oxford; but also went to Belgium to record Flor Peeters at Mechelen Cathedral. He plays his own works on two LPs – *Lied Symphony, Variations & Finale on a Flemish Song* [Volume One]; *Three Preludes & Fugues, Partita on 'Lord Jesus has a garden', Aria,* Two *chorale preludes* and *Elegy* [Volume

Sir George Thalben-Ball on Vista Records

Two]. One label, Pilgrim, produced LPs of Eric Thiman at the City Temple and Gerald Barnes at Bloomsbury Baptist church; another non-conformist church organ at Central Methodist Hall, Westminster, and its organist W S Lloyd-Webber, were recorded by Welkyn Records.

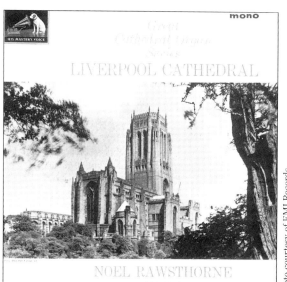

Meanwhile the larger firms were making strides with the leading series being *Great Cathedral Organs* from HMV. This began in August 1963 at Liverpool [Anglican] Cathedral with Noel Rawsthorne and ended with Roger Fisher at Chester in December 1970. These nineteen discs form a landmark in organ recording, produced by Brian Culverhouse. The players' ages range from mid-thirties to late seventies at the time of recording and their instruments are of course representative of all our major builders plus varying amounts of pipework remaining from earlier centuries. Music comes from several centuries and countries reflecting all types, though there were very few transcriptions or arrangements. During the period of the series stereophonic recording became more popular; the final volume was only issued in stereo. Philips, on their *Fourfront* label issued recordings by Nicolas Kynaston, Jean Guillou, Pierre Cochereau, Barry Rose, Martin Neary and Karl Benesch [on the charming organ of the 'Silver Chapel' in Innsbruck] among others. RCA Victrola's output included Harrison Oxley [St Edmundsbury], Caleb Jarvis [St George's Hall Liverpool], Philip Dore [Ampleforth Abbey], Melville Cook [Leeds Parish church] and Alan Spedding at Beverley Minster.

Between 1953 and 1959, the ten volume *History of Music in Sound* was issued by HMV. It contained excerpts from Ancient Asia to the twentieth century including choral music from Byzantine, Ambrosian, Gregorian and Mediaeval sources. Organ music is represented by works from the fifteenth to eighteenth centuries played by Susi Jeans [Marienkirche Lemgo] Geraint Jones [Steinkirchen] and Henriette Roget [St Merri Paris].

In the late 1950s and early '60s the number of visiting choirs and organists grew, both to and from Britain – as did the number of people hearing Continental sounds for the first time. The long traditions of choirs such as the Kreuzchor Dresden and St Thomas Leipzig, the latter having earlier made records under Karl Straube and then Günther Ramin, could be heard and compared to other well-known long-standing choirs such as the Vienna Boys choir. Choral training in British institutions could also be judged, whether in college traditions like King's or St John's or cathedrals such as Westminster under George Malcolm. Some attempts from the early '60s, for example, at authenticity now sound idiosyncratic in some timbres and rhythms, rather like the exaggerated sounds of certain 'neo-Baroque' organs built in that period, where extreme upperwork and rasping reeds represented a new generation of sound after smooth trombas and heavy wind-pressures, etc. The listener has over the years had a great choice in musical style, from Bach played on the piano by Edwin Fischer to the early music ensembles of David Munrow.

Organ builders brought out records of their instruments; J W Walker with St John Islington, Merton College Oxford, Wimborne Minster, Brompton Oratory, St Joseph Wembley and St Bernard Northolt among others – players include Jane Parker-Smith, David Blott and Brian Trant. Aeolian-Skinner, Möller & Wicks, all in America, and Walcker in Germany did likewise – Aeolian-Skinner's *King of Instruments* ran to thirty volumes of many of their famous organs such as Symphony Hall Boston [Pierre Cochereau at the organ], St John the Divine New York [Alec Wyton] and Grace Cathedral San Francisco [Richard Purvis]. Volume One has G Donald Harrison as narrator with excerpts from several organs.

There was an explosion of music by composers whose work was previously little known [apart from early pioneering efforts by a small number of players]. In the *Great Cathedral Organ* series Conrad Eden recorded Schoenberg's *Variations on*

LP from J W Walker Ltd, Organ Builders.

a Recitative and Karg-Elert's *Homage to Handel*, and Christopher Dearnley, at Salisbury, played Carl Nielsen's *Commotio*. During the latter part of the LP era, i.e. until the mid 1980s, the scene was set for even greater growth with the coming of compact discs. By this time firms thoughout Europe were issuing recordings which were generally available here i.e. not only in shops specializing in imports. Oryx for example introduced European recordings on famous organs such as Arlesheim [Silbermann 1761], Frederiksborg [Compenius 1612], Neuenfelde [Schnitger 1685] and Weingarten [Gabler 1750].

Other companies included Erato, whose most long-standing artiste is Marie-Claire Alain; her first LP was issued in 1954 – a recital from St Merri & Ste Clotilde, Paris, of music by her brother Jehan and Jean Langlais, with Langlais also playing some of his own work at Ste Clotilde. M-C Alain is still recording for Erato almost half a century later – with one break to make a CD for Gallo on the Alains' house-organ which had been rebuilt at Romainmotier, Switzerland; the other early Erato players, Langlais and André Marchal went on to record for several other companies. Erato issued a collection of *Encyclopedie de l'orgue* which was far-reaching in players, organs and compositions – it was intended that the list would include sixty volumes, but several apparently were not issued. Of those that were, most of course represented France, including Vol.45 – the Duruflés playing Maurice's compositions at St Etienne du Mont [Paris] and Soissons Cathedral. M-C Alain had a part in sixteen volumes, and other organists included Luigi Tagliavini, Anton Heiller, Gabriel Vershraegen, Montserrat Torrent and Susan Landale who plays early English music at Framlingham.

At times a company produces recordings which are a 'one-off'; one example which resulted in players not otherwise heard on disc as soloists comes from the First International Congress of Organists of 1957, held in London – excerpts were recorded by US firm Mirrosonic and include C H Trevor at St Sepulchre and John Dykes-Bower at St Paul's. Susi Jeans from her home Cleveland Lodge plays both the Baroque organ [with Ahrend pipework] and the three-manual Hill, Norman and Beard instrument.

Before the last years of the LP era two firms, Motette in Germany and Priory in England, started issuing several series which continue today. Whereas Motette concentrate on organs, Priory has become renowned for organ and choral discs. One of Motette's most enterprising projects is a seven LP set *The Art of Cavaillé-Coll*. This demonstrates 27 organs, many otherwise unheard on record as well as the builder's more famous examples – choir organs, some less-known instruments and some tracks of Leonce de Saint Martin at Notre Dame de Paris [taken from an earlier LP on the Studio SM label].

Incidentally, this is one area where an organ which has undergone major rebuilds has been recorded at each stage – Vierne [1928], Saint-Martin, [1953/4], Cochereau [1956 on L'Oiseau-Lyre, including Vierne's *Second Symphony* and Dupré's *Symphonie-Passion* and later on Philips [1965-8 after the major alterations of the early 1960s], and through to Solstice, ending with the moving improvisations of Lent 1984 just before his untimely death. The titulaires since Cochereau have all recorded, up to those discs dating from after the latest rebuild of 1990. The organiste-adjoint for many years, Pierre Moreau, recorded music by Vierne and Tournemire in 1967 and in 1969 Dupré was recorded improvising in Notre Dame – this disc was issued by the Association des Amis de l'Art de

Marcel Dupré, which has issued LPs by Dupré, mainly improvisations from services at St Sulpice in 1970/1. Similarly at St Sulpice, Widor and Dupré were succeeded by Jean-Jacques Grunenwald and Daniel Roth who also both made recordings there.

In America the Organ Historical Society recorded many rare instruments and in East Germany VEB put on discs twenty Silbermann organs, some of which were later issued on other labels in Western Europe.

Just as the advent of the long-player meant longer sides, so with compact discs a single side lasts up to nearly 80 minutes. Digital recording

Photo courtesy of Francis Jackson

Francis Jackson and Marcel Dupré

has led to yet higher standards, where it is possible to edit very small sections, even separate notes, into a piece. It is therefore good when a programme note states that music has been recorded in one take and left unedited. In the case of the organ there may be noise, perhaps a historic tracker action or escaping wind, and compact discs have been returned to shops because of these honest sounds!

Priory's CD catalogue has more breadth and depth than any other such recording project of the last few decades, indeed in church music it is unrivalled. From its inception [on LP] by Neil Collier and Paul Crichton in 1980/1 – the first commercial recording was Michael Overbury at Newark parish church [PR109], but the very first, PR 101, was a private recording from Tring parish church. The catalogue for 2000 has a total of 95 choral discs and 130 organ with at present another 22 planned. Among choral series are *Great Cathedral Anthems*, *Magnificat & Nunc Dimittis* [now complete in 21 volumes], ten volumes of *Psalms of David* and *Te Deum & Jubilate*. Other miscellaneous discs centre around a particular cathedral, a section of the liturgical calendar, or music by one composer. The latter include Bliss, Stanford and Bairstow as well as William Lloyd Webber and Whitlock, who both figure in the organ catalogue.

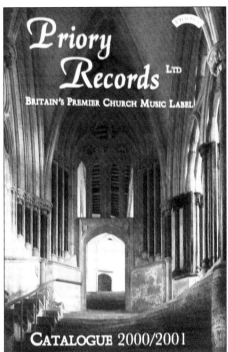

Photo courtesy of Neil Collier

The series *Great European Organs* runs to 55 discs with others added regularly – indeed, all are currently available as those deleted can be duplicated by special arrangement. The organs range from the really great, such as St Jacobi Hamburg, St Ouen Rouen and St George's Hall Liverpool to lesser-known instruments such as the two-manual Cavaillé-Coll/Schwenkedel in Notre-Dame-des-Champs Paris and organs in Iceland and Finland. Music is often equally little-known, but like the organs worth getting to know!

The recording of relatively unknown instruments forms part of the raison d'etre behind the Benchmark label. On each CD, Paul Derrett [who was one of the players in the Priory series of works by one composer – in his case Henri Mulet and Guy Weitz] plays six organs in one area. The first three such areas are Cheltenham, Newcastle-under-Lyme and Brecon and organs vary in size from four stop chamber to four manual and date from an early Bevington to a 1986 Blank built in Holland.

Today it is independent companies like the above that listeners rely on – large multi-nationals release very few new organ CDs, often simply reissuing older material [such as Walcha on Deutsche Grammophon], or recording a few titles from artists under contract.

Reissues of historic players are of course important, yet again it is to smaller firms like Amphion that one must turn. Among examples from this label are CDs of 'cleaned-up' 78s by several groups of organists, and single discs of others. Some contain not only old records, but also excerpts from acetates and tapes of radio broadcasts and unpublished test recordings. Single organist/composers include Bairstow, Whitlock, Weitz and Jackson, each being heard [however briefly] interpreting their own work. Some choral music is included on certain discs, such as sections from Bach's *B minor Mass* from a Royal Albert Hall concert of April 1926 by the Royal Choral Society and Royal Albert Hall orchestra conducted by Bairstow – an early electrical recording. Other Amphion issues contain tracks from EMI *Great Cathedral Organs* and several CDs by Francis Jackson, the only British organist to have recorded on 78, LP and CD.

Organs may be very well-known but hardly recorded; one instance of note is the Willis in St Bees Priory, Cumbria. Five 78s were made by William Coulthard for C P Waterhouse, including music from Bach to Weitz and Whitlock, and later one cassette by Roger Fisher who has now made a CD of the organ, again demonstrating how small concerns – in this case David Lane [DRL recordings] fill gaps left by the larger commercial enterprises. Of companies concentrating on the organ, interesting discs have come from Festivo, Solstice and Editions Lade among others on the Continent and Gothic and Pro Organo in USA. More and more instruments are being put on disc from all over the world and music by previously unknown composers.

Today the art of the transcriber is renewed, with Lemare arrangements and recitalists' own works being heard, exemplified by David Briggs' transcription of Mahler's *Fifth Symphony* from Gloucester Cathedral [Priory label] and in another field his transcriptions of Pierre Cochereau's recorded improvisations. Briggs is also one of the present day's greatest improvisers, with improvisations of his own on the Kevin Mayhew label [Gloucester and St Paul's Cathedrals], Delos [First Congregational Church Los Angeles], and his own label [Gloucester/Birmingham Oratory]. Thus one of the most vital uses of organ recording – the capture of ephemeral music unwritten and generally only heard by those in the 'live' audience – is now much in evidence throughout Europe and USA. The recording of improvisations is not new; an early acoustic 78 is on Odeon by Omer Letorey [Paris Opera's chorus director] and another early 78 comes from Warsaw, played by Mieczyslav Surzynski.

One of the most enterprising of recent projects is Briggs improvising a soundtrack to Cecil B de Mille's 1928 silent film *King of Kings* – 110 minutes of music on a double CD – which was enacted in front of a full cathedral in March 1999. This, the last recording before the rebuild of the Gloucester organ, is a fitting event for the last year of the millennium, and from here we look forward to a continuation of the same – new music, exciting recitals by great artists, new instruments and at the same time reminders of an equally exciting past in newly-found historic gems recreated and enhanced by whatever new technology may be invented to serve the listener.

KING OF KINGS

An improvised soundtrack to Cecil B de Mille's classic film of 1928

Recorded by
DAVID BRIGGS
on the organ of
Gloucester Cathedral
during a live showing of the film on 24th March 1999
(The last recording of the organ before the 1999 rebuild)

Photo courtesy of David Briggs

Bibliography

The Gramophone Shop Encyclopedia of Recorded Music [1948].
The World's Encyclopaedia of Recorded Music –
F Clough & G J Cuming [1952].
Doner's Discography – W H Doner [1952].
Music on Record – F W Gaisberg [1947].
The Guinness Book of Recorded Sound – R & C Dearling [1984].
The Organ on Record – T Hoyle [1985].

Acknowledgements

Ruth Edge – EMI Archives
Timothy Day – National Sound Archive
Dr Francis Jackson
Neil Collier – Priory Records
David Briggs – Gloucester Cathedral
Martin Monkman – Amphion Records
Paul Derrett – Benchmark Records
Sylvia Parker – Audiosonic Gloucester

Contributors

STEPHEN BICKNELL was born in London in 1957.

As an organ builder he worked with N P Mander Ltd and J W Walker & Sons Ltd, becoming head designer at Manders 1990-93. In 1993 he left organ building to pursue a free-lance career.

In 1996 CUP published Stephen Bicknell's prize-winning and much acclaimed *The History of the English Organ*. Stephen Bicknell also wrote three chapters for *The Cambridge Companion to the Organ* (1998).

Stephen Bicknell now works as a writer, designer and consultant, and lectures in Organ History at the Royal Academy of Music. His interests include architecture, engineering and gardening.

ROY BINGHAM, a University educated Chartered Engineer studied organ at Nottingham under Charles Pickard FRCO. A founder member of the Cinema Organ Society he had an ex cinema Wurlitzer organ installed in his home for 25 years. He has broadcast, recorded, and since the late 1960s been writing occasional articles relating to cinemas, organs and music in general. One of his recent contributions is a detailed biography and discography of Albert W Ketèlbey.

He was once told that his Amens were too slow and he has been stopped in Chicago for driving too fast.

KEVIN BOWYER was born in Southend in 1961 and has made a name for himself as a player of unusual repertoire and contemporary music. He has won first prizes in five international organ competitions and has released many organ CDs. His travels as a concert organist have taken him to all the usual places and one or two others besides. He is a popular teacher, active on the staff of the St Giles International Organ School and at the Royal Northern College of Music. During his moments away from the organ Mr Bowyer reads, drinks (real ale and malt whiskies) and takes the odd pinch of snuff. He sleeps less often these days but still enjoys dozing when the chance presents itself.

DAVID BRIGGS is renowned as an improviser. After winning all the prizes at FRCO aged seventeen, David became Organ Scholar of King's College, Cambridge, studied with Jean Langlais, and was the first British winner of the Tournemire prize for improvisation at the St Albans International Competition.

After four years as Assistant Organist at Hereford Cathedral and five years as Organist and Master of the Choristers at Truro Cathedral, he moved to Gloucester Cathedral, where he is centrally involved with the Three Choirs Festival. He composes, gives concerts all over the world, and has made many acclaimed recordings.

PATRICK BURNS began work as a tuner's assistant for HNB. He then became a general organ builder with installation work in both the USA and Canada. On his return he was privileged to work on the restoration and installation of the organ in Buckingham Palace. He then became the youngest tuner HNB ever appointed which has led to him being only the fourth tuner in 100 years to represent the company in South Wales. His passion is to fire express steam locomotives.

JOHN BUTT was organ scholar at King's College, later studying articulation markings in the music of Bach for his PhD, and subsequently having four books published by CUP. He joined the faculty at UC Berkeley in 1989 as University Organist and Assistant Professor in Music. In 1997 he returned to Cambridge as a lecturer and fellow of King's College. He has several essays in the *Oxford Companion to Bach* (for which he is consultant editor) and *New Grove 7*.

Active as a player and choral director in Britain and the United States, Dr Butt's ten recordings on organ, harpsichord and clavichord have been released by Harmonia Mundi; his next recording will be the complete organ works of Edward Elgar.

LIONEL DAKERS was born in 1924. Following five years war service in the Army he studied at the Royal Academy of Music. He was assistant organist at St George's Chapel, Windsor from 1950-54 and then organist of Ripon and Exeter Cathedrals. From 1973-89 he was Director of The Royal School of Church Music where his work involved worldwide travel, as did his examining for The Associated Board. His writings include 15 books. He is a CBE and an honorary Doctor of Music of Lambeth and Exeter.

PAUL HALE has been Editor of **Organists' Review** since 1992, having previously been Reviews Editor. A cathedral organist by profession and currently President of The Cathedral Organists' Association, he trained as Organ Scholar of New College Oxford and was Assistant Organist at Rochester Cathedral before moving in 1989 to Southwell Minster as *Rector Chori*. He leads a richly varied life, giving organ concerts and directing choral events internationally, acting as organ adviser to two dioceses and to several cathedrals, schools and colleges, being an examiner for the RCO, and recently preparing twenty-three articles on twentieth-century organists for *New Grove 7*. He has a passion for collecting antiquarian books on the organ.

TERRY HOYLE, born in Derbyshire, is an artist and teacher who studied painting and stained glass design, taking a BA in Fine Arts at Durham University. He is the author of *The Organ on Record*, has broadcast on BBC Radio about organ recordings, and is organist at St John's Northgate Methodist Church, Gloucester.

THOMAS MURRAY, Professor of Music at Yale University, joined the faculties of the Yale School of Music and Institute of Sacred Music in 1981. He performs and teaches on the renowned Newberry Memorial Organ (E M Skinner) in Woolsey Hall at Yale during academic terms, touring for recitals and lectures during the remainder of the year. A recipient of the American Guild of Organists International Performer of the Year award (1986) he is widely known for his interpretations of the Romantic repertoire. Prof. Murray's interests also include the playing of transcriptions, which he views as a thoroughly justifiable extension of the *bona fide* organ literature. Prior to accepting his academic post he trained one of the most respected American choirs of men and boys at the Cathedral Church of St Paul (Episcopal) in Boston. He is an avocational  student of architecture and organ case design, a life-long collector of antique furniture, prints, books, early recordings of classical music, and a keen researcher and devotee of pre-World War II Rolls-Royce motorcars.

JOHN NORMAN is a professional organ consultant and a founder member of the Association of Independent Organ Advisers (AIOA). His work has included the supervision of over a dozen new organs. He is also editor of *The Organbuilder* and has written the *Soundboard* column for the **Organists' Review** for almost twenty years. John studied acoustics at Imperial College, London, and organ under H A Roberts. At Hill Norman & Beard he learned voicing from Robert Lamb and tonal finishing from Mark Fairhead, working on seven cathedral organs before leaving in 1974.

RICHARD SHEPHARD is Head Master of York Minster School and Chamberlain of York Minster. At York University he is a Visiting Music Fellow and a member of the Court. After Selwyn College Cambridge he became a lay-vicar at Salisbury Cathedral where he taught in the Choir School and became noted for his choral compositions. His services, responses and anthems are now sung in numerous cathedrals and churches in the UK and the USA; larger commissions such as the opera *Cædmon* have been received with acclaim.

NICHOLAS THISTLETHWAITE is Canon Precentor of Guildford Cathedral. He is author of *The making of the Victorian Organ* (1990) and co-editor of *The Cambridge Companion to the Organ* (1998) besides other monographs, articles and reviews relating to the organ and church music. He was Secretary and later Chairman of the British Institute of Organ Studies, and was Organs Adviser to the Diocese of Ely from 1992-99. As an organ consultant he has advised on a number of major projects including Birmingham Town Hall, Eton College Chapel, Chelmsford Cathedral and Buckingham Palace.

PETER WILLIAMS, chairman of the British Institute of Organ Studies, held the first British university chair in Performance Practice Studies (Edinburgh) and is currently revising his three-volume book *The Organ Music of J S Bach*. Professor Williams is a jury member of the *International Bach Competition*, Leipzig, July 2000.